Unrig the Game

Unrig the Game

What Women of Color Can Teach Everyone About Winning

Vanessa Priya Daniel

RANDOM HOUSE
NEW YORK

Published in the United States by Random House, an imprint and division of Penguin Random House LLC, New York.

RANDOM HOUSE and the HOUSE colophon are registered trademarks of Penguin Random House LLC.

Excerpts from "Trashing: The Dark Side of Sisterhood" in chapter 16 appear with permission of the author, Jo Freeman, and *Ms.* magazine.

LIBRARY OF CONGRESS CATALOGING-IN-PUBLICATION DATA
Names: Daniel, Vanessa Priya, author.
Title: Unrig the game / Vanessa Priya Daniel.
Description: First edition. | New York, NY: Random House, [2025] | Includes bibliographical references and index. |
Identifiers: LCCN 2024035561 (print) | LCCN 2024035562 (ebook) | ISBN 9780593596210 (hardcover) | ISBN 9780593596227 (ebook)
Subjects: LCSH: Minority women—Political activity. | Leadership in women. | Women political activists. | Social change. | Social justice.
Classification: LCC HQ1236 .D36 2025 (print) | LCC HQ1236 (ebook) | DDC 303.48/4082—dc23/eng/20240903
LC record available at https://lccn.loc.gov/2024035561
LC ebook record available at https://lccn.loc.gov/2024035562

Printed in the United States of America on acid-free paper

randomhousebooks.com

1st Printing

FIRST EDITION

Book design by Ralph Fowler

For Kwali, Ifetayo, Tricia, and Mom.

My Wonder Women.

Sometimes people try to destroy you precisely because they recognize your power—not because they don't see it, but because they see it and they don't want it to exist.

—bell hooks

Contents

PART ONE

Winning in the Clutch

1 The MVPs and Their Three Superpowers   3

2 What Shapes Us   32

PART TWO

Superpower #1
360-Degree Vision

3 The Whole Truth   69

4 The Power in Belonging   86

5 Barriers to Bring Down   116

6 Two Generational Shifts   143

7 Bridges to Build   167

PART THREE

Staying Well Within the Work

8 Burnout   185

9 Rejecting the Call to Mother and Mammy   202

10 Setting Boundaries   217

11 Healing Ourselves   226

12 Healing Within Organizations   240

13 We Are Not a Monolith   246

PART FOUR

Superpower #2
Boldness

14 Staying On-Key   269

15 Feminism's Problem with Power   300

16 Haters and Toxic Power   320

17 Recovering from Attack and Burnout   358

18 Playing Big   368

PART FIVE

Superpower #3
Generosity

19 Rising by Lifting Others   379

20 Advice for Our Younger Selves   389

Acknowledgments   393

Notes   397

Index   403

PART ONE

Winning in the Clutch

1

The MVPs and Their Three Superpowers

"Mommy, can we go to Saturn this weekend?" My three-year-old, Ifetayo, looked up from pushing around her toy fire truck. She had perched a model of the solar system on top of it. Ife is the most confident person I have ever known, and her self-assurance was on full display that morning. During her previous obsession with Baby Shark, we had taken her to the aquarium to satisfy her curiosity. So, it stood to reason that we would now bring her to Saturn at our earliest convenience.

It was one of the last days of summer 2021 and I was making my way downstairs to cook breakfast for my two kids. I paused on the last step, feeling the soft carpet underneath my bare feet, and taking in the sunlight streaming through the trees to land in Ife's soft curls. It was my favorite time of year in the Pacific Northwest, when the rain and gloom have given way to warmth and blue skies, and everything has opened up—flowers, front doors to let in the breeze, and people who, after scuttling past each other during the long fall and winter months, now lifted their gazes to smile and look one another in the eye. I couldn't see it from our house, but I knew that a few minutes away, the Salish Sea was already shimmering in deep blue, beneath the evergreen hills and snowcapped mountains.

Ife stared at me intently. "Saturn, huh? Maybe we can ask the fairies how to get there after breakfast," I suggested. She nodded solemnly, then looked out the window at the fairy garden our family had built around a magnolia tree in our front yard. It was already abuzz with magic, Black and Brown fairy figurines gently twirling in the breeze, a riot of vibrant purple flowers swaying above the dewy green moss below. Nestled in the moss was a host of fantastic items one might need on adventures to never-before-seen places.

I loved the wild possibility of our fairy garden, sitting in the middle of an ordinary neighborhood in Tacoma, Washington. It was a sanctuary for the unbounded wonder of children's minds, and a symbol of the tenacious joy of two queer women of color making way for our family in an overwhelmingly white and straight city. Given the troubling state of the world, Tricia and I were determined to provide our two daughters with the seeds for creative thinking and faith in possibility that they would need to survive the coming years.

Our ten-year-old daughter, Kwali, bounded up to me with bright eyes. I waited for her usual morning questions about whether she could play with her neighbor friend, eat a Popsicle, or have screen time. Instead, she had just one question. "Mommy, is the world coming to an end?"

"What made you think about that?" I asked, buying time for my uncaffeinated brain to pivot from Saturn to the end of times and try to think of a solid parental answer. Kwali explained that she and her friends had been talking about the hurricane battering New Orleans, the wildfires engulfing the West Coast, the murder of George Floyd, and abortion rights being attacked in Texas. I listened as she ran down her list of disasters. I looked at her expectant face awaiting my response.

I wrapped my arms around my firstborn and tried to offer her a comforting answer. "Well, love," I said. "There are a lot of good people fighting for a better world and to save our planet. We are a part of that fight. We hope we'll win."

The truth is no one is coming to save us.

The MVPs

These are apocalyptic times. No generation has faced stakes this high or a responsibility this large. There is no guarantee that there will be enough time for future generations to accomplish the work we were too afraid to undertake, to be bold where we were timid, to act where we hesitated. All of us who are alive and able to take action today, *we* are the team on the court. This is our shot, and we can't afford to miss.

I think about this daily as I look at my two daughters and feel how much I want them and their children to have clean water to drink, clean air to breathe, and the ability to lead safe and fulfilling lives. I think about it as I reflect on my twenty-five years working in social justice movements, and the gravity of what those movements face today. Social justice victories are no longer just about who lives well or not. They are about how long human beings as a species will have a planet on which to survive. And given the outsize role the United States is playing in harming the earth, whether these movements succeed or fail has global implications.

No team worth its salt would bench its MVPs (most valuable

players) during the final championship game. Yet, in the rapidly closing window of time that we have to realize the promise of democracy, to save our rights and the planet, when many of our MVPs are women of color (WOC), that is exactly what progressive movements are doing. If movements don't figure out how to value their skills and quit benching them by leaving them underestimated, overburdened, attacked, and undefended, it will continue to negatively affect the scoreboard for everybody.

This is not a book about how *all* WOC are MVPs who know the way to freedom because . . . Nikki Haley. As movement elder Linda Burnham said, "Clarify your politics and we can talk from there. I don't care what color you are. You can be wrong as two left shoes." Nor is it a book about how everyone else needs to go quiet and get out of the way so that progressive WOC can lead. As Rajasvini Bhansali, executive director of the Solidaire Network, put it, "The points of unity cannot just be identity. They have to be political, principled, to have a movement-building orientation, and honor shared strategies for power building." The United States is a diverse nation, and it will take people from many walks of life to ensure our collective survival. There is both a moral and tactical imperative for kindhearted people of all races, genders, and backgrounds to be active in social justice movements, as constituents, leaders, and MVPs. It's a both-and. As in, we can put all these good people together, and without our WOC MVPs, we still don't win.

The immense and looming forces threatening the planet, democracy, and, increasingly, the well-being of even the most privileged are not new to WOC. In a speech I gave in 2017 in San Francisco, as Donald Trump was being sworn into office on the other side of the country, I said, "As we prepare to face the dual-headed monster of misogyny and white supremacy, women of color—who have for hundreds of years in this country been battling that same monster for our very survival—have something to teach America about how to fight."

This remains true.

WOC—and Black women in particular—have repeatedly demonstrated how essential they are to the success of every major social justice movement. Black women voted in higher percentages against Trump than any other demographic group. They founded Black Lives Matter, #MeToo, and the U.S. reproductive justice movement—three of the most influential social change efforts in decades. In the 2020 election, Black women in Georgia, through sheer grit and determination and flanked by other people of color, and Black men in particular, changed the fate of the state and the country. That same year, Black women led countless uprisings for Black lives across the country—the largest protest movement in U.S. history that sparked demonstrations attracting thirty million people around the globe.

Overall, WOC are the country's most progressive and civically engaged voting bloc, with higher voter-turnout rates than any other group. From the streets to the ballot box and to Congress, no other demographic group in the nation stands up more strongly against hate and more clearly for freedom, climate action, and human rights.

To name just a few examples:

- Take "the Squad," women of color in Congress who form the most progressive flank in the U.S. House of Representatives.[1]

- Consider the drivers of the Green New Deal—a Black woman, Rhiana Gunn-Wright, wrote it; a Latina, Rep. Alexandria Ocasio-Cortez, was its first high-profile supporter in Congress; and a Desi (South Asian American) woman, Varshini Prakash, led the Sunrise Movement,

which prompted a groundswell of young people to push
for it.

- Think about the architects of Oregon's best-in-the-nation
reproductive justice law, which expanded access to full-
spectrum reproductive health care for all, including those
who are undocumented and transgender. And the WOC
who led the fight to protect abortion access locally—
a lifesaving backstop in many cities and states now that
Roe has fallen.

- Think of Pramila Jayapal, Alexandria Ocasio-Cortez, and
others in the top leadership of the Congressional Progressive Caucus who fought successfully alongside grassroots
organizations to ensure that the 2022 Inflation Reduction
Act, the largest allocation for energy and climate in the
history of this country, a) benefited low-income and
environmental justice communities, including $27 billion in
direct appropriations and excluding controversial oil and
gas infrastructure projects, b) capped the cost of insulin for
seniors on Medicare at $35, and c) gave Medicare the power
to negotiate prescription drug costs.

- Consider the WOC elected officials who teamed with
groups like the National Domestic Workers Alliance to win
gains for women and children in the American Rescue
Plan, which expanded the Child Tax Credit for forty
million families with sixty-five million children and allocated over $1 billion for survivors of domestic violence and
sexual assault and $28 billion for home- and community-
based care (benefiting eight million families and the domestic workers who provide care).

- Take the electoralizing[2] of racial justice movements from Arizona to Pennsylvania to Georgia, and the historical and present-day leadership of trans WOC in busting gender norms that harm us all.

- Recall that today, 30 million children in this country receive free or reduced-price meals in public schools as a result of the Black Panther free breakfast program, which was designed and run by Black women.[3]

- Examine the fifteen years of polling showing that women of color are the strongest supporters of climate action,[4] a fact demonstrated by those who led and won the fight for the Justice40 Initiative, a Biden-Harris 2021 Executive Order that mandates 40 percent of *all* federal climate and clean energy investments (including the Inflation Reduction Act, as well as the CHIPS and Science Act, and the Bipartisan Infrastructure Law) benefit "disadvantaged" communities.[5] This would not have happened without WOC leaders from grassroots organizations like the Asian Pacific Environmental Network, which served on the White House Environmental Justice Advisory Council, and state-based frontline alliances like the NY Renews coalition.

Most of all, we see it in the disproportionate number of WOC-led organizations willing to tackle problems intersectionally[6]— from the term *intersectionality*, coined by Kimberlé Crenshaw, and introduced by the Combahee River Collective of Black women— simultaneously dismantling the forces of white supremacy, patriarchy, capitalism, and colonialism.

And then there's Meghan Markle. If a Black woman hadn't

called bullshit and decided to save her own life, Prince Harry would still be having high tea with a splash of brainwashing in the royal palace. If that isn't a microcosm of how WOC save our own lives and free others in the process, I don't know what is.

This is not about some false romantic notion that WOC are magical beings striving to "save us all." It's the fact that the obstacles that WOC must remove—in order to survive and thrive—are the same ones that keep all people from being free. When WOC fight and win for ourselves and our communities, everyone else benefits by extension.

At ninety-three years old, former United Farm Workers union leader Dolores Huerta is a feminist and social justice icon and one of the living legends of our time. When I asked her how many of her biggest victories, for farmworkers and other communities, were possible because of her lived experience as a woman of color, her response was, "Most, if not all of them."

People began to realize the importance of WOC during the 2020 elections. In state after state, the numbers were undeniable: WOC in general—and Black women especially—*created* the margin of victory that kept the country from careening over a cliff into fascism. They did it with strategies such as year-round, long-term, door-to-door grassroots organizing with voters, which had long been derided as inefficient by everyone from electoral donors to the Democratic Party leadership. They did it through community-based organizations that had for years been written off as too small and too marginal to be serious. They did it with a multi-issue approach—tackling abortion access alongside climate justice, police reform, and other issues—that had been widely dismissed as diluting the potency and focus of single-issue fights.

When Kamala Harris stepped forward to accept the Democratic nomination for president of the United States on August 22,

2024, her candidacy represented both a historic achievement and a flashpoint for the ongoing racial and gendered challenges that women of color in leadership continue to face. From the grassroots WOC leaders who helped secure major electoral victories to Harris herself, their leadership has been met with targeted attacks designed to undermine their legitimacy.

Harris, a Black and South Asian woman, will undoubtedly continue to encounter intensified scrutiny as a prominent leader— her identity used against her in ways that echo and surpass the struggles of her predecessors. Trump and his supporters have already given her the nickname "Laffin' Kamala," deliberately mispronounced her South Asian name, cast her as "the DEI candidate," and questioned her Blackness in front of the National Association of Black Journalists. This gives greater license to those who make gendered and racial attacks on the grassroots WOC leaders who are critical to ensuring that the next administration is held accountable to deliver meaningful improvements in people's lives, from climate justice to reproductive freedom to support for Gaza.

These attacks mischaracterize Harris's qualifications, reduce her to a symbol of diversity, and question her belonging, reflecting deeper issues with how our society responds to women of color in power. Yet, Harris's nomination also stands as a testament to the power of grassroots organizing and leadership among women of color, who remain central to electoral success and advancing progressive agendas.

Women of color understand something crucial about social change that was essential to 2020's landmark electoral wins and to reenergizing the electorate's sense of possibility with a Harris nomination. They know the factors that will be essential for countless other victories in the future.

The Three Superpowers

At the heart of what WOC bring to leadership are three super-powers that shine like megawatt bulbs, lighting the path to liberation for all people. They are:

- **360-degree vision:** The ability to look at things intersectionally, to innovate solutions that address white supremacy, patriarchy, capitalism, and colonialism simultaneously, pulling up from the roots the interlocking tangle of oppressions that hurt us all.

- **Boldness:** The tenacious drive to push beyond safe, timid, incremental change to make the brave demands required for people to thrive and for the planet to sustain human life.

- **Generosity:** The conviction that we rise by lifting others, encouraging and collaborating rather than competing and tearing down, so we can build a deep bench of leadership beside us and behind us that embodies the value of interdependence.

As a group, WOC hold a disproportionately higher concentration of this kind of thinking and praxis in their work for social change than any other segment of society, making them a triple threat in the fight for freedom. These qualities are not present in every leader who is a woman of color, nor are they absent from every leader who is not.

Disproportionality is not the same as universality.

Ninety-five percent of Black women voted against Donald Trump, whose campaign included attacks on women, immigrants, Muslims, disabled people, the LGBTQ community, and people of color, among others. That is a stunning level of political and moral clarity. Yet, Candace Owens, an ardent Trump supporter, is a Black woman. There are WOC who are terrible leaders. Tokenizing stereotypes that cast all WOC leaders as progressive and visionary is as much a denial of our humanity as negative stereotypes that label all of us as aggressive or victims. On the flip side, no group votes more consistently for hate at the ballot box than white men, who are followed very closely by white women—both voted in clear majorities for Trump in 2016 and 2020—as just one example. Yet, Jane Fonda and Steve Kerr are two white people, among many others, who work diligently alongside people of color to free all of humanity. To buy into universality is to endorse bigotry. But to not acknowledge disproportionality is to ignore the odds.

As I have often said to high-net-worth donors who give to "social change," you can continue to allocate the vast majority of giving to white men and less than 1 percent to WOC, but you don't get to call it strategic. Clarity is also contextual. In the twenty-first century in the United States, WOC have a lived experience surviving the major oppressive forces in our society simultaneously. That results in a high degree of lucidity. In another time and place, it might well be another group that drives toward freedom with the greatest clarity.

We have to start talking about the three superpowers to truly value them. And we must start talking about the forces that keep WOC on the bench.

The Bench

There are many things that people do to rig the game and bench WOC leaders by making leadership positions treacherous for us, but the top four are:

1. *Assume she is incompetent,* a setup requiring her to work four times as hard and be four times as good to be taken as seriously as her white male counterparts.

2. *Expect her to mother and mammy,* a demand that she either expend energy nurturing and caretaking at a level that isn't required of any other kind of leader, or be cast as cold, unfeeling, mean—labels that block her access to resources and opportunities.

3. *Allow her little to no margin of error,* leaving her less room to fail, to experiment, to innovate without risking her career.

4. *When she is attacked, leave her alone and unprotected, and gaslit when she attempts to defend herself.* The thoroughness and consistency with which women of color leaders are abandoned when they are attacked prompts the question posed by Carolyn Jess-Cook: "Why were we taught to be afraid of the witches and not the people who burned them alive?"

It costs all of us when many of our best movement leaders are bleeding so much precious time and energy navigating and surviving these dynamics instead of dreaming, strategizing, innovating, and leading.

These are not new problems. Nor are they resolved by wealth or status. Tony Award–winning actor, writer, director, and comedian Sarah Jones is a leader in advancing social justice movements through the arts. I first saw her in 1999 when her breakthrough one-woman show, *Surface Transit,* premiered at the Nuyorican Poets Café in New York City. I was blown away. Jones has been called "a master of the genre" by *The New York Times* and praised by the best in the industry, but there is nothing Hollywood about her.

Speaking about the leading WOC in Hollywood, she told me, "You don't graduate out of racism and misogyny. I had a show for a major network that a bunch of white men killed in their racism and ignorance and misogyny. They bought it from me and destroyed it and me for a couple of years. This is my journey in Hollywood. You get well paid and there are certain trappings, but it's incredibly racist and misogynistic to the bone. The last few years, notwithstanding #MeToo and Time's Up—God bless Tarana [Burke]—and the progress there has been, it is overwhelmingly still a site of a lot of pain and trauma. I've talked to A-list Black women and they say, 'Yeah girl, me too, absolutely. This is happening to me too with all my millions and visibility.' "

This parallels statistics that prove that, despite controlling for every other factor, women of color with higher levels of wealth and education still experience disproportionately worse health outcomes (such as high maternal mortality rates among Black and Indigenous women) driven by the stress and "weathering" of racism.[7]

For decades, WOC were simply shut out of leadership positions in most industries. Against all odds, and thanks to the tireless work of many generations, a breakthrough occurred in the past decade, and more WOC ascended into leadership than ever before in U.S. history. In the social justice sector, we took the helm of scores of organizations, including some of the largest national legacy institutions. We began working in solidarity with one another and, despite the rigged game, scoring wins for millions of people. What a relief to finally see our MVPs on the court at a time in history when we need them most!

Now, just a few years later, an exodus of these leaders is underway.

One foundation colleague of mine who manages a large gender justice portfolio of mostly WOC-led groups told me that more than 70 percent of her grantees had seen leadership transitions in 2021—higher than in any year she could remember. By the end of 2021, I had lost track of the number of Zoom calls I had been on with WOC executive directors—tough, excellent, and seasoned leaders—who were in crisis about the level of attack they were under.

One call weighs heavily in my memory, when every WOC leader on the line named a serious health problem she was managing due to the stress of being attacked from all sides. The call ended with someone sharing that they had heard separately from eight different WOC leaders that they planned to leave their positions and would never consider an executive director or CEO job again because of the impact on their bodies and psyches. Leaders were departing mid-career, taking with them decades of wisdom, skills, and relationships, an incalculable loss for movements.

I have worked in social justice movements for twenty-five years, and though I've spent enough time in predominately white and male environments to have a point of comparison, WOC have been at the heart of my work for most of my career. I've been a researcher and freelance journalist covering a range of issues, from domestic violence survivors fighting welfare reform, to Chinatown sweatshop workers unionizing to improve working conditions, to women's health advocates calling out racial disparities in breast cancer treatment. I've worked as a community and labor organizer supporting home care and other predominately low-income, WOC workforces. And I was founder and leader—for seventeen years—of Groundswell Fund and Groundswell Action Fund, two of the largest funders of WOC-led grassroots community and electoral organizing in the United States. I have dedicated most of my career to supporting WOC leaders to kick open doors and lead and have had a front-row seat to their strategic brilliance. When I sat down to write this book, I didn't have a solution to the exodus that was occurring. In my own leadership journey, I have succeeded beyond my wildest dreams, and failed spectacularly. There is still so much I am learning and figuring out. What I did have was the drive to find a solution, the time to seek it, and a wide set of relationships with the kind of wise leaders who could help piece together the answers we all need.

Over the years I've spent hundreds of hours talking to leaders, listening to their stories, what they see as their strengths, their greatest barriers to success, and what keeps them up at night. I have known many WOC leaders for fifteen or twenty years, as peers and friends. I began reaching out to them. One by one, I sat down with more than forty-five leaders, including beloved elders like Dolores Huerta, Adisa Douglas, and Bernice Johnson Reagon. Dr. Reagon, a giant of the Civil Rights Movement, the founder of Sweet Honey in the Rock, and a guiding light to so many of us, passed away just before the publication of this book, may she rest in power. I spoke with elected officials like Representative Pramila Jayapal, artists like Sarah Jones, and grassroots leaders like Ash-Lee Woodard Henderson, former co–executive director of the historic Highlander Research and Education Center, where Rosa Parks and other iconic civil rights leaders once trained. Their deep insights are woven throughout the pages of this book. Their wisdom has, for me, been a master class in leadership and a sister circle of support. I hope it is that for you too.

Social movements are tough terrain for any leader of consequence. Anyone who has seen the film *King in the Wilderness* (which chronicles the final three years of Dr. Martin Luther King, Jr.'s life) knows that even those of his stature, who are widely accepted as heroes in the present day, suffered greatly from the anguish of attack from all sides. However, there is something distinct facing WOC leaders.

In his book *Whistling Vivaldi,* sociologist Claude M. Steele recalled how as a young Black man he would strategically whistle a melody from the popular composer Antonio Vivaldi while walking through the predominately white neighborhood near his college campus. He noticed that when he did this, the white people passing by were less likely to grab their purses or cross the street. Their fear of him, programmed through the stereotypes of Black men as violent and dangerous, lessened, and with it the grave dangers that white fear could mean for him. By changing his own presentation, he protected himself from what he called "stereotype threat."

Stereotype threat for WOC leaders is a potent blend of racism and misogyny that comes at us from people of all races and genders. It makes leadership exceptionally treacherous. It shows up in how the world receives our leadership, how some WOC treat one another, and even how we see and think of ourselves. There are myriad ways in which WOC leaders "whistle Vivaldi" to put others at ease, to protect ourselves from being annihilated. Like expending energy to reassure people who are threatened by our power and success that we are not monsters. Many of these strategies sap our time and energy, putting a substantial drag on the velocity of our leadership, which in turn hinders the success of social change movements.

MINI MASTER CLASS
Gloria Walton

Gloria Walton is the president and CEO of the Solutions Project, which is globally recognized for uniting the fields of climate change and racial justice. Gloria was most recently acclaimed as being among the most powerful women in U.S. philanthropy by *Inside Philanthropy*.

"Conforming our shape and our presence to mitigate or respond to people's conscious and unconscious bias is exhausting," she shared. "I'm experimenting with giving myself permission *not* to do that, and if someone is uncomfortable, I'm also permitting myself to name what is problematic about their discomfort—in a compassionate but honest way. It's not easy. It creates uncomfortable conversations, but if I don't hold up a mirror and gently educate a well-meaning person, they're not going to see it, and then they're going to do it to the next woman of color."

The benching is worse now, with the rollback of diversity, equity, and inclusion,[8] attacks on critical race theory, the SCOTUS dismantling of affirmative action, and the extremely heightened levels of conflict within movement organizations. For decades, the laugh-to-keep-from-crying running joke among WOC leaders has been that unless we founded an organization ourselves, we were usually only invited to lead one if it was a fixer-upper. Now, a historic number of WOC are being invited to take the helm of prominent social change organizations when the entire field of social justice feels like a fixer-upper. Separate and distinct from the constructive push for organizations to evolve, a generalized anti-authority teardown of organizational leaders is sweeping across progressive movements writ large. A rising trend among nonprofit workers to conflate all authority and positional power with abuse, all boundaries with oppression, and all discipline with exploitation, is a quagmire for leaders and organizations. Right-wing attacks have also become more dangerous. All of these are hitting WOC leaders with particular force, compounding the existing racist and patriarchal notions that Black and Brown women who are assertive rather than placating are aggressive, mean, and need to be put in their place.

On January 6, 2021, Trump incited an attack on the nation's Capitol in which throngs of armed extremists and vigilantes stormed the building, threatening to kill people and forcing lawmakers—especially progressives—to hide for their lives in offices, under desks, and anywhere they could. One of these lawmakers was Alexandria Ocasio-Cortez, who shortly after surviving the January 6 attack talked to *GQ* magazine about the challenges of surviving vicious attacks on a regular basis both from the right wing and from members of her own party. "Others may see a person who is admired, but my everyday lived experience here is as a person who is despised. Imagine working a job and your bosses don't like you and folks on your team are suspicious of you. And then the competing company is trying to kill you. . . . So many people in this country hate women. And they hate women of color. And that weighs very heavily on me. And it's not just the right wing."[9]

Ash-Lee Woodard Henderson captured the sentiment of many WOC leaders I interviewed, saying, "It often feels like we are building the plane while flying it—and being shot at both from the outside and the inside."

We are living in a time when it is not unusual for WOC to simultaneously receive death threats from white supremacists, be undermined by white coalition allies, and be unfairly attacked by their own staff—including people of color. People in this country are in pain and for good reason. Globally, authoritarianism is rising, climate disasters are mounting, and war is raging, with more armed conflicts happening now than at any time since World War II.[10] Our rights are being taken away and income inequality is increasing. As an attorney colleague of mine who represents hundreds of nonprofits recently said to me, "It is one of the worst times to be a nonprofit leader because everyone's mental health has gone down two or three notches. Leaders are having to manage through this as people bring all of that to work."

Part of the offering of this book at this time in history is the reality check that we in the movement have got to get ourselves together. As my longtime friend African feminist activist and writer Jessica Horn said of those working within social justice movements, "It's not a time to be fighting each other when it's so serious outside. We are weakening the possibility of a democratic future. This is a good moment to pause and have a think about us."

And we have to talk about all of it, even the parts that have been considered taboo to speak about in the public square. Some of the forces benching WOC away from leadership and power are external: white people, cis men, and the institutions they control. These forces are real and formidable. I will examine their impact and how WOC navigate and triumph over them. But I will also explore the powerful ways in which the internalization of white supremacy, patriarchy, unbridled capitalism, and the relentless messaging that we are not and should not be leaders can manifest itself in the suspicion and tearing down of our leadership efforts by our own sisters, our own communities, and, most tragically, even ourselves.

As Audre Lorde once wrote so poignantly, "It is easier to crucify myself in you than to take on the threatening universe of whiteness by admitting that we are worth wanting each other." This is often the greatest heartbreak: when our own people attempt to tear us down or stand idly by to allow it. Without vigilance, the internalization of oppression works to police us back into more passive and submissive stances and ultimately into silence. These dynamics can be the most painful, and when we dare to lead, they function in mighty ways to keep us from achieving the victories that we, our children, and the world at large sorely need.

Understanding who we are as leaders, what works for and against us, how we both enable and undermine ourselves and one another, is all critical to getting off the bench and in the game.

The Price of Silence

As a former labor organizer, I know that workplaces don't get safer until problems are brought out of the shadows and into the light of public discussion, where behavior and systems can be confronted and changed. It was once socially acceptable and legally permissible for most workplaces to use child labor, to demand an unending norm of fifteen-hour days and seven-day workweeks, to allow workers to be maimed or killed on the job, and to fire employees for being pregnant. None of these conditions improved without a public discussion that named them and organizing that transformed them. As James Baldwin reminds us, "Not everything that is faced can be changed; but nothing can be changed until it is faced."

Today, many racial and gender stereotypes have been put under the bright light of public discourse, which is a critical step in reducing their power. This is not so for WOC leaders. Beyond leaders talking quietly with one another, the public discussion of what happens to us in these positions is almost nonexistent. When I asked a prominent organizational development consultant who works primarily with WOC leaders why none of her clients were talking or writing publicly about what they were experiencing, she answered with only one word: fear.

I know the fear of telling the truth firsthand and have at times kept silent about the hits I took in leadership, which were so much worse than those experienced by any of the white or male leaders I knew. There are the old fears: WOC have to work four times as hard to prove we can hack leadership. Speaking out about the beating you are taking once in the position will only be bandied about as proof that you couldn't hack it after all. If the hits are coming from other people of color—which they often are—there is the fear of airing our dirty laundry in front of white folks and funders. Then there is the new fear, in the era of cancel culture, of standing up to bullies who may become further enraged and drag us online. WOC know the margin of error for us is razor-thin. White leaders and even cis men of color can often survive false accusations and unwarranted attacks in ways that we cannot. We can present all the evidence and data to disprove baseless rumors and mean-spirited lies, but who would believe us? So, we keep our mouths shut. And when the pain and damage become too great, we quietly exit the movement.

Most leaders I spoke to about this book emphatically urged me to write it, citing the need for an authentic discussion—especially now. Still, a few cautioned me against it. "What will funders say?" they wondered. "Why make yourself a target?" I weighed this carefully. I decided to write it anyway, all of it, including the challenge of lateral violence between and among women of color.

Library shelves are full of books by white men and women examining their imperfections and struggles without their reputations being harmed. Airbrushed representations of realities WOC leaders face may serve respectability politics, but they certainly don't serve us. The fear of negative stereotypes keeps WOC trapped in performances of perfection. We worry that we will be destroyed if we reveal our imperfect, three-dimensional selves.

This fear is toxic to us. It robs us of our humanity and steals our right to grow and evolve. It roots us in shame and traps us in pain, which is a perpetuation of the white supremacist project that demands we orient ourselves toward a judgmental white gaze rather than toward one another.

I love us, and so I reject these taboos. Instead, I embrace the example of truth tellers like Zora Neale Hurston, who dared to write in a way that celebrated the full and imperfect humanity of Southern Black folks—their authentic vernacular, their triumphs, and their failures. For WOC to love ourselves wholly is to tell the whole truth about ourselves.

I also have some practice in telling hard truths to get free. I was five years old when I told the truth to get free from my sexual abuser. I was twenty-two when I came out of the closet as queer. I was twenty-seven when I went to work in philanthropy, telling the truth loudly about the redlining of funding to the most marginalized communities, willing to be fired if that's what it took to get dollars flowing in the right direction. Truth telling is not theoretical for me. It has meant real and sometimes painful consequences. But it has also led me to where I am today, freer, more whole.

As Hurston told us, "If you are silent about your pain, they'll kill you and say you enjoyed it." Well, here goes breaking the silence. If the raw truth of what many people expect from women of color leaders were a job description, it would read something like this:

Position Description: Woman of Color Leader

JOB DUTIES:

1. *In every new space you enter, deal with the assumption that you are incompetent* with a positive attitude. Produce work that

is four times as good as your white female or male counterparts to be seen as equally credible.

2. *Satisfy the mothering and mammying needs of others as needed.* Provide a level of nurturing and emotional labor that would never be expected of your white or male counterparts.

3. *Be likable at all costs,* even when it requires giving up the decision-making power that any effective leader must exercise in order to have actual impact. Understand that when people assume that every woman of color with positional power is unapproachable and mean, it's not their problem, it's yours. Fix it. Work harder to convince them that you are a human being and, even more important, a nice girl who doesn't think too much of herself and knows her place.

4. *Work with zero margin of error,* knowing how easily you can be discarded for any major mistake, real or perceived. Invest in a mouthguard for nighttime teeth grinding, and various other pharmaceuticals and herbal remedies for the hypervigilance that this requires and the toll that it will take on your body and mind.

5. *If you realize you've been invited onto a glass cliff (an organization in crisis) be nice about it.* Hustle to clean up the mess that preceded you, and work your Black or Brown girl magic to save the organization. Let the knowledge that you are the only one they will blame if things fail put a fire under you to do whatever it takes to get the job done.

6. *When called a bitch for setting limits that would be considered normal for any other leader, ignore it.* Anything else will be

considered defensive and proof that you are, in fact, a bitch.

7. *Be a willing screen onto which your staff can project the other women authority figures who ever disappointed them in life:* their mother, their grandmother, their great-grandmother. Do not react or respond as they unload the rage they have for these people onto you. Weather this with a cheery disposition.

8. *If your work is especially high-impact, know that you will receive more death threats than your white and male counterparts.* Understand that neither the public threats on your life nor the security detail on your house will inspire enough compassion to deter others, including people in movement work and even some members of your own staff, from piling on with their own attacks. Weather this stoically and quietly.

9. *Apologize profusely whenever staff members accuse you of perpetuating white supremacy culture* for asking them to show up to work on time or to do their jobs well. Anything less on your part will be considered defensive, unaccountable, and probably white supremacist.

10. *Apologize and admit fault immediately if accused of any kind of discrimination, bias, or other misuse of power—ageism, transphobia, xenophobia, antisemitism, anti-Blackness, retaliation, etc.—even if there is ample data and evidence to prove the accusation is false.* Remember that data itself is white supremacist— not generally, but definitely when it is used by you, and that evidence, when delivered by you, is just defensive and mean.

Also, remember that few things put people more at ease than seeing a powerful woman of color apologize.

11. *Follow the terrible advice of most of the organizational development (OD) firms and practitioners in the sector,* that the best way to handle destructive staff is to give them more decision-making power and room to break everything in the organizational house. Understand that many OD providers also have a problem with women of color using their power and need you to know your place and be a nice girl. They also need to get paid, and creating unnecessary amounts of structure and process in which even more chaos can flourish pays much better than supporting you to follow your gut instincts to draw healthy boundaries. Don't trust your gut. What do you know? *They* are the experts, do what they say!

12. *If you are dragged publicly for some baseless rumor, prepare to be abandoned by nearly everyone and treated as if you are radioactive.* Reread *The Scarlet Letter,* understand that the same ancient rules still apply, and accept this inevitability. Be gracious with gutless people. Smile when they put a hand on your shoulder and express their sympathy to you in side conversations while doing absolutely nothing to have your back in public. Try your best not to despair in wondering how an army comprising so many chickenshit individuals will defeat a well-financed, rapidly advancing authoritarian machine.

13. *Take it in stride when other women of color who you have lifted and supported stab you in the back* because of group pressure, competition for resources, internalized racism

and patriarchy, jealousy or spite, or for the rewards the system gives them for taking other sisters out. Understand that heartbreak about betrayal is unprofessional.

14. *Be affable about tokenizing.* Welcome the saccharine praise by those who are more concerned with appearing support- ive of a woman of color leader than giving you the critical feedback and information you need to avoid being hit by a train headed your way.

15. *Never talk publicly about job duties 1–14 above.* Know that if you break the code of silence people will call you hysterical and bitter. They won't believe you. They will assume you are exaggerating because leadership is just too much for you to handle.

16. *If you don't succeed in leadership after following the rules above, listen to those who remind you that not everyone is cut out for these positions.* Don't worry about the system being rigged. Instead, stew about how *you* failed and how it was all *your* fault. Accept the fact that you must not have known what you were doing after all. Step down and go quietly. Get back in your fucking place.

If progressive women of color leaders wrote an equally honest cover letter in response to this job description, it would begin: "Dear Movement: We could all be winning more if you took your foot off of our necks."

No effective woman of color leader abides by everything on this list—she would never accomplish anything if she did. But *every* woman of color leader working to make change in political, social, or cultural movements has to expend energy navigating *some* aspect of this list on the daily. We need people around us to unrig the game by chucking the list in its entirety, along with the punishing behavior that so often targets a leader who refuses any part of this toxic and all too common job description.

A Gift for My Sisters

When I was a young leader in my midtwenties, I wished for a book that would remind me that I was not alone, that others faced the same challenges I was confronting, and that they had found a way through—and that I would too. I longed for a resource that shared the wisdom of WOC in movement, of how they thrived as leaders—making meaningful contributions to a better world—amid so many obstacles. I want this to be that book. I think of it as my gift to my movement sisters, who I love dearly, and I offer it with the heartfelt hope that it will help our superpowers shine.

There is one comfort I hope every woman of color leader who reads this book will take away: You are not alone. For us, this book does several things: It affirms our brilliance, names the obstacles in our way, and collectivizes our wisdom on how to navigate them. It is a balm for the painful challenges we often encounter as we dare to lead. It is a reminder that there is a wellspring of knowledge and wisdom among us for how to lead in ways that transform the world while honoring our own well-being and the well-being of others. It is also a reminder that the responsibility for changing the systemic oppression we face does not rest with us alone.

One day, I was at my daughter Kwali's swim meet when I spotted a middle-aged woman in the crowd, likely a fellow mother, sitting in a folding chair apart from most of the parents. She had fallen asleep with her mouth open. She was clearly exhausted. Resting on her chest was a book titled *What to Do When He Won't*

Change. It struck me as a perfect metaphor for what often happens in movement. The fact that those who participate in and benefit from systems that exhaust WOC leaders to their core are allowed to not change—while we study up on how to work around them and somehow survive—is bullshit. The notion that WOC leaders can escape our predicament by just trying harder at leadership is magical thinking. It makes about as much sense as telling Black folks during Jim Crow to try harder to vote when literacy tests and poll taxes were making that impossible.

WOC leaders can lift our voices to speak out about what needs changing, but those who work with us must also take collective responsibility to change norms and unrig the game.

For WOC who are not in leadership positions, and for non-WOC, including and white folks, this book presents two opportunities. First, to strengthen your own praxis by learning from the creative innovations WOC leaders are bringing to social change strategy and organizational leadership. Not all, but many of the challenges WOC leaders face are supersized versions of those being felt by leaders of all races and genders in these times. The strategies WOC use to surmount these are helpful additions to any leader's toolbox. Second, this book is an opportunity to more deeply understand the experience of WOC leaders so that you can, in the interest of all of us, step up to help make leadership a less treacherous place. As the great Maya Angelou reminds us, "When you know better, you do better." The responsibility lies largely with you.

My most fervent intent is that this book opens a conversation in the public square that radically shifts how people view and treat WOC leaders. May the leaders of today—and those in my daughters' generation—have a clearer, less obstructed runway from which to take flight with their best strategies and ideas. My vision is that we meet these end-of-times challenges with the radical imagination and confidence that is so needed to save our democracy and the planet. If my daughters decide to lead, shoulder to shoulder with grassroots communities, toward a better world, I want to be able to tell them honestly that enough people will see them, protect them, and unrig the game of the barriers that attempt to block their light. I want them, with their remarkable empathy and confidence, to have the best possible shot at taking us to the never-before-seen places, the metaphorical Saturns: the new ways of being that humanity must reach to evolve and thrive.

Finally, my heartfelt gratitude to the more than forty-five inspirational leaders (listed in the appendix) with whom I conducted formal interviews during the writing of this book. We rise by lifting one another.

2

What Shapes Us

When I was five years old, I had a regular morning routine. I pulled a pair of yellow construction-paper wrist cuffs over my hands and pushed a matching crown down gingerly over my jet-black curls. All the pieces of paper were fastened together with crooked staples and adorned with red, white, and blue designs I had scrawled with Crayola crayons. To me, they felt like magic. I picked up an old jump rope that I had knotted and turned into a lasso. Then I headed out into the middle of our front lawn. Standing tall, chest puffed out, I twirled the lasso in circles high above my head, shouting as loudly as I could, "I am Wonder Woman!"

It was 1983, and Lynda Carter's *Wonder Woman* was big. I spent hours staring into my family's tiny rabbit-eared TV as she fought her way out of countless seemingly insurmountable situations. Carter was a superhero, and there was no one she couldn't defend herself against or protect herself from. I was obsessed with her, and especially her golden lasso. Because it had the power to make people tell the truth. There was a truth sitting heavy on my heart that I desperately wanted to tell, and I wanted truth-telling power too.

That year, my parents and I lived in a suburb of Seattle, Washington, surrounded by my close-knit Sri Lankan family—my dad's people, who had immigrated to the United States in the late 1970s, fleeing a civil war. Priya was the middle name my parents gave me. In Tamil, it means "beloved," and I was. When I wasn't on the hip of an auntie or older cousin, I was being doted on by my grandparents or running through the house with my little cousin Enosh, who was like a brother to me. We would dash through the kitchen, where my favorite auntie was chopping coconut, each of us grabbing a juicy piece from her outstretched hand. My bond with my family was strong. From birth, my relatives were my entire world.

And that's what made the truth—hidden within me—so hard to tell. That's why I was out there every morning, spinning that lasso, working up the courage to tell it. I knew that most everyone in my family loved and cared for me. I also knew that one of the men in our family kept doing something to me that I didn't like, something that confused me and filled me with shame. Something he threatened me not to tell anyone about. One morning, I woke up and didn't head out to the front lawn. Instead, I told. I had no idea that it would change the trajectory of my entire life.

My father and his family turned their backs. They said they didn't believe me. It would take decades before I would realize that believing me had very little to do with it. I had turned on a light in a room where many of the women in my family had hidden away their own pain. A room they needed to keep dark. The rule was clear: Either keep that light switch flipped off, in denial, or you were out of the family. Who did I think I was? Only one person stood with me: my mother. When she saw no one else was willing to protect me, she packed me up and we left. When she walked out, she left behind the only support system she had.

It wasn't easy. We struggled for money. The man who had sexually abused me left death threats for her on our answering machine. Some nights I would wake up and find her sitting at the end of her bed, crying and praying for the money she needed to provide for us and keep me safe. It wasn't until years later, when I was a mother myself, that I realized the courage of what she had done.

This is how, at age five, I learned superpower number two: My mother taught me to be bold. If you want to be free, you have to be willing to speak the brave truth. You have to be willing to lose the people who want to stay in the lie. They will break your heart, but freedom is worth it.

At first glance, the situation was a painful but simple one: A daughter had been harmed and a mother had done what she needed to do to protect her child. In reality it was anything but. Because I was Brown and my mother was white, and this was America.

We rented the basement unit of a house in Seattle's north end, near the naval base. The house was modest, with outdated appliances and wood-paneled siding. My bedroom had a rust-colored carpet and a window that looked out at a brick wall. But the place had one major redeeming quality: a backyard that opened up onto a thin, pebbly beach on Lake Washington. The lake was a wonder. Its slate gray waters turned blue farther out, and in the distance, evergreen hills were topped by snowcapped mountains. My mom and I spent so much time staring at the water. I believe that watching it wash against the shore, day after day, helped us eventually heal.

Not long after we moved in, the bright sunlight of summer waned and became the heavy gray overcast of fall. We were alone now, just my mother and me. She was loving and attentive. And yet, during those first weeks in our new home, it felt as if someone had pressed a mute button on our world. Gone was the laughter and hubbub of a bustling family life, gone were the love and care of cousins and aunties, the bursting color and glint of batiks and gold bangles, and the smell of curry and dahl balled together with fragrant basmati rice between brown fingers and lifted into waiting mouths. My family ate with their hands, as is the custom in Sri Lanka. In this new place, there was quiet and solitude, and the metallic taste of forks on teeth. Here, the only people I saw were white.

A few family members visited infrequently. I learned that many things could be true at the same time. They loved me. And they considered me a traitor. They gave me gifts and nourished me with the familiar foods of home. And they were beginning what would be a decades-long campaign to pressure me to recant, to turn that light switch back off. Papa (my grandfather) and Granny came to visit first. "Come, da-ling," Papa called to me, patting my shoulder firmly with his hand. "Open the parcels we brought for you, eh?" He motioned to the plastic Payless Drugstore bags they had brought, each double knotted at the top. Inside were tins full of my favorite foods—dahl, curry, rice—and usually a fresh, uncut mango that I would devour every inch of, scraping the peel and seed clean with my teeth as if it were the last mango on earth. The flavor of the curry chicken on my tongue seemed to restore balance to something deep down in my soul. I loved seeing Papa and Granny, but it felt different—formal and stiff. My mom made small talk about the weather, and my grandparents asked me rote questions about school. Papa was kindness personified. As a toddler I used to hold his eighty-year-old hands in mine, marveling at the contrast of them. One side the color of dark coffee beans, and soft in that comforting way that only the skin of elders is. The other side, cream-colored with deep, dark lines, and calloused in that way of those who have done hard labor. Kind of like the man himself, I would reflect later in life. Someone who had toughened up enough to survive the brutality of British colonization but managed to keep his heart soft and kind. I adored him. I wanted so much to just climb into his lap like I used to do, resting my head on his chest. But there was a weird pall over the room that made me hesitate. After their visits, my stomach would ache with anxiety and I'd curl up in a ball on the living room floor.

My favorite cousin, Enosh, once visited with his sister, Shanaya, and their parents. The moment they arrived, the queasiness in my stomach doubled me over. There was no one I missed more than Enosh. I asked about him daily, and the distance between us had put a crack in my heart that only deepened with his visit, which felt neither friendly nor familiar. After a while, my stomachache eased up, and I tried to interact. "Akka!" I said, calling Shanaya by the Tamil word for sister that Enosh and I had always used for her. She turned to me with a sharp reprimand: "Akka means sister. I'm your cousin." With my family, I felt something I had never sensed before. Instead of cupping my face in their hands and pulling me into their warm embrace, they stood at a distance and chatted about mundane things. Instead of shouting "You're it!" and chasing me in our usual game of tag, Enosh looked at me with a bored and aloof stare. It was as if a glass door had been closed and locked. I was on the outside, looking in.

When I asked my mom why our relatives felt so far away, she simply said, "Blood is thicker than water." I didn't understand. She also told me, "What happened, it's not your fault." But all I knew was I had told the truth. And as a result, my family had gone away. My mom and I were all alone.

My family came to visit less and less. I kept waiting for them to come back, to reappear on the horizon. I looked for them wherever I was—at the grocery store, the mall, the library. Where had they gone? When would they return? Every day I would come home from school, plunk down on the couch in front of the TV, and turn the dial past all of the cartoons and kids' shows until I found *The Jeffersons* or *Good Times* or *Sanford and Son,* all featuring Brown people who looked like my family. "Would you like some water, Mr. Jefferson?" asked Florence, the housekeeper. "Why, yes, Florence, I would, thank you," answered Mr. Jefferson, strutting across the living room. "Good, me too," Florence clapped back, a glint in her eye. "Get me some while you're at it, will you?" The studio audience erupted in applause. I cracked up, alone in my living room. I stayed glued to the screen, spending quality time with my favorite TV families until my mom called me for dinner.

Being alone was an unfamiliar sensation. So was the constant presence of fear in our household. Terrified that the man who had hurt me would harm us or kidnap me, my mom and I were forever on edge. An extremely private person, my mother had no choice but to reluctantly tell my schools and day cares to be careful not to release me to anyone who was not on the pickup list. If life was terrifying at home, it was mortifying at school. In the first grade, my teacher called me to the front of the class, gave me a clipboard with a note on it, and asked me to walk around to every class and show it to the teachers. At first, I beamed with pride. She had chosen me to be her special helper! I diligently performed the task. Each teacher I handed it to read the note, then looked at me very intently after they read it. Later, I learned that the note instructed teachers to take a good look at me and make sure that no one but my mom picked me up because a relative had abused me and I was at risk of being kidnapped. When one of the teachers made a comment revealing what was in the note, I wanted to disappear. I knew the teacher who had written the note meant well, but I felt exposed and humiliated. I learned to read and write quickly, vowing to never again shop around a set of words on a page without knowing what they said.

Most days, my anxiety was high. I dealt with it by clinging to my mother like a barnacle. She was, in my mind, all I had left, the only thing between me and the abyss of utter loneliness and desolation. In the grocery store, especially, I was careful not to let her out of my sight in case she decided to abandon me (like Punky Brewster's mom did on the TV sitcom). I had quiet conniptions inside my head when I was the last kid picked up from day care— which was often because Mom was rushing from work. My worst anxiety came at night. In our new house, I set up camp in my mother's bed; graciously, she didn't protest. At night I lay awake, listening to the clanging of her doing the dishes. When she finally came to bed, I pressed myself to her like a starfish, tightly holding handfuls of the red velour bathrobe she slept in, as if we were spinning in outer space and I could at any minute be tossed into oblivion. Sometimes she couldn't stand it. "Enough, child!" she'd say. "Give me some space to breathe!" She seemed even more alone than I was. She had no close friends, no real support from her family. My father's family had been her world. When we left, I had her, but she had no one. I remember asking her, years later, "Mom, who was your rock when we were going through all of that?" She responded simply: "I was my rock."

My mother grew up an army brat with parents from Selma, Alabama. Her parents believed in Ronald Reagan, the Republican Party, and America's right to bomb whatever country it pleased. They believed if you weren't Christian, you were going straight to hell, and they believed in an extreme version of spare the rod spoil the child. The severity of the beatings meant that she and her siblings often went to school covered in bruises. When she left home at seventeen, she rebelled against all of it. She became the

first woman in her family to call herself a feminist, to marry outside of her race, to pursue graduate studies and a career outside
the home. She left the church, lived in India for a time, and em-
barked on a New Age quest for spiritual meaning. Few obstacles
deterred her. Worried her parents would pull all financial support
if they discovered she was engaged to marry a brown-skinned
man, she finished her undergraduate studies in three years instead
of four. She plowed forward to complete her doctorate, facing
down a level of sexism that drove many of her female classmates
to drop out. That sharpness and toughness carried her and us
through life.

As a child, I witnessed her, as a single mother, start and build
her own business and buy our first home. I went with her to bank
after bank, watching white male loan officers size her up, a single
unmarried woman with her own business, and turn her down. It
had been less than fifteen years since the law changed that required women to have their husband or male relative sign off to
obtain even a credit card and discrimination was still commonplace. She persisted until she found someone who would give her
the loan. Growing up, I watched her put more stock in brains than
looks, reject the notion that she needed a man to be complete,
transgress the norm of preserving family ties at all costs (we visited her family on a total of three occasions my entire childhood),
and break the cycle of generational violence by parenting me
with a lot of love and kindness. I was her only child and she never
once beat me. From my mother I learned that good communication is not just about what you say, but about the quality of how
you listen. There was something about the calm in how she listened that inspired everyone—from a truck driver to a brain surgeon—to open up and talk about the most tender parts of their
lives. One of the biggest gifts of my childhood was being raised
by a mother who I could talk to about almost anything. My

mother is also the least conformist person I have ever known. She paid little to no attention to the opinions and judgments of others and had an unshakable commitment to trusting her own instincts. As a parent, she was in most ways an incredible role model and my fiercest protector. There is no question in my mind that I would not be the person I am without the good that she gave me. And like every parent, she had her limitations. Unfortunately for me, a Brown child born into America, race was hers. As a girl child, I was seen and supported to the fullest. As a child of color, I was utterly alone.

My mom moved us into a world of white liberals and New Agers. She might as well have taken me to another planet. As a tour guide, she left out a lot of pertinent information. Notwithstanding her years in India, and a decade as the only white person in the Sri Lankan family she had married into, she, like most white people, had spent most of her life in all-white environments. She lived on Planet White and thought about things largely from that perspective. It's an odd thing, when I think about it. I mean, if you were from Alaska and had some visitors from the tropics, wouldn't you warn them about the cold? Wouldn't you tell them to bring a coat and some layers? Wouldn't you warn a Brown kid you're bringing to Planet White to expect bland food and micro-aggressions?

Some white people treated me well. There was also a lot of racism. I didn't understand why people always asked me, "Where are you from?" I didn't understand why my white teachers punished me and the other Black and Brown students in my class for things that I saw our white classmates doing with no consequence. I didn't understand the pain and suspicion I sensed in the hearts of my Black schoolmates—the only people I saw who were Brown like me—who looked at me sideways and asked me why I talked like a white girl.

Like most white liberals in the eighties and nineties, Mom believed that the best way to avoid being racist was to never talk about race. She described herself as "color-blind." *More like a blindfold*, I thought years later, marveling at the racism that socked me in the stomach throughout my childhood while she looked on cheerily, utterly oblivious. We lived in Seattle, so it wasn't the overt slurs and burned-crosses-on-your-lawn type of racism one encountered in other parts of the country. Rather, it was the smile-in-your-face microaggressions—death by a thousand cuts.

One day, when I was about seven, my mom and I walked into a New Age bookstore. The air was filled with incense, and the shelves were stacked with books between wood and stone carvings of various gods and goddesses of the world. A large smiling Buddha sat by the entrance. The clerk, a white woman, stepped out from behind the counter to get a closer look at me. She clasped her hands together and exclaimed to my mother, "Oh, she's beautiful! Where'd you get her?" I squirmed. I didn't know why, but this lady made me uncomfortable. I felt she was eyeing me like just another statue or "ethnic" artifact that some white person had picked up during their world travels and deposited in her store. "I hatched her!" my mother replied to the woman's astonishment. Later, on the way to the car, I asked my mother, "Why did that lady ask where you got me?" My mother expressed her annoyance. "People are ignorant," she said. "They can't imagine that a white person and a Brown person could actually have a child. I spent days in labor!" She was irritated, but mainly because the woman lacked imagination and hadn't given her due credit for the labor of childbirth and the status of birth mother. She seemed oblivious to how the exchange had affected me.

Like so many classes I was in, my second-grade class had few students of color. The teacher was Ms. Smith, a white woman who, for some reason, couldn't stand me. When I colored on paper at my desk during story time—something I saw many other children doing—she stopped the class to admonish me, warning that if I did it again there would be consequences. When I wrote an assignment in cursive, which I was eager to learn and had asked Mom to show me how to write at home, Ms. Smith scolded me for working ahead. "Cursive doesn't come until next year," she snapped. "Don't do it again." When I did well on another writing assignment, she accused me of plagiarizing, unable to believe that I had the capacity to write well.

I shared these various incidents with Mom. She found nothing remarkable about them. I decided that I would win over Ms. Smith. I had recently seen the movie *Pollyanna* and figured if Hayley Mills could kill them with kindness, well, so could I! The writing assignments Ms. Smith gave us were usually short, so I sat down and handwrote a ten-page story and presented it to her as a peace offering. She corrected it in red ink and gave it back. I was baffled. She hadn't even thanked me for the present! I was out of ideas. Then, one day, a Black girl named Keisha who sat near me raised her hand to use the bathroom. Ms. Smith kept refusing her until she couldn't hold it anymore and a pool of urine appeared on her chair, spilling onto the floor while the entire class looked on. I looked at Keisha. She sat quietly, staring straight ahead, tears rolling down her cheeks as Ms. Smith told her sharply to go clean herself up. After that I decided Ms. Smith was just a horrible person. I stopped trying to win her over.

At no point did my mother notice that this woman was a racist. At no point did she intervene. Years later, as a grown woman, I burst into tears while watching footage of fourteen-year-old Venus Williams being interviewed by a white male reporter—and the ferocity with which her father came to her defense when the reporter attempted to cut her down with microaggressions. In the interview, Venus smiles proudly and expresses total confidence that she can beat her opponent. The reporter presses again and again about whether she is actually that confident—and why? Richard Williams descends on the reporter like a lion: "She said it with so much confidence the first time. But you keep going on and on. You are dealing with the image of a fourteen-year-old child, and this child going to be out there playing when your old ass and me gonna be in the grave. You're dealing with a little Black kid—and let her be a kid. She done answered it with a lot of confidence. Leave that alone!"

When it came to gender, which my mother understood from personal experience, she was my greatest defender. She had suffered the stings of sexism her whole life. She had risked her life to save mine. When it came to race, though, I had all the vulnerabilities of a Brown girl but none of the protections. When we left my Sri Lankan family and first arrived in "Whitelandia," I had no one blocking for me. I had no one who even noticed the painful ways in which I didn't belong. Even worse, when I did express my experience and pain at home, I had a parent who gaslit me, denying the reality of what I was encountering, leaving me wondering if I was crazy and if it was all in my head.

Lost at Sea

My mother never told me what race I was. To her, it was unimportant. Left to my own devices, I looked around for the people who looked most like me, whose culture felt most like where I had been raised. The only people I saw who were Brown like me, and who seemed to talk and laugh a little more freely, like my Sri Lankan family—and not the more reserved white people around us—were Black people. I decided I must be Black. I knew my people were from another country, but not understanding the relationship of race to geography, I just figured I was Black—the international edition!

On one of their rare visits, my Sri Lankan family added to the confusion by bringing me children's books with pictures of Black people. One day, they brought me a large one titled *The People Could Fly: American Black Folktales.* A family of brown-skinned people was pictured on the cover, flying above the clouds in the blue sky. Inside, they had written, "To Vanessa. With Love, From Granny and Papa." I stared at the cover and pored over the pictures inside. The book was full of Brown people, just like my family. I didn't have words for it, but when I looked at the people in that book, just like when I watched *The Jeffersons,* something in me settled and calmed. I felt like I was closer to home.

Now that I think about it, my grandparents were probably having a similar dilemma. No doubt they wanted their granddaughter to see herself in the books they gave me, so they grabbed the only one in the store with brown-skinned people on it. Similar reasons must have motivated many of my Sri Lankan relatives to marry into the Black community. For reasons I wouldn't fully understand until I was an adult, most members of my family rejected the path of assimilation into white society that was popular among many middle- to upper-class South Asian immigrants and instead aligned themselves with the Black community. Several of my cousins married Black people and had kids who were a mix of Black and Sri Lankan. Sometimes, I'd see them from a distance when my cousins dropped off Granny and Papa for a visit.

My case of mistaken identity lasted for years and was a setup for eventual disappointment. The whole ordeal was both tragic and hilarious. When I asked my mother why I was Brown and she was white, she told me a magical story, knowing I liked sweets, that I had been made by mixing chocolate and vanilla together. If I ever seemed skeptical, she would point to the birthmark on my arm and say, "See, that's where they didn't stir it in all the way!" This explanation was not helpful on the playground.

At school, the first question most Black kids asked me was "What'chu mixed with?" I gave my standard answer: chocolate and vanilla. They would look confused and try another tack. "You got Indian in you?"—which was their polite way of asking why I didn't have Afro hair. "I don't think so," I would answer slowly, puzzled. Mind you, I was also benefiting from the wonders of American public school geography lessons. I had not made the connection that people in South India and Sri Lanka are essentially the same, racially, and that my grandfather was Dravidian, from South India—so technically I did have *actual* Indian in me. But by Indian, of course, these kids didn't mean from India; they meant Native American, since a lot of Black folks with straighter hair can trace that trait back to mixing with Blackfoot, Cherokee, and other tribes.

Eventually, I figured out where India was, but I still didn't get the connection to race. My mother confused me further. During the New Age journey of self-discovery that she was on for most of my childhood, she became for some time a disciple of an Indian guru named Sai Baba, who, for some reason, had a gigantic Afro. My mother had a life-size, full-length picture of him in our downstairs basement that she and other disciples would meditate in front of during Thursday night gatherings. *Ah, yes,* I thought to my eight-year-old self knowingly as I looked up at Sai Baba. *Black, the international edition! Just like me!*

A Life Raft

Sometimes, the universe intervenes in ways that are inexplicable. When my mom bought us a house in a predominately white area, the only Black family in the neighborhood lived next door. They had a daughter who would become one of my closest childhood friends. What are the odds? Sometimes I crack up thinking about it. When it came to race, my childhood was like a bizarre version of the TV show *Survivor*. The announcer's voice in the show trailer would have boomed: "She's eight years old and she's been dropped off in American apartheid with only *The Jeffersons* and the Black family next door to help her. Will she make it?" Generously, the universe gave me even more than this. By another stroke of luck, the elementary school I went to had a Black woman principal, Black students on campus due to mandatory busing programs, and several Black teachers who taught about civil rights. I was in second grade when one of my teachers showed us footage of protesters facing dogs and fire hoses in Birmingham. At assemblies, the entire school sang the Black National Anthem.

I was hopelessly confused about my identity during these years. But damn if I wasn't active. I did a book report on Harriet Tubman, and she became my hero. I was in our school production of *The Wiz*. I joined a group of kids who made friendship bracelets that we sold to benefit the anti-apartheid struggle in South Africa. The walls of my room were covered with my heroes and sheroes: Michael Jordan, arms outstretched beneath the word WINGS, Judith Jamison in her iconic pose from *Cry*, her leg reaching high-high-high. I was Black and proud.

Lucky for me, the group I had mistakenly assumed I was a member of also happened to be the one that was best equipped to help me with my predicament of being stranded alone in the morass of American race relations. It would be Black women, the mothers of my friends, who would tell me the anguish I often felt as a brown-skinned girl moving through white space wasn't just in my head. It wasn't some chocolate-and-vanilla fairy tale or some light thing I could simply ignore, as my mother would suggest. It was something called racism. It hurt. It could be deadly—it had the power to kill people and to harm their spirits. Their message to me was clear: I had better listen up, get with it, and learn how to navigate the world in the skin I was in. I got the message loud and clear and took in the advice they gave me.

Some of this came in the form of correction. Once, in the grocery store, I tickled the feet of my friend's baby brother, who was sitting in the front of the shopping cart. He was tall and chunky for a one-year-old. Playfully I said to him, "Are you gonna be a football player when you grow up?" His mom intervened: "Now why would you say that, Vanessa? Why not a doctor or a lawyer? Don't stereotype Black boys into sports." Other lessons came from observing. Once, in the early nineties, I accompanied my neighbor friend and her mom to a neighborhood meeting about break-ins. The white neighborhood safety committee announced that the suspects were Black and urged everyone to call the police if they saw anyone who fit that description. My friend's mother stood up like a shot and admonished them. "This is unacceptable," she said. "I am not going to have the police called on every Black friend and relative who visits my house." Black women were schooling me. Still, my confusion about my own race persisted.

It wasn't until I was nine years old that some friends of mine, who were actual Black girls, realized my confusion—and set me straight. I was playing in the backyard with my next-door neighbor and best friend Aisha and her friend Kianna. There was a gap in the fence that Aisha and I could slip through to get to each other's yards, and the three of us were balancing on top of a red brick wall near the gap. Somehow the topic turned to skiing.

"Those skiers in the Olympics be *flyin'* down that hill," said Kianna. "*Ooowee,* I would be scared."

"Yeah, cuz Black people don't ski anyway," said Aisha.

"Yeah, we don't," I said, thinking that I had never been skiing.

"Watchu say?" said Kianna.

"I said, 'Yeah, we don't,' " I repeated.

"Why you say 'we'?" she asked. "You said 'we,' like you Black or something. You ain't Black."

"What are you talking about?" I clapped back, incredulous. "Yes, I am!" I held my brown arm next to hers. "I'm the same color as you."

Aisha chimed in. "It's not about you being the same shade of brown."

I thought about it for a moment, puzzled. Maybe she meant it had to do with the skin color of people in your family.

"My grandfather is darker than anyone in your family," I said defensively. I thought of his dark, Dravidian complexion, which was as black as some of the darkest people I had seen from Africa.

"It's not just about color, silly," Kianna said. "Black is when your ancestors are from Africa. And yours ain't. You from India or something, right? That's a whole other country than Africa." (Her geography was better than mine, but not by much.) "And yo mama white," she said firmly, as if that decided it.

I was devastated. Who was I, then? Where did I belong? And who were my people? I resolved that if I wasn't Black—and I knew I didn't feel at home in most white spaces—then there was only one logical thing to do. It was obvious! I had to become Sri Lankan. The next time my mom and I were in the bookstore, I ducked over to the help desk and asked for books on Sri Lanka. There was just one in the entire store: a Fodor's Travel guide. While my mother shopped for New Age books, I tried my best to download an entire culture from that guide. I quickly realized it was futile: I couldn't learn a culture without being around the people who were a part of it. And how would that happen? The only Sri Lankans I had ever seen were my relatives—and we were estranged from them. My mother wasn't exactly taking us to Sri Lanka anytime soon. It would be another seven years until, at sixteen years old, I would briefly reconnect with my family before moving out of the state for college and adulthood. At nine years old, I was stuck.

The few times I talked to my mother about my predicament, she was too mired in her feelings to be helpful. With a hurt expression, she would say, in all sincerity, "But you're part of me! You're half-white. Why can't you just be a part of my culture?" She didn't understand. Out in the world, no one saw me or treated me as white. More important, I didn't *feel* white. I loved my mother dearly, and I got along well enough with many white people in our community, but I had spent the first five years of my life immersed in Sri Lankan culture. In the white world, I felt like a fish out of water.

With nowhere else to go to find anything remotely resembling my experience—or anyone who looked like me—the Black community continued to be the closest thing I had to a sense of belonging. And Black women and girls—my friends, their mothers, and their big sisters, along with the freedom fighters and feminists I read about, like Harriet Tubman, Assata Shakur, bell hooks, and Audre Lorde—continued to be the only ones who taught me how to navigate and survive America as a girl of color. It was, at times, a tenuous belonging. I was welcomed and embraced most of the time, which was a godsend for me as a kid, but periodically I was shut out and put in my place. I learned at a very young age how to code-switch into Black vernacular around Black kids to survive socially. Talking "like a white girl" was a major liability—and the best way to get clowned and rejected. The anguish of feeling like a complete outsider hit the raw nerve of the rejection I had felt from my family. I bent myself into new shapes, conforming to avoid the pain. Still, I never passed. It would have been easier on the playground to just pass as Black, but as soon as I understood my race and heritage, I couldn't bring myself to disrespect my family or lie about who I was just to belong. When people asked me what I was mixed with, I always told them the truth: I was white and Sri Lankan. This made me more of a target.

The older I got, the more racism bore down on me. My friends' youthful innocence was disappearing.

"You have the white man's nose," one of my Black friends told me teasingly. "All pointy and shit."

"Your hair looks like a horse tail," Aisha said one day, giving my ponytail a hard pull that felt more angry than playful. That comment stung. Especially after all the times I had sat behind her while we watched *A Different World* or *The Cosby Show*, taking out her braids and extensions one by one when she was ready to switch styles. I played it off in the moment, but when I got home, I cried. She was my best friend. We spent nearly every day together after school. We spent Thanksgiving and Christmas at each other's houses. With her, I had felt accepted.

And now I started to feel shame about my appearance whenever I looked in the mirror. (As an aside: Looking back now, with an adult perspective, the irony is not lost on me that while I was busy feeling like a freak and a weirdo growing up in Seattle, across the ocean, one of the most densely populated regions on the planet—South Asia—was chock-full of people who looked just like me!)

Growing up, I saw Black women as the epitome of strength and beauty—something I could never attain. It didn't occur to me that as we all became teens, my Black girlfriends were in their own pitched battles with a white standard of beauty. The marginalization so many Black girls felt in a country that placed a higher value on straight hair, narrow features, and light skin led some of my friends to resent me in the same way they resented lighter-skinned Black girls with features that met those false "all-American" standards of beauty. I saw the pinched look of pain on the faces of my dark-skinned friends as lighter-complected girls cracked jokes: "She so Black, when she walk in a room, she cause a Blackout." American racism was doing a number on all of us and we, in turn, were doing a number on each other.

Years later, an elder Black woman friend, whose complexion was the color of coffee beans, said to me, "Colorism cuts all of us differently, Vanessa. There is pain in being dark. And while there are privileges in being light, there is pain in that too." Then she shared with me the story of a light-skinned Black woman she had known who gave birth to a beautiful chocolate brown baby girl. The woman told my friend that the first thought that popped into her mind when the doctor placed her lovely newborn baby in her arms was "Thank God. At least no one will call her a high-yellow bitch." Years later, when in my late teens I reconnected with my favorite Sri Lankan auntie, I would realize that colorism had poisoned people the world over. A stunningly beautiful woman at seventy, my auntie appeared as a young woman in an old photo I used to gaze at. She leaned against a palm tree, knockout gorgeous. But for most of her life she never knew it. Because she was dark, like my grandfather, Papa. She was told, everywhere she turned, that she was ugly. She recalled her shame when in grade school the teacher asked her, as the darkest kid in the group, to step to the side when they took the class photo so that she wouldn't "ruin" it. Ironically, the first time she considered the possibility of her own beauty was when she arrived in the United States in the 1970s, at the height of Black Pride, and saw the slogan "Black Is Beautiful." Her face lit up as we sat at her kitchen table and she shared this memory with me. "I loved it!" she said, smiling.

Amid the painful dynamics of colorism among Black girls of

different shades, my concerns weren't particularly special. But I felt vulnerable all the same; I was of a different race, and more than a few people routinely took satisfaction in reminding me that I was an outsider. Thankfully, despite the periodic stings of exclusion, most of my experience among Black women and girls was one of love, care, and support. I would never fully understand what it was like for them to grow up as Black girls in America. They would never fully know what it was for me to grow up as a Brown girl in the wilderness, without a people to fully claim me, without a culture that wasn't a mismatch with my race. But we offered empathy and love to each other. They didn't have to extend this compassion to me, but many did, and I was grateful for it. I would never forget that when I was a child and at sea, they could have let me drown. Instead, they threw me a life preserver. This support, generosity, and love would be graciously extended to me by Black women throughout my entire life—in the form of sisterhood, a helping hand, a loving challenge, an encouraging word, and in the intersectional feminism created by Black women, which felt wide enough to shield more of me from most of the arrows society shoots at Brown girls. Many of the most important doors I have walked through in my life and career have been opened for me by Black women.

That's how I learned superpower number one, 360-degree vision: Black women taught me to see race, class, and gender simultaneously. To think intersectionally and act in solidarity.

I became a kid who traversed and code-switched between different communities—between my mom's white New Age friends, my Sri Lankan immigrant family (once I reconnected with them in my late teens), and the Black community—each of them home to people I loved and cared about. I was the kid who could make dahl, tell you the healing properties of crystals, and cornrow your hair. I could switch up my language, mannerisms, and vernacular on a dime—sometimes authentically, as I relaxed and vibed with the people I loved and felt most comfortable with, and sometimes performatively, to avoid being socially annihilated. I felt I could survive anywhere. And yet I fundamentally and painfully belonged nowhere. I was racially ambiguous in a place where few others were, so I was often regarded with uncertainty. My body was a constant site of mistrust, exotification, and othering. The older I got, the more I felt there was not a single place where I could fully relax and know that I wouldn't at some point be treated as an outsider, an impostor, suspect. At fifteen, I wrote in my journal, "I feel like I'm swimming in the ocean without any land to rest on. I am so tired."

As a teenager, I found comfort in writers and organizers who gave me words and frameworks to understand what was happening. I sat in the back corner of city buses devouring the writing of James Baldwin, bell hooks, Langston Hughes, Zora Neale Hurston, Cherríe Moraga, Howard Zinn, Gloria Anzaldúa, Toni Morrison, Arundhati Roy, Assata Shakur, and countless other thinkers whose words and worldviews felt like life preservers. I threw myself headlong into ethnic studies, adrift in confusion but grasping for clarity. At one point in my first undergrad year at the University of Washington, two of my African American studies professors took me out to lunch to thank me for volunteering in their offices all year. They asked me what my mother thought about my strong interest in ethnic studies. "Well, my mom is one of those white people who just doesn't see race. She's color-blind," I said with complete earnestness. I saw their eyebrows fly up as they exchanged looks, no doubt understanding my ravenous appetite for literature on race in a new light. Thinking back on that moment now, I chuckle. They must have been thinking "*Mmmhmm,* and *that* is exactly why this child is sitting right here."

Even as a teenager, I could see that so many people I loved

were excluded from belonging in ways that fundamentally limited their rights, opportunities, and joy. My immigrant family faced discrimination for their accents and brown skin. My Black friends and their families faced it for their race. My mom faced it for her gender. And the Black and Brown women in my life faced it on multiple fronts. If belonging didn't exist in any of the structures around me, I reasoned that I would need to create my own. I was fifteen when I started creating spaces where I could belong with fewer conditions and from which I could help advocate for a world of greater belonging for everyone. In high school I created a club and newspaper run by queer kids and kids of color organizing for ethnic studies. I left my home state and the University of Washington and transferred to Smith College in Massachusetts for my sophomore year. There, I and a group of mostly queer artists and activists created a student club called FIRE, which stood for—wait for it—Feminist Intercultural Revolutionary Encounter (Encounter because we needed the E). Only in your late teens can you be this dramatic and take yourself this seriously!

My classmates and I traveled to Philadelphia to march to demand freedom for the political prisoner Mumia Abu-Jamal and to Seattle to protest the WTO (World Trade Organization). We held campus teach-ins about the evils of the IMF (International Monetary Fund) and World Bank and hosted mixed-media art shows about Black and Brown resistance. We organized a rally on campus and took a group to the Bronx building where a classmate's family lived—and where the unarmed African immigrant Amadou Diallo had been gunned down days earlier by plainclothes police. The police said they thought he had a gun. The only thing they found in his hand was a wallet. He had been trying to give it to them, thinking he was being mugged. We stood in the vestibule and looked at the bullet-riddled walls. The police had fired forty-one shots. We were trying to make sense of the world, trying to face up to the pain in our communities, trying to make things better.

I expanded my own understanding of race in the United States. I read about the internment of Japanese Americans, the kidnapping of Native children who were forced into mission schools, the ongoing struggles for Hawaiian and Puerto Rican independence, the burning of Chinatowns and Black Wall Street that dared to prosper, and how the border crossed many Mexican people, not the other way around. I wrote my senior thesis on the connection between the Black Power movement and the Cuban Revolution. I interviewed members of the Black Panther Party and traveled to Cuba, where I saw how race as a construction moved differently in other colonial contexts. Most of all, I learned about the strength, creativity, and resilience of people of color.

An Outsider, Again

And then, just as I started to feel some comfort in my life, I was pulled out to sea again. From a young age, I had known I was attracted to women. But I had always suppressed and denied it. *God?* I remember thinking when I finally admitted to myself that I wasn't straight. *Did you feel I needed more things to make me an outsider?* At twenty-two, I came out of the closet. My mom didn't talk to me for a year. Aisha, my childhood neighbor who now had two kids who were my godkids, gave me the world's weirdest version of reassurance. "It's okay. God forgives even rapists and murderers, so I'm sure you'll be all right." Soon after, she broke off all contact.

During this rough time, the queer community did what it does best and held me in the embrace of chosen family—a tradition that has saved the lives of countless young queer kids whose blood family has shut them out. My queer elders were a calm and steady presence when I needed one, reminding me that "This too shall pass," their presence proof that we can survive, that we can grow old. My peers and I held each other up with a lot of love and the limited skills that most people in their early twenties can muster in processing loss. Holidays were hard and despite our attempts to numb the pain, the grief many of us held about our estranged families spilled over. At one holiday party, a friend let out a guttural wail for her estranged mother while vomiting tequila into the bathtub. Outside, another yelled about family members who had passed away before relationships could heal, insisting she wanted to die to be with them. She chased me in circles around her truck cursing me for refusing to give her the keys. On those heavy days the anguish felt like too much for our young hearts, and we did our best to save one another's lives. On lighter, summer days, we went to the clubs—Club Mango and Club Papi and Mami in San Francisco, and Butta in Oakland—and danced to the pounding rhythms of hip-hop, salsa, rap, dancehall, reggae, and house until we were drenched with sweat. In those moments I felt free. I felt liberated too, when I looked at my community and the many ways people expressed gender. Even as a cis woman, I had never felt comfortable for long on the super-femme end of the spectrum. My presentation fluctuated from soft butch to femme. With my queer people, in so many ways, I found the space to just be. My chosen family broadened, and eventually a few members of my Sri Lankan blood family came back into my life in positive ways too.

I was back on dry land for the most part. The pain of rejection around my queerness didn't linger. The community of support lifted it off of me quickly. But all the years of feeling like a freak and a weirdo because of my race stayed with me in powerful ways. In my thirties, Tricia and I wanted to have a child. I tried for over a year to get pregnant. Tricia is Jamaican and we wanted the child's race to reflect both of us, so we used Black sperm donors. I was unable to get pregnant. When our last known donor moved out of state and our money ran out to buy any more sperm from a bank, we hit a dead end. A friend of a friend stepped up to help. He was tall, ruggedly handsome, and kind. He was also white: Irish, straight from Ireland, in fact. We both liked him, but I refused to accept him as a donor if I was the one carrying the baby. My heart couldn't take the idea of bringing a child into the world who would look like me, who might suffer the same torment of living in U.S. racial apartheid in the wilderness without a shared community of people of their same race to claim and protect them. And that's how Tricia became the birth mother of our elder daughter. The experience of race and gender shapes our destinies in powerful ways. The journey to loving and accepting ourselves is not a linear one. We learn the lessons we need along the way. As a young person, I marveled at the wondrous resilience of the queer community: a people who had been shamed and shut out but had innovated to create pride and inclusion.

That's how I learned superpower number three, to be generous. Queer people of color taught me to rise by lifting others. If you want freedom for all people, look to those on the margins. If you want to build an inclusive society, listen to and lift the wisdom of those who have been shut out.

After college, I watched many of my Smith College peers head out to jobs making six figures on Wall Street. I headed for Oakland, California, the birthplace of the Black Panther Party, to make $23,000 a year as a community organizer. When I wasn't organizing, I was writing to support or document the work of movements.

Veteran organizer Gary Delgado sent me out to meet organizers across the country. I traveled to the rural, cotton-field-lined community of Tunica, Mississippi. There, I met Black organizers who were still battling the ghosts of Jim Crow, which were depriving their children's public schools of resources. They pointed out the small wooden churches along the road—one for each plantation. Most had been there since slavery. They were designed to keep enslaved Black people, and later Black sharecroppers, worshipping separately, rather than at a larger church where they could potentially organize in larger numbers. I walked down dusty desert roads in New Mexico's pueblos with Native American organizers Laurie and Sonny Weahkee. I learned about their fight to stop developers from running a major road through their sacred petroglyphs, an area of rock formations with fifteen thousand painted images where their ancestors had prayed and held ceremonies for thousands of years.

Standing in the twilight, at the place where the road was poised to be built, I talked to the developer, a white man in a cowboy hat. "Why not just route the road around the sacred site to not disturb it?" I asked him. The blood rose to his face. His eyes darted back and forth across the land in a frantic mix of fear and fury. "If we give in to them on this road," he said, "where does it end? What's to stop them from taking everything?" I looked at him standing there, against the backdrop of a mountain range, every inch of it covered with the lights of Western civilization, with everything the white man had already taken. I understood something then about those who are sick with the illness of white supremacy: their obsession with scarcity, their terror that others will do to them what they have done all over the world, the twisted logic that justifies their greed and dominance.

Reproductive justice leader Eveline Shen called me in to write a story on Asian girls organizing in Oakland. I listened to their stories about living hand to mouth on the meager wages their mothers earned working in sweatshops throughout the city's Chinatown garment district. Their families bought groceries at a store near where I lived. It sold goods that other stores considered not fresh enough to stock. It had almost no vegetables, but featured an entire case of malt liquor. These young women were strong, proud, and fierce, organizing for better pay and safer working conditions alongside their mothers.

I stood in the backyards of Latinx farmworkers, listening to the roar of crop duster planes that sprayed carcinogenic pesticides mere yards away from where their children were playing—children suffering serious asthma and other health problems as a result. In the tradition of Cesar Chavez and Dolores Huerta, they were courageously fighting and sometimes winning David-and-Goliath battles against agribusiness. I sat in living rooms, in Memphis, Tennessee—like that of the wonderful and only recently departed environmental justice organizer Doris Bradshaw—where Black women wept as they shared stories of losing their newborn babies, spouses, and other loved ones to health conditions caused by an old defense depot that had polluted the entire area.

In each of these places there was pain and suffering, but there was also strength, ingenuity, love, and resistance. These communities and the brave warriors fighting for their dignity had my heart. They changed me. My first year as a union organizer, I visited a home care worker named Maria at her house. We sat down across from each other at her kitchen table. Maria was a Chicana single mother who was also caring for her elderly father. Recently out of college, my mind was awash in theories and Audre Lorde quotes. Maria looked me dead in the eye and said, "This month I'm deciding between putting food on the table or buying medicine for my dad. How's the union going to help me with that?" I got it. It wasn't that she wasn't interested in theories; she was. It's just that whatever I was doing and saying needed to relate to her gaining the power to change her day-to-day material conditions. Ultimately, she became a powerful leader who did just that. That's what I love about real organizing. You can't ride on theories, concepts, and language in isolation. It cuts through the bullshit.

I spent over a decade working as a student, community, and then union organizer before entering philanthropy and founding Groundswell Fund, which grew into a pair of organizations— a 501(c)(3) and a 501(c)(4)—with a combined annual budget of $26 million, and one of the nation's premier funders of grassroots organizing led by WOC and trans and gender-nonconforming people of color. Like so many other WOC, my experiences drove me toward the superpowers—to see things from a 360-degree perspective, to act boldly, and to be generous in lifting others.

In my movement work, I met inspiring and effective freedom fighters from all walks of life. Still, when I think about the breadth of people in my life who are dearest to me—my white middle-class mother, my Sri Lankan immigrant relatives, my Jamaican co-parent, our two daughters (one Black and Irish, the other Black, Alaska Native, and Arab), my queer community (including my trans and non-binary loved ones)—there is one set of leaders whose ideas and praxis most often chart a path to freedom for everyone I love: WOC. Disproportionately bold in their truth telling, intersectional in their visioning, fighting in a way that leaves no one behind. The leadership that many WOC are bringing to movements for social change is not just important to us and our communities, it is important to everyone and every community. Supporting their leadership would become my life's work.

PART TWO

Superpower #1
360-Degree Vision

T he most critical leap in the evolution of the human species is not AI or commercial space travel. It is an evolution of consciousness that shifts us from fragmentation to wholeness. Wholeness is not sameness. It is not reducing the current cacophony of difference into a single uniform note. It is a harmonizing of infinite unique notes. It is about human beings coming into right relationship with the planet, with one another, and with ourselves. It is, at its beginning, a complete reversal of the colonial project of disconnection and at its end, a new way of being that humans have never fully realized before.

This is not a new idea. The concept of wholeness, oneness, right relationship, and mutuality is as old as time. Human beings of every color, creed, and generation have uplifted it. Most religions refer to it. Many Indigenous societies lived and live in ways that were and are in far greater alignment with it. Yuri Kochiyama, the Japanese American freedom fighter who held brother Malcolm X's head in her hands as he died, called us into it this way: "We must never forget that we belong to each other."

Humans have always struggled mightily to achieve wholeness due to our proclivity to categorize, divide, and extract in order to dominate one another. In every corner of the earth, we organize and rank ourselves by countless identity markers according to race, caste, gender, class, sexual orientation, age, ability, religion, and other characteristics. Western colonialism turbocharged this tendency toward fragmentation in every conceivable area of life. The United States was studied and many of its practices of racial oppression and segregation adopted by both Hitler's Germany and apartheid South Africa. Western medicine compartmentalizes the body so profoundly that one must go to different medical doctors to deal with ailments impacting different parts of the body, often receiving disjointed treatment plans that tackle each organ, each issue, in isolation. In this paradigm, mind and body were, until very recently, viewed as irrelevant to each other. Mainstream Western medicine has yet to acknowledge what so many cultures have taken for granted for centuries through the study of the chakras, Chi, and other such elements: that the physical body of muscle and bone is powerfully affected by the energy body. In British colonies, where traditional drumming, singing, and dancing were banned among African and Native peoples, and puritanical values extended much of this to the broader population, there was a concerted attempt to cleave human beings from their most basic channels of human expression through the body, voice, and music. So many of us have had to fight our way back into connection with even our ability to *feel* in a society geared toward numbing out through shopping, medicating with drugs and alcohol, overworking, and otherwise distracting ourselves from what hurts. How might our behavior shift toward kindness and justice if we remembered how to *feel* and empathize with the joy and pain of the earth and all of its living beings? If we remembered how to process and release, instead of just stuffing down the pain in our bodies and minds?

Even the Western social justice movements that are ostensibly operating to lessen divisions and promote unity operate (with great encouragement from philanthropy) in stark issue silos, tackling climate change, reproductive rights, police brutality, and other causes with little shared analysis about the tight interrelationship of the systems that harm the earth and the beings living on it.

So much of the fracture of humanity is about our seeming inability to upgrade away from two bugs in the original factory settings of our species: greed and dominance. A lot of people in movement talk about revolution but are fundamentally operating from these same factory settings. They are not trying to break out of the habit of dominance, they just want to change who gets to dominate. They want the group they are a part of to have its turn on top. It's about as revolutionary as rearranging the chairs on the deck of the *Titanic*.

People who try to upgrade often become targets. Said movement ancestor Bernice Johnson Reagon, "There was a time when folks saw the major movement force coming out of the Black community. Then, the hottest thing became the Native Americans and the next, students' rights and the next, the anti-war movement or whatever. The movement force just rolled around hitting various issues. Anytime you find a person showing up at all of those struggles . . . one, study with them, and two, protect them. They're gonna be in trouble shortly because they are the most visible ones. They hold the key to turning the century with our principles and ideals intact."[1]

MINI MASTER CLASS
Norma Wong

A slight yet strong figure with eyes that sparkle with humor and wisdom, Rinzai Zen Buddhist teacher and social justice leader Norma Wong is one of the most influential elders guiding movement leaders today. I have yet to attend a Zoom meeting she hosts where less than one hundred people show up and stay—sometimes for four hours at a time—and like many leaders, I've had the privilege of learning from her in person. Of Native Hawaiian and Hakka ancestry, she has been a grassroots organizer, a Zen Buddhist priest, an elected state legislator, and the right-hand staffer to the governor of Hawaii. Among her many historic victories is the successful negotiation for the munitions cleanup of Kahoʻolawe, an island sacred to native Hawaiians that was used as a bombing target by U.S. and allied forces. Many of her teachings are shared in her recent book, *When No Thing Works: A Zen and Indigenous Perspective on Resilience, Shared Purpose, and Leadership in the Timeplace of Collapse.* She described the importance of wholeness this way: "The Tao Te Ching and most Indigenous narratives echo each other in flagging the breaking of humanity from the universe. We have strayed from the source. Conflict is the place where you understand where things are not whole. You can see, feel, taste where things are not right. The extent to which mending this becomes a collective responsibility, rather than one in which you count on a singular figure or leader, the better. All under heaven intact is the mother strategy from which all other strategies emanate. If it does not have all under heaven intact you are entering the binary and the state of war. You must go to the place where the universe is less broken."

If we make this evolutionary upgrade to wholeness, we will stop destroying one another and the planet. We will survive, and even thrive. If we fail to make it, our species will go extinct. The time left to leap is dwindling. Many of the most important innovations about how we come back together come from the people who human societies have done the most to break apart. Who these people are varies across time, space, country, and culture. In the United States, WOC, who live in the crosshairs of patriarchy, racism, classism, and colonialism, are one such people, and the 360-degree vision we bring to dismantling these is an essential tool.

3

The Whole Truth

The School Dance

For women of color, 360-degree vision starts at the micro level of our families and daily lives. My daughter Kwali was in the second grade when she came home from school one day crying. She held a bright pink flier that her teacher had handed out at the end of class. DADDY-DAUGHTER DANCE! it proclaimed in large bubble letters. "All my friends are going," she said, sobbing. "And I can't go." The obvious reason being that there was no daddy to be found in our two-mom household. My wife, Tricia, and I exchanged looks and sat down at the kitchen table to talk it over with her.

This was just the latest in a series of unfortunate events at Kwali's new school. We had moved from Oakland, California, to a small city just outside Tacoma, Washington, to be closer to my aging mother and to settle in a place where we could afford to buy a house. To say the move was a culture shock would be a huge understatement.

Oakland is a mecca for queer families of color. Tricia and I had lived there for seventeen years. We thoroughly enjoyed being in the city that had more lesbian couples per capita than any other major city in the nation.[1] When we began planning to have kids, there were so many other queer women on the same journey that the local queer mamas' community support group, called Baby-buds, was full, prompting us to launch another chapter with other mothers. For years, our Babybuds chapter of queer women of color—about six couples and a few single women—gathered in folding chairs in living rooms and around potlucks at kitchen ta-bles to share our hopes and dreams, our anxieties, and our tri-umphs. We traded notes about sperm banks, doctors, and midwives to use or avoid. We held tree-planting ceremonies for miscarriages and showers for babies on the way.

When you are queer, pregnancy often takes a lot of time and money. Tricia and I had to pay thousands out of pocket for a stan-dard doctor-administered intrauterine insemination (IUI) proce-dure that was entirely free to insured straight couples with fertility issues. This is because most insurance companies, including ours, required nine to ten months of "attempts" at conception before covering the procedure's cost. Straight couples could just walk in, say "We've been trying for a year," and have everything covered. Their word was enough. Tricia and I had to produce a paper trail that proved that we had, under the observation of a doctor, been trying for that same length of time via IUIs—which cost several hundred dollars a pop.

By the time Kwali was born, we had drained all of our savings and had run up our credit. Nest eggs that many straight couples put to use after their kids are born—to buy a house, set up a col-lege fund, pay for quality childcare—are empty by the time many queer families finally welcome our kids. The process can be over-whelming. I was working in philanthropy when we were trying for Kwali, and one day I had baby making so thoroughly on my brain that I had an entire conversation with a colleague about donors before realizing, as an uneasy look slowly spread across her face, that she thought we were talking about philanthropic donors when in fact I was discussing sperm donors. Whoops! The infrastructure in the Bay Area still had a long way to go to support queer families, but our community was strong. No matter what we came up against, we knew we could at least go to a Babybuds meeting to laugh and cry about it all.

After a time, there was a whole set of kids among the Babybuds crew. Our children grew up together like a sprawling extended family, seeing one another on camping trips, at Easter egg hunts, holiday parties, playdates, and everything in between. Many of our kids would attend the same schools together over the years. Hetero norms and sexist thinking didn't have much oxygen in that environment. When a boy at my daughter's school claimed that girls couldn't be firefighters, he was quickly corrected. One of his classmate's two moms was training to be a firefighter. It was such a fabulous gay world that we had actual conversations about what we would do if and when our kids told us one day that they were straight. How we would make sure they weren't made to feel like outsiders or weirdos, and that they knew they were loved and accepted for who they were. By contrast, Kwali had been stung by anti-Blackness by the age of three, even though she was in an environment where most of the kids were Black or Brown. One day, I found her crying in front of the mirror as she tried to brush her Afro hair straight so the girls would let her play Elsa, from *Frozen,* on the playground. Despite this, she had zero concept of any stigma attached to people being LGBTQ.

All of that changed in 2017, when we moved to Washington State. Like so many others, after seventeen years in our beloved Oakland, we were gentrified out. The housing crash of 2008 hit the East Oakland neighborhood where we had bought our first home hard. At night we lay awake, listening to the pop-pop-pop of gunshots, the screech of tires, and the sound of police helicopters overhead. Three young brothers were shot and killed on our corner. Yellow caution tape blocked off streets. Flowers and candles remembering the slain were the norm along sidewalks. When our first daughter was born in 2011, Tricia and I thought long and hard about whether to move or stay. We loved our neighbors and the beauty and resilience of the community. But the violence was wearing on us. As a young child, Tricia had been affected by gun violence in the ghettos of Kingston, Jamaica, before moving to her grandmother Ruby's house in the countryside, and then again after immigrating to a rough part of Dorchester, Massachusetts. I had grown up fairly sheltered in a quiet, middle-class neighborhood in Seattle, but I couldn't help thinking that my Sri Lankan family hadn't traveled across oceans to save their necks from a civil war only for me to be shot in the United States. Tricia and I sold our house and rented away from the gun violence, hoping to save up enough money to buy in a safer area of the city. Soon it became clear that affording a house in Oakland was a pipe dream. Tricia convinced me to move to the Pacific Northwest, about an hour south of Seattle. The cost of living was lower there and, most of all, she reasoned, we would be closer to my mom, who was getting older and who I knew would need the support of her only child at some point.

We chose to move to a city just outside of Tacoma, because it was one of the most racially diverse cities in the area, had highly rated public schools, and was near the natural beauty of the Salish Sea. We failed to realize that it was diverse because it was a military town, which meant the population was largely socially conservative. Compared to the Bay Area, it felt like we had boarded a time machine and been transported back thirty years. Kwali's school, like many in the region, had a student body that was majority kids of color being taught by a nearly all-white staff.

During her first week of school, Kwali informed us that she needed only one of us to pick her up at her bus stop after school. This struck us as odd. She had always happily declared, "Two mommies! Two mommies!" whenever we showed up together to pick her up. Tricia and I both juggled busy schedules, so when the stars aligned for us to turn up at pickup together, it was rare and special. Kwali later told us that one of the girls on her bus had warned her that if other kids found out she had two moms, she would be bullied. A few weeks later, at lunch, a kid decided to do a poll at her table. "Who here wants to be gay when you grow up?" No one raised their hands, and some kids, to show just how much they did not want to be gay, ducked down to put their hands on the floor. The lunch monitor watched the entire exchange and did nothing. More tears after school from Kwali.

Tricia and I talked to the principal, the teachers, and the district. We pushed until they added books on same-sex families to the library and the teachers' circle-time reading, put up rainbow flags in the office, and committed to training staff. By the start of the following year, Kwali had the confidence to introduce herself to another kid by saying, "I have two moms, and there's nothing wrong with that." A bit of a shell-shocked introduction, but an improvement on hiding out in shame. The kid said back to her, "I know there's nothing wrong with it. My grandma is gay." This was a big deal—up until that point, Kwali had been the only kid at her school who was out about having queer family.

Unfortunately, homophobia was only the beginning. When race came up in a conversation with her classmates and a kid happened to say, "Kwali is Black," one of her white friends jumped to her defense as if she had just been insulted. "No, she's not! Don't say that about her!" Thankfully, our daughter was unfazed. She had such a strong dose of Black pride at home and from her time in Oakland, where even the most elite private schools have units on the Black Panthers. As her parents, though, we were worried about the drip, drip, drip effect of it all.

And the drips continued. One winter evening, the school held a "multicultural fair." A circle of folding tables in the lunchroom featured some beautiful displays about the Philippines, Samoa, and Ghana, from families proud of their roots. Alongside them was an exhibit titled "America." It was a random collection of miniature objects: a Ferris wheel, American flags, hamburgers, Twinkies, bottles of Coca-Cola—and figurines of white people.

Then, in preparation for Veterans Day, the school choir began learning a military song about bombing and shooting people that included the lines "At 'em boys, give 'er the gun! . . . Hands of men blasted the world asunder . . . Souls of men dreaming of skies to conquer . . . With scouts before and bombers galore."

Soon after, during the third-grade unit on European colonialization of the Americas—a time that witnessed the genocide of twenty million Indigenous people—I happened to pass by Kwali's computer (during Covid). Her teacher cheerfully and unironically asked the class over Zoom, "Who here would have liked to be a conquistador?"

With each drip, we spoke up and demanded change from teachers, the principal, and the district. We challenged the principal on the wisdom of elementary schoolchildren singing lyrics about bombs and guns when school shootings were at an all-time high and the district had already had two recent lockdowns due to threats of gun violence. He said the military families would revolt if he nixed the song this year (we kept her home that day), but he agreed to pull it the following year. I asked the teacher who was surveying the class about being conquistadors if she thought it might also be appropriate to poll the class on who would have liked to have been a Nazi, since both groups committed genocide. She dropped that slide and the question from the curriculum. We secured agreements from the school and district to adjust the curriculum around race and queer families.

It wasn't easy. At one point, the principal—a white man—hoped we would understand the tough position he was in trying to keep all of the parents happy when on the one hand he had parents like us in his office, wanting more attention to equity, and on the other he had parents who didn't believe white people and people of color were equal to each other at all, and were adamant that being gay was a sin. What was he to do? We reminded him that he was legally required to ensure the taxpayer-funded tent of the public school he ran was big enough to be inclusive for all students, but not so large that it met the standards of raving bigots. Tricia volunteered weekly in Kwali's class. I did a presentation for her class about feminism and racial justice. Then we took Kwali to the Family Dance—the former Daddy-Daughter Dance, renamed in response to our demands. Kwali danced her heart out and had a ball.

Eventually, we moved to Tacoma, which was more progressive, but our leadership and advocacy in that first city left Kwali's school a different place than it had been when we arrived. The problems we felt compelled to fight to keep our kid safe—racism, sexism, homophobia, gun violence, colonialism—were hurting other kids too. Queer kids, Native kids, kids from queer families, and kids of color can now see themselves more reflected and less disrespected in the books their teachers read, the events their school hosts, and the curriculum they learn. By extension, all of the kids now have a better shot at being exposed to ideas about inclusion and equity. Kids of all genders who don't have dads around—including the many kids being raised by single moms, grandmothers, or other relatives, as well as the many kids whose dads are away on military deployments or lost their lives on active duty—now feel welcome at the Family Dance.

On a hyperlocal scale, this is what I think of as 360-degree vision in action. It's a vision that millions of women of color have from living our daily lives in the crosshairs of multiple forces of oppression. In the face of separation, exclusion, and silence, this vision looks toward wholeness, belonging, and truth telling. It's a vision that begins in the family and spreads to communities, benefiting everyone in their ecosystem.

Women of color movement leaders are doing the same in changing systems and policies at every level of society. Using a multi-issue approach, they tackle problems simultaneously and holistically.

The Identity Coat Check and Telling the Whole Truth

Beginning in the mid-1990s, I spent ten years working at the grassroots within various social justice movements, from labor to racial, economic, and environmental justice, to immigrant and LGBTQ rights. In each of these movements, I felt the pressure to check parts of myself at the door in order to enter: my gender, my race, my queerness. It was as if there were an unspoken coat check where you were politely (or not so politely) invited to hang up pieces of yourself upon arrival at the union meeting, the rally, the strategy session—then collect them when you left.

Unity and wholeness produce strength. Division and fragmentation foster weakness. The coat check is a form of divide and conquer for both the individual and the collective. It has two consequences for movements: First, it reduces the number of people who participate in them because there are entire swaths of the population who would rather turn around and leave than coat-check pieces of themselves as a condition of entry, or to work in movements where they don't see their lives and the issues they care about reflected. Second, it creates points of weakness that the right can easily exploit to tear down rights for everyone. When you pretend, for instance, that women and transgender people don't exist, you refuse to protect them. In doing so, you create an opening through which the right can drive bad policy and other attacks that impact everyone.

When organizations pretend that any issue—from climate to healthcare—isn't raced, classed, and gendered in powerful ways, it leads to fighting for wins that leave many people behind. It yields wage fights that fail to address the gender pay gap, which as we know is worse for Black women than white women, even more egregious for Latinas and Native women, and worst of all for transgender women of color. It fuels negotiations over health benefits that neglect reproductive and transgender healthcare, allowing employers to get away with not covering contraception, abortion, midwifery, and gender-affirming care. It results in messaging to the public around carbon reduction that is focused on wonky language about "parts per billion" that makes the average person's eyes glaze over—instead of issues that people understand and care about, like high asthma rates that affect people in their neighborhoods, especially neighborhoods of color. Unsurprisingly, those who are left out turn away from movements. And just like that, movements cut themselves off from their greatest power source: the populations most impacted by injustice and most motivated to fight with all their might for the boldest solutions.

When women of color refuse the coat check, they push movements to tell the whole truth. This is not an easy task because there are a lot of "progressives" out here telling half-truths. They're telling the truth about climate change but denying the existence of white supremacy. They're telling the truth about economic inequality while glossing over the problem of patriarchy. And they're telling the truth about homophobia yet ignoring transphobia and xenophobia. We can't get to freedom if we're not fully honest about all problems that confront us.

Like most feminists of color, I was greatly influenced by Black feminist thought generally and the 1977 Combahee River Collective Statement in particular, which noted:

> Black feminist politics also have an obvious connection to movements for Black liberation, particularly those of the 1960s and 1970s. Many of us were active in those movements (Civil Rights, Black nationalism, the Black Panthers). . . . It was our experience and disillusionment within these liberation movements, as well as experience on the periphery of the white male left, that led to the need to develop a politics that was anti-racist, unlike those of white women, and anti-sexist, unlike those of Black and white men. . . . We also often find it difficult to separate race from class from sex oppression because in our lives they are most often experienced simultaneously.

Telling the whole truth is not purist politics that cancels or discards those who aren't "woke" or aligned on every issue. Every single one of us is in a constant state of evolving our thinking and connection to others. Smart organizing requires us to meet people where they are at with love, and team with them where alignment exists. This offers them opportunities to expand their empathy and solidarity, just as they will surely offer us opportunities to expand ours. Telling the whole truth is how we can bring a fragmented humanity back into wholeness. It is also about playing good defense.

The far right knows where we are fractured. They know the areas where we lack the backbone or language or political will to stand with certain communities. And, like spotting a hole in our defense, that is exactly where they drive the lane to score points that diminish the rights and liberties of everyone. They knew it in Houston in 2015, when they used the image of trans people and bathrooms to repeal a nondiscrimination ordinance that would have protected many groups, including cis women and people of color, from bias in housing, employment, and other areas, a strategy that has now been exported to many other states.[2] Because progressives were unwilling to stand with trans people, the ordinance was defeated and everyone lost out.

For decades the far right has also known that they could count on most progressive organizations to leave reproductive rights and justice groups alone, with no backup, when challenges to abortion came up. Antiabortion rhetoric was never about just one policy here or there; it was a way for the right to energize their base to elect people who would then vote against a whole host of progressive values, including economic justice, climate justice, and immigrant rights. It is only now, after the fall of *Roe,* that the Democratic Party has stopped treating abortion as a political third rail, beginning to center it in its party platform and the messaging of candidates.

Telling the whole truth is also about playing good offense. Half-truths don't energize the largest progressive base. We must stop thinking we can't walk and chew gum at the same time, that we can't talk about issues like race and gender at the same time. We have to stop underestimating the capacity of the average person to deal with complexity.

In my early twenties, I worked as a union organizer for the

Service Employees International Union (SEIU, Local 715), supporting home care workers. I loved the workers, who were mostly middle-aged or older immigrant women. They reminded me of my favorite auntie, who had also been a home care worker after she came to this country. The workers treated me with great affection. I think I reminded them of their own daughters and nieces. After the attacks of 9/11, the union advised us to stay out of any protests against the U.S. invasion of Iraq, urging workers to focus instead on bread-and-butter issues like wages and benefits in their contract negotiations. They thought geopolitics would be too hairy and complex for workers to understand, that it might undermine the unity and focus needed to win contract fights. But the war was on everyone's minds and kept coming up in union meetings.

I found the home care workers I represented to be quite astute on the topic. Many of them came from countries that were suffering because of U.S. military involvement. One of my shop stewards was from El Salvador and lived there during the U.S.-backed military operation in her country. Her eyes were riveted to the floor as she told me, "I remember walking out the door of my house to go to the store. I had to step over dead bodies in my garden to get to the road." As a result, she felt for the Iraqi people and wanted to stand in solidarity with them. Also, many of the workers had children or grandchildren who had enlisted in the U.S. military because the public schools in the ghettos and barrios where they lived had failed to provide them with a way out of poverty. College was out of reach. For many, the military felt like the only way out.

The workers were worried about their children being sent into harm's way to fight this war. Some wanted to join an anti-war demonstration in San Francisco. I supported them. We marched together carrying the SEIU banner. Far from distracting, dividing, or alienating people from engaging in union fights, the experience of talking together about this other dimension of their lives—and taking action together in solidarity with people in a global context—deepened the bonds between the workers and their trust in the union. Instead of being a distraction or dilution, it was yet another point of connection and fortification. They were stronger and more united in labor fights as a result, which made them more of a force in union campaigns.

The whole truth doesn't scare people away—it draws them in. Most people prefer it. As Audre Lorde said, "There is no such thing as a single-issue struggle, because we do not lead single-issue lives." People like a vision that they can see their whole selves in, and the whole selves of their loved ones and their communities. When movement efforts dare to fight with this kind of vision, they attract support, and they win.

The Power of Bold Demands

The Reproductive Health Equity Act, established in Oregon in 2017, is arguably the best law in the nation protecting reproductive freedom. And it wouldn't exist if not for the leadership of women of color who brought their 360-degree vision to the issue. Like most states, Oregon has long been home to a pro-choice coalition consisting of Reproductive Freedom for All (formerly NARAL), Planned Parenthood, and the ACLU. Over the years, this coalition had some victories on abortion and contraception. But it was a mostly white group, and it hadn't been able to put together a multi-issue or multiracial coalition. This weakness began to hurt its ability to win on even its core issues. For several years the coalition put forth a bill with a narrower set of demands, without coverage for trans or undocumented people, and lost resoundingly. They tried again. This time, though, women of color got active in the coalition and proposed a radical new idea: expand the bill to include public funding for full-spectrum reproductive health care—including abortion and postpartum care—and cover everyone, including people who are poor, undocumented, transgender, or gender nonconforming.

This new bill reflected 360-degree vision, accounting for race, class, immigration status, and gender in a far more expansive way. But in a policy landscape littered with laws that are drafted to cater to the political middle—and exclude the most vulnerable communities—the original coalition members strongly opposed the new legislation. They raised their concerns. If they had failed in passing a bill that asked for less, how on earth would they pass a bill that asked for more? The women of color, however, were adamant: More was needed to make the bill meaningful in the daily lives of the communities they represented. They refused to abide by the usual politics of expediency and incrementalism and made the case that a bold and holistic bill could draw support through grassroots organizing. The coalition agreed to give it a shot.

It is important to note that the coalition was willing to lend its support to the new bill only after considerable effort on the part of activists who had long been overlooked. For years, several organizations led by people of color had been tilling the soil for reproductive justice in Oregon. A relatively new national organization led by women of color—All* Above All—worked directly with NARAL, providing political education and training to activists to work effectively and respectfully with organizations that were staffed predominately by people of color.

"White-led organizations often come in with their agenda and assume everyone will move that agenda without any input," recalled Destiny Lopez, then the co-director of All*. "The train is already leaving the station and you are inviting people on board for the ride without talking to them about the itinerary. We helped them understand the history of why reproductive justice groups existed, and the history of oppression of people of color within the movement."

One of the organizations All* prepared them to work with was Western States Center, a multiracial regional powerhouse and reproductive justice (RJ) champion in ten western states. In partnership with the Bay Area–based RJ organization Forward Together, All* supported BRAVE, a cohort of people of color–led grassroots organizing shops that wanted to integrate RJ into their work. Patiently and diligently nourished over many years by phenomenal RJ leaders like Aimee Santos-Lyons, Kalpana Krishnamurthy, Eveline Shen, and Dana Ginn Paredes, BRAVE included a growing number of organizations that were becoming steeped in an analysis of race, class, gender, and reproductive justice. Some of these were among the organizations that ultimately joined the pro-choice coalition and pushed for the new version of the Oregon bill. "NARAL had the access to the state legislature and was able to open doors, but ultimately the BRAVE cohort was who was seen on the Hill," Lopez explained. "At their peak, BRAVE had a lobby day of 150 people of color."

Although the new bill alienated some people, it attracted far more, securing the support of immigrant and LGBTQ rights organizations, as well as healthcare reform organizations, all of whom had an interest in backing it. The groups galvanized their constituents, who could now see themselves and their priorities reflected in the bill and created the tipping point needed for its successful passage. Backbone, solidarity, telling the whole truth, and organizing paid off and continued to do so when, the following year, voters decisively rejected a constitutional amendment meant to challenge the bill and restrict state funding for abortion.

Amy Casso, Western States Center's program director at the time, said, "When you ask for what you want and refuse to let others drive a wedge to privilege one community over another, you just might win."[3]

We've also seen what it costs movements when women of color face too many barriers to bring their 360-degree visions through. My friend and colleague Katherine Grainger, managing partner at Civitas Public Affairs Group, was a young lawyer when she wrote the marriage equality bill in New York. Katherine is a Black lesbian and a diligent student of long-arc strategy toward winning transformational change many generations into the future. She thinks expansively and cares deeply about queer and trans people of color. On winning marriage equality in New York she said, "It's something I feel very proud of. My critique is, what if we started the marriage fight with a larger understanding of what it would take to reach gay liberation and how marriage could be a tool or tactic to get us one-quarter of the way there? My older self would be able to have those conversations. My younger self was writing forty-five versions of religious-exemption language to get the bill passed."

The critique on gay marriage by many in the LGBTQ community is that it was myopic as an end goal. Indeed, after its passage at the federal level, many LGBTQ-rights efforts closed down and funding for LGBTQ rights dried up overnight, leaving the most marginalized members of our community (queers of color, transgender people, low- or no-income queers) still out in the cold on key issues like housing, employment, medical care, and violence. A segment of the gay rights movement, largely driven by affluent white gay men, celebrated and went home. Katherine acknowledged the importance of the marriage win and some of its unexpected outcomes. "However you feel about the policy of marriage itself, it helped to destigmatize being queer. This is a very powerful tool." Her nieces and nephews, she said, are having a vastly different experience growing up in a world with far less stigma around being LGBTQ. I agree with her wholeheartedly on this point. She told me, "If we had really thought about a long-arc version of what comes after marriage, we could continue to use the power of that destigmatization to win future fights, starting with trans [rights]. Young people are very open on the gender nonbinary and trans rights, but we didn't keep the political power in place for that to play out at scale. This is the kind of thinking movements need to include in their strategies." Katherine now leads and supports policy work for long-arc change, especially around expanding gender justice and dismantling patriarchy.

Women of color making bold demands—by tapping into 360-degree vision and organizing a grassroots base to fight for them—is a growing trend in American politics. While prevailing political strategies go narrow and calculate victories by throwing people under the bus, 360-degree strategies win by going broad and leaving no one behind.

4

The Power in Belonging

Belonging is a core human need. It's right up there with food, water, and shelter. Belonging is about safety and love and well-being. Those without it often have higher stress, more illness, and shorter life expectancies. There are many places that people, even marginalized people, can feel a sense of belonging: in a support group, at a book club, on a team, at a place of worship, or in a house in the ballroom scene. Movement isn't necessary for this. Movement spaces are necessary as places in which we find some degree of belonging within a group/organization *and* from which we can kick open the doors for more people to belong in the larger society: to access housing, healthcare, education, employment, safety, and the full right to participate in civic life.

This expansive desire to create more belonging in society—for ourselves and our loved ones—is at the root of why many women of color work for social change. At its best, it is the act of composting pain into something positive. Poet and actor Sarah Jones voices the sting of social exclusion that drives many people into movement work. "My mother's skin was white, my father's skin was black, and there was a sense that something was wrong with us walking around in the world in Washington, D.C. I felt afraid, like I didn't belong, couldn't belong, and could not quite understand why. That inquiry—why don't I fit? Where do I fit? And are there other people who are also suffering?—there was a real sense of wanting to have more freedom not just for myself but for anyone else who could relate. That is at the root of anything I've tried to do."

An Organizer's Dream

The power of a movement is directly related to the number of people in its ranks. Organizations that foster an environment of belonging attract more people. Building those ranks—recruiting and retaining people—is hard work! Any organizer who knows the painstaking work of going door-to-door and phone banking—to motivate even twenty people to turn out to a community or union meeting—knows what a remarkable moment we were in post-Trump. Rooms that would have taken days of door knocking to fill prior to Trump are packed without much effort at all.

Never before has such a large percentage of the U.S. population flocked to social activism. The Women's March was the largest rally ever on U.S. soil. The racial uprisings of 2020 were the largest protest movement in the country's history. Just two years into the Trump presidency, a poll showed that most Americans had attended some type of protest or demonstration—many for the first time in their lives. Movements have the chance to bring millions of new people into their ranks to power a much-needed sea change in policies, systems, and culture. The opportunity to scale and sustain the grassroots base of support for social justice has never been as ripe as it is today.

To seize this opportunity, movement organizations must do two things effectively: organize and unify. Organize to transform what might otherwise be one-off activism—attendance at a single march or rally—into sustained engagement over the long haul. And unify to build solidarity in the face of forces that seek to divide and conquer, to help people link arms across various differences—race, class, gender, immigration status—to protect the most vulnerable communities and win liberation for all people. Neither of these can happen without organizations that can properly welcome people into environments of relative inclusion and belonging. Grassroots base-building organizations need to make people feel welcome.

To do this, organizations must avoid toxic belonging. Toxic belonging can develop if the bar is too low and conditions for belonging are too few, allowing people who willfully and carelessly harm others to stay in the group with no intervention—for example, letting the sexist who belittles and harasses women to go unchecked. At the other end, toxic belonging can exist if the bar is too high, conditions for belonging too numerous, holding people to an unreachable set of standards—and shaming and tossing them out when they can't meet them—for example, publicly shaming rather than kindly calling in a well-meaning elder who uses language like "minorities," "Hispanic," or "ladies and gentlemen" because they are not up on the latest racial justice or gender non-binary lingo. This results in a climate of fear and silence instead of care and learning.

More than one movement organization has been reduced from a larger number of people that could have accomplished something together to a handful of liberal arts majors who talk to one another in social justice jargon, agree on almost everything, complain about everyone else, and are too small in number to effect much change. Too high a bar equals 100 percent self-righteousness and 0 percent power to do anything of consequence in society. As author and racial justice leader Rinku Sen said, when building a coalition, it's not enough to have member organizations that are ideologically aligned, they must also have people power, "otherwise zero plus zero equals zero."

Few things give good organizers more anguish than to watch the movement respond to one of the single best organizing opportunities in the history of this country—when crowds of people are ready to roll their sleeves up for social change—by making the barrier to entry impossibly high. We are living in an era of barriers.

I was raised in a community and labor-organizing culture in the era of bridges. When I think back on some of my comrades who have made transformative changes in our world, very few would have survived today's environment. I think of Cindy Hernandez, a Chicana and Apache woman and shop steward in SEIU's home care division. When her site organizer, a white guy, quit and I was hired, she told my boss, "I don't want no bitches." Without missing a beat, my boss, a quick-witted woman from Mexico City, replied, "Well, how about a gay bitch?" Cindy was tough as hell, and we locked horns more than once, but she was a great organizer. We spent hours driving around in my car to the homes of other workers, the union hall, and legislative visits in Sacramento. She lives in Pacifica, a remarkable neighborhood in that the developers didn't snag land in time to build massive resorts and so the simplest, working-class row houses stretch for miles, with stunning views of the Pacific Ocean. We would sit on her sofa and chat about the union, her kids, our survivor stories, all of it. We rolled up our sleeves and built a relationship based on respect for each other. And we helped home care workers win tangible improvements in pay and benefits. She grew, and I grew.

I think of Cathy Lerza, a white woman roughly thirty years my elder, who was my supervisor when I first entered philanthropy. One of my first encounters with Cathy was in a meeting that I was facilitating when a few minutes in, she interrupted me and took over facilitation. I felt completely undermined. For a moment I was furious. Being young and hotheaded, I thought seriously about telling her off as soon as the meeting wrapped up. Then I took a deep breath and decided to get curious about where things would go if I took the time to get to know her. After working together for a while, grappling and giving each other feedback, she became a mentor and one of my biggest supporters as I built Groundswell Fund. When Groundswell had just begun to take off but was still quite fledgling, I was down for months with a serious back injury. Despite my protests that it was far too much for me to receive from her, Cathy insisted on diligently churning out scores of funding proposals that I didn't have the physical strength to type. Even more astounding, she did this while sitting by the bedside of her dying mother. With this act of kindness, she helped to save the organization that I cared so much about and that would offer so much support to WOC and trans people of color. Cathy would have my back again and again over the years, becoming one of my most trusted confidants and dearest friends. What I felt from her was more than just kindness, it was love— love for me and love for the communities Groundswell was supporting. I felt the same love and care for her. It was true solidarity. We learned and continue to learn so much from each other. The lesson wasn't to go quiet, but to have the hard conversations with a good measure of grace, for long enough, to see if growth, empathy, and connection were possible, to see if hearts could open. I cringe to think of the friendship I might have lost had I acted rashly and just called her out after that first encounter.

I think of the two thousand mostly affluent donors who gave to Groundswell my last year there, putting money into the control of WOC and trans and gender-nonconforming people of color to distribute. They stayed in it through difficult conversations to bridge vastly different life experiences, and over time, *love* developed to build the kind of trust to move $100 million to the movement over the years. I don't think any of it would have happened if my spirit of engagement was what is becoming the norm in so much of movement today. I fear that I would have written off all these people without a second thought. Today, even people who have worked in movement for years, who are steeped in the ideology and lingo of social justice and savvy at navigating differences, are struggling not to be pulled up and dragged down for some small infraction or another, real or imagined.

There is a brand of almost academic elitism in the purist language and jargon that people are expected to know and practice under penalty of callout and cancellation. It's not that language and terms shouldn't evolve—they should. It's the extreme, punitive demand of instant uptake and conformity under penalty of public shaming and humiliation that is the problem. Most movement people will admit that their family members, the people who know and love them and sit around the dinner table with them daily, could not be in movement spaces without being skewered for some mistake. We can't build a base of ordinary people like this. When I spoke with LaTosha Brown, co-founder of Black Voters Matter and the Southern Black Girls and Women's Consortium, she nodded with understanding. "It's a gotcha culture."

It's as if we have lost the ability to tell the difference between someone with ill or lazy intent who is dangerous to us and someone with goodwill who is just in a different place on their learning journey with less skill or fluency. Countless organizations are missing out on the best organizing opportunity in U.S. history as a result of this dynamic. Organizer and strategist Ejeris Dixon wrote, "Just as punishment does not transform behavior, neither does judgment. When we make judgment into one of our primary organizing strategies, we reduce the trust needed to create safety."[1]

How do we know when to build a bridge and when to build a wall? How do we meet people where they are with love, rigor, and encouragement on their path to liberation? It begins with facing and having compassion for ourselves for our mistakes on the evolutionary path to greater consciousness. In her seminal essay, "Coalition Politics," a young Bernice Johnson Reagon recalled a song she once wrote in which she referred to Vietnamese people as having "slanted eyes" and Indian people as having "straight black hair."[2] "Did you see what I did?" she recalled. "Reduced these people to the slant of their eyes. If I ran into a Vietnamese who didn't have slanted eyes, I'd be in trouble. . . . [I] reduced all of the people in India to straight hair! Then I ran into some of them who were so black and some of them got kinky hair. Do you understand what I'm talking about?" We don't always get it right, but our principles carry us to greater heights. Writes Reagon, "The thing that must survive you is not just the record of your practice, but the principles that are the basis of your practice."

It's not about giving people a pass to continue to speak and behave in ways that are ignorant and harmful; it's about calling them in with a firm but kind invitation that's not mired in purist politics. When did we decide to stop reaching for people and start shutting them out? How did it get so bad?

The Frenzy of Fear

As much as we might hate to admit it, one of the central projects of the Trump administration was a smashing success: driving a majority of the population into a frenzy of fear and division. For his supporters, this fear deepened the already well-worn neural pathways that allow people to skip over facts and evidence to scapegoat others for their problems and derive a sense of belonging by marginalizing others as an external threat. The tired refrains—"Mexicans are taking our jobs," "Black people are draining the public coffers," "Queers are destroying family values," "Arabs are terrorizing us"—grew day by day, culminating in the January 6, 2021, attack on the U.S. Capitol. What the left is loath to admit is that Trump's project has worked not just with the right. It has been wildly successful with progressives too. People working in social justice movements and our constituents are in a frenzy of fear. There is an apparent amnesia about the paranoia and infighting between people of color that, fueled by COINTELPRO and other right-wing forces, contributed greatly to the unraveling of important movement organizations like the Black Panther Party. History is repeating itself as many of us are increasingly at one another's throats.

By the end of 2020, many people working in movement were no longer led by their heart; they were controlled by their amygdala—the fight-or-flight part of the brain. This response is useful in jacking up our adrenaline and cortisol when, say, fighting off an attacking bear, but not so much in a staff meeting. For many, the ongoing nightmare of kids in cages, police killings, the ban on Muslims, the gutting of transgender rights wasn't just happening on the news. It was happening to our friends, families, colleagues, and organization members. The terror of the Trump years—compounded by the anguish of George Floyd's murder, the intensity of a long-overdue racial reckoning, the advent of Covid-19, and the increasingly apocalyptic impacts of climate change—have been taking their toll. The fact that we now so often answer to our amygdala is understandable. But it doesn't make it any less damaging. Operating from the amygdala, out of electric levels of fear, without the benefit of curiosity, logic, or discernment, is incredibly corrosive to belonging—the glue that holds together so many of the critically important relationships upon which the movement is built.

In the fight-or-flight scramble for safety, people are weaponizing the blunt instruments of judgment, blame, callout, cancellation, and performative takedowns to establish who belongs and who doesn't, who is in and who is out, who is a threat or not. We are increasingly unable to tell the difference between healthy boundaries that protect us from harm and walls that keep even our strongest allies out.

I met Loretta Ross in 2005, when I began engaging with the reproductive justice movement. She had co-founded the RJ movement eleven years prior, and although I didn't know it yet, I would spend the next two decades funding it. We were in a hotel ballroom full of funders in Washington, D.C. Notwithstanding the few warm and heartfelt people in the crowd, the place felt stuffy and stilted. Standing behind a wooden lectern dressed in regal African fabrics, long dreads flowing from behind a purple headwrap, with a clear and direct voice, her presence was unapologetic in every sense. She didn't hedge, she didn't pander, she didn't equivocate. To me, a Brown woman who was new to the funder environment, she felt like an infusion of oxygen, of fresh air. I was deeply moved by her story of growing up as a Black girl in the South and how she had gone on to change the world. A powerful survivor, Loretta has a fire to fight for reproductive justice that was ignited by her own experience as a teen girl in the 1960s who had no choice but to have a baby conceived through incest, and later as a young woman who was sterilized against her will by the Dalkon Shield—an intrauterine contraceptive device aggressively marketed in Black and Brown communities before being found to have a dangerous design flaw.

Now in her seventies, Loretta is an author, a MacArthur Foundation "genius grant" recipient, a recent inductee to the National Women's Hall of Fame, and associate professor of the Study of Women and Gender at Smith College. Her latest book, *Calling In,* focuses on untangling society from the negative aspects of cancel culture. When we last talked, she gave me a clear example of the tangle. She told me a reproductive justice organization recently called her in to tell their staff the story of how the RJ movement was founded. Answering their call, she shared with them how, in June of 1994, twelve Black women met in a hotel in Chicago, coined the term, and launched the movement.

What happened next is one of the reasons she said she is more discerning these days when deciding which movement organizations to work with. "Someone spoke up and proclaimed that I was being transphobic because I had written trans women out of the history," Loretta recalled. "I said, 'I know the twelve women who were in the room and none of them were trans then, and none of them are trans now, so how could I have written them out of the history?' I literally got attacked for being transphobic." Actual facts didn't matter; feelings did, and feelings were the new facts. What Loretta described is the type of manufactured offense that is happening in every corner of movement.

Social Media

Barriers have also gotten worse in the digital age. Social media, in general, and Russian bots, internet trolls, and right-wing governments in particular have heightened distrust and aggression. As Anand Giridharadas noted in his book *The Persuaders,* Russian troll farms made millions of posts on social media platforms to get "Americans to regard each other as immovable, brainwashed, of bad faith, not worth energy, disloyal, repulsive."[3] Nothing is greater kryptonite to organizing than people who have written each other off.

One glaring example of this was exposed in September 2022 by *The New York Times* in its article "How Russian Trolls Helped Keep the Women's March Out of Lockstep." It proved that Russian hackers and bots targeted Women's March leaders Linda Sarsour and Tamika Mallory (both WOC) to deepen divisions—particularly racial divisions—within the movement. This was a major factor in cutting the engines of the Women's March organization, which had in 2017 organized the largest demonstration ever held on U.S. soil.

Another example is the attempted takedown of the country's largest abortion justice electoral shop, All* Above All, which was dragged online when one disgruntled staff member lobbed claims of anti-Blackness, and staff from organizations throughout the repro rights and abortion fund fields immediately crusaded in solidarity. Roughly half of the organizations that came after All* online were white led. One Black woman repro leader, who preferred to remain anonymous, wrote to me, "It looked like many organizations were trying to use this as a way to virtue signal online. Whether it's out of fear that they would be called out next or not wanting to be the person/group left out of the thrill of collective dragging online, this collective takedown, regardless of facts, has left our movement fractured, ineffective, and bleeding leadership, which is often WOC." The claims turned out to be baseless, but major damage had already been done. Instead of marshaling its strength and momentum going into 2024, arguably one of the most critical election years for reproductive issues in decades, the organization started the year having to rebuild itself from the ground up.

Tech ethicist Tristan Harris pointed out that the core incentive that social media was built around is grabbing as much human attention as it can. Since the human brain is wired to pay less attention to harmony and more attention to threats such as conflict, negativity, and division, social media skews content in this direction. Said Harris, "A more addicted, outraged, polarized, narcissistic, validation-seeking, sleepless, anxious, doom-scrolling, tribalized . . . society [is] a direct consequence of where the incentives in social media place us."[4]

Those who play into this are not only harming those under attack, they are feeding a much larger and more dangerous beast. One of the classic ways authoritarians rise to power is by fanning the flames of tribalism, dividing people along lines of race, caste, gender, religion, and other differences. In social media, they have a new, powerful tool to supercharge division. In countries around the world, the path to authoritarianism has nearly always been paved with the eroded rights of female, queer, and trans people. This is bearing out today.

Authoritarianism is on the rise globally. According to *Politico,* the 2023 report issued by the International Institute for Democracy and Electoral Assistance (IDEA) on the Global State of Democracy shows democracy on the decline. Seema Shah, who leads IDEA's Democracy Assessment unit, wrote, "The six-year decline is the longest consecutive period of deterioration—in which countries with net declines outnumbered those with net advances across a range of metrics—since records started being kept in 1975."[5]

It takes discipline and clarity to not be drawn into building walls and participating in the fracture of belonging; to not do the work of our opposition for them by turning on one another—whether the threats or mistakes are real or imagined. It's harder still when we are in pain and when social media algorithms encourage it. But it's a discipline we must exercise.

MINI MASTER CLASS

Cindy Wiesner

It was a sunny afternoon in June of 2022, the day after SCOTUS overturned *Roe v. Wade.* Having worked for nearly two decades in the repro justice movement, I had spent the morning fielding calls from several colleagues who were in tears. Things felt bleak. To maximize our power, the repro movement needed to align around a unified strategy aimed at something tangible. Instead it was in a tailspin of purist politics and competition: people out-woking one another, clawing down anyone with a good idea who looked like they might gain power (or funding), and deadlocking in nonsensical battles over terminology.

I happened to have a call with Cindy Wiesner, executive director of Grassroots Global Justice Alliance. I first met Cindy in 2001, in a hot, crowded hotel basement in Washington, D.C., before a direct action of welfare moms fighting against the ongoing effects of former president Bill Clinton's massive cuts to the social safety net. I was a green twenty-year-old organizer sitting shyly at the back, and Cindy was at the front of the room, writing the action plan on butcher paper and commanding the crowd like a general. The daughter of a single immigrant mother who was a domestic worker, Cindy is well traveled and deeply studied in social movements around the world, having learned beside revolutionaries like the late Honduran freedom fighter Berta Cáceres. She is a skilled strategist and her work stands out for connecting intersectional, feminist organizers across borders. Contrary to walls, she is the ultimate bridge builder.

Cindy doesn't work primarily in the repro movement, but she's a lifelong feminist organizer who I respect deeply.

She told me that lately she asks those who reject power in favor of purism, "Do you actually want to win? Are you operating from the politics of victimization or the politics of power? Power in the capitalistic, hetero-patriarchal system looks a particular way and that is not the power that movement is talking about. People conflate that. We need to be more rigorous about defining what power means. If we're actually saying we want to change the world, have systemic alternatives to what currently exists, material changes in people's lives, we have to be able to be sober and clear that purism is not going to make those types of changes."

Creating Belonging for Our Teams

The great irony of belonging for WOC leaders is that we often rise into leadership positions because we are very good at creating belonging for others—leading winning campaigns that don't leave people behind, cultivating organizations in which people can be their full selves—only to find that these positions offer little belonging for us. In fact, they are often places of isolation, exclusion, and othering. It can feel like a cruel joke that takes us full circle. Most of us started our movement journey because something in us responded to the sharp pain of societal exclusion—of ourselves or the people we love—with the brave impulse to forge a more inclusive world. It is demoralizing to have worked so hard toward this end, only to end up right back in that same pain.

It was this way for me. Movement, in my greatest hopes, meant the promise of a society and a world without the toxic conditions of belonging that had long plagued me and those I loved. I also had the hope of working together for this goal with like-minded people who would value rather than ostracize me for my differences, as society had done.

I spent years as a community and labor organizer, working on campaigns that won more belonging for poor and working-class people. When I founded Groundswell Fund, a public foundation that raised dollars from wealthy individuals and foundations (mostly white) and granted them out to multi-issue, grassroots organizing efforts (nearly all led by people of color), my own experience of being an outsider led me to center some of the most marginalized groups in our work. Foremost among them were Black women, who, as grantees, consistently received the largest share of resources from every fund and program we ran. We included transgender people in the organizational mission statement from the very beginning and eventually became one of the leading funders of trans-people-of-color-led organizations in the country. The U.S. south, which is woefully neglected by most of philanthropy, received a greater share of our resources than any other region in the country.

Groundswell was fueling the agency of those who belonged the least in society, and it was also attempting to model the kind of beloved community in which people from all walks of life could see themselves and, to some degree, belong. For a long while, and in many ways, it achieved this model. Fifteen years in, millions of dollars were moving through structures where grassroots leaders held supermajorities at every level of decision-making. Millionaires might be at the table some of the time, but they were listening and collaborating rather than dictating and dominating. It was a space where a wealthy white woman might say, "I've talked to my friend at Harvard and I think what will solve Black maternal mortality is a research report better documenting the problem"—but be willing to hear and follow the guidance of the Black woman community midwife sitting next to her when she said, "The last thing we need is another research report! There is more than enough documentation of the problem. What we need is funding for a new policy that organizers are already mobilizing around that will enable Medicaid coverage of expanded pre- and post-natal care for Black mothers."

The Groundswell community was a space where a Latina leader in the repro justice space could say, "The repro movement needs to build more capacity to engage voters," and be delighted to hear a male donor—who had recently funded grassroots groups in the environmental movement to build this capacity—offer to connect her to enviro leaders to hear what supports they felt were most important to succeed. Groundswell was a space in which a donor could arrive interested in protecting abortion rights and become inspired by a grassroots environmental activist to get their family foundation to divest from fossil fuels.

The model was in many ways a shining success. The funders and donors were deeply influenced by the work and inspired to help open up more resources across philanthropy more broadly for WOC-led organizing. Around the time I left, the org had grown from an annual budget of $300,000 to $26 million, from two to two thousand donors, from one to forty foundation partnerships, and from twenty to nearly two hundred grantees. Our grantees were scoring hundreds of progressive policy wins that expanded rights and access for groups most excluded by society. Even more important, they were successfully building a vibrant, sustained, and growing grassroots base of supporters capable of defending and implementing those gains and taking on the next fight to win even more ground. We were also running robust capacity-building programs that were seeing major success in helping grantees scale up their organizing muscle to engage and mobilize voters—an arena women of color and queer and trans people had been consistently shut out of by traditional electoral efforts. It was a team effort on the part of our entire staff and board, and we were making an impact!

The organization itself was an expression of trust and solidarity toward a vision of belonging across difference. It began as a staff of one—me—just talking to people as I had done when organizing workers and in communities. At first, I was genuinely puzzled as to why I seemed to have a knack for inspiring white millionaires to give over dollars and decision-making power to grassroots leaders of color, or to coalesce groups of people where millionaires sat beside community organizers to chart the course of strategy. Eventually, I realized, my childhood experience of moving between very different groups had been boot camp for this.

Bernice Johnson Reagon reflected on working across differences as akin to functioning at a high altitude: "There is a lesson in bringing people together where they can't get enough oxygen, then having them try to figure out what they're going to do when they can't think properly. . . . That is often what it feels like when you're *really* doing coalition work." She added, "There probably are some people here who can breathe, because you were born in high altitudes and you have big lung cavities."[6]

I am one of these people. I had operated at the altitude of race, class, and cultural dissonance from the age of five, navigating wildly different norms and worldviews in spaces where my sense of belonging was constantly in question and where I keenly felt the differences between myself and others.

For me, the lung capacity for coalition building that Johnson Reagon references came down to the ability to do two things in the face of behaviors that threaten one's sense of safety and comfort: Love people and tell them the truth. The knowledge that each human contains multitudes was something I understood viscerally. I knew my white mother loved me enough to risk her own life to save mine. I also knew she was so deeply programmed by the white supremacy culture that permeates our society that she lacked the will to understand or validate how I experienced race. I loved her and I challenged her thinking head-on. I loved and also confronted my Sri Lankan aunties, who during my early adult years were incredibly generous with their home-cooked meals and family stories and calls to see how I was doing, but who were so deeply programmed by patriarchy that they could not abide that as a child I had spoken out to protect my body from an adult male abuser. I loved and spoke the truth to my childhood best friend, who generously shared her Black girl survival kit with me, even though, at times, her own distress led her to other me painfully for being Brown.

I could find and love the good in just about everyone, and I was fearless in talking with people authentically about difficult things. At the end of the day, most humans appreciate authenticity. I found that white donors and funders who were used to being fluffed up by an endless line of people who told them what they thought they wanted to hear—while holding them in contempt behind their backs—were relieved to meet someone who genuinely saw and cared about them as human beings and was willing to challenge them on their thinking. Grassroots leaders who were used to philanthropists either romanticizing or infantilizing them were happy to sit down with someone who truly valued their wisdom and experience and was also willing to ask and grapple with difficult questions in order to understand.

Internally, with the Groundswell staff team, the project of creating beloved community also appeared to be going well in many respects. Staff were generally supportive of one another. They had significant creative control over their areas of work and ample space to shape organizational strategy and policy. We worked staff-wide to co-design organizational values and ground rules, and a twelve-person volunteer committee of staff from every department and level worked to develop many aspects of organizational policy. Since working conditions are a part of belonging, we strove to make them exceptional. All staff (except for the top two executive positions, including mine), no matter where in the country they were located, were receiving salaries at or above the seventy-fifth percentile of the Bay Area nonprofit sector (one of the highest in the nation) and between $2,000 and $20,000 per year for professional development.

We reasoned, if standard health insurance plans weren't inclusive of full gender-affirming and reproductive health care, we would fill in the gaps. So, on top of 100 percent employer-paid family medical coverage and roughly $3,000 for reimbursement of alternative healthcare and co-pays, we offered each staff member $20,000 per year for fertility care, $30,000 per year for gender-affirming health care, and $10,000 per year for support with adoption. Work-life balance was a constant work in progress, but everyone worked from home with flexible schedules and had between seven and ten weeks of paid time off, plus an additional three-month sabbatical after every five years of employment and four months' paid parental leave upon the birth or adoption of a child. During Covid, we paid for people's in-home childcare and for staff in the New York area, who wanted to escape the round-the-clock blaring of ambulance sirens, we offered to pay the cost for them to relocate to other places temporarily.

Things were by no means perfect, but Groundswell was many times more humane than any place I had ever worked. My 360-degree evaluations from staff about how well I was leading had been stellar year after year—the main critique being about my pacing sometimes being too fast. The same was true for most of the other WOC in leadership positions on staff. Belonging seemed to be going along well, but there were major fires developing.

When Things Fall Apart

Brushfires of conflict that threatened the sense of belonging within the organization occurred a few times over the years. Each time, attacks on women of color leaders based on stereotypes were a major spark. Each time, we were able to put out the blaze before it burned out of control, allowing the team to re-harmonize and the work to hum on. In some instances, during a flare, there were periods when the us-versus-them sentiment from staff toward WOC leaders heightened until it felt worse than nearly any other type of social exclusion I had endured in my life. In these moments the irony was not lost on me that an organization whose mission it was to support the leadership of WOC across movements had itself become a place where WOC in leadership were profoundly not allowed to belong.

Most people of color have experienced building a relationship with a person of another race where you think there is trust and respect and then, bam! Out of nowhere, they say something ignorant that reveals that they see you as a stereotype, a caricature. It can be so disappointing and hurtful. Increasingly that is what leadership began to feel like—like being typecast and ostracized. The opposite of belonging.

In these difficult times, the more I felt excluded and othered, the harder I stretched myself, working long hours to hold down the fundraising, on top of parenting young children—all while striving to spend more time with staff, hoping that people would get to know me beyond the stereotypes they held, and see that I was trustworthy. With very few exceptions, I didn't confront, challenge, or draw healthy boundaries regarding unkind behavior. My method for dealing with the couple of people who were gossiping and trashing me throughout the organization was to extend myself further in their direction, trying to meet their needs and demands to win them over.

I had been taught early on as an organizer to decenter myself to focus on advancing belonging in the world for others. But these periods of dissonance between the vision of belonging we were working to actualize externally and the profound marginalization I felt within the organization internally began to wear on me. I thought we were doing all the right things, that the fires were par for the course for an expanding organization and would keep being put out, and maybe eventually stop happening to the degree that they were. I was blissfully unaware that I was making a series of major mistakes as a leader that would later hurt belonging for both me and the organization. I was diligently putting out the fires but missing that something needed to be done about the dry grass. It was only a matter of time before something would spark a wildfire that would be very difficult to contain.

The year 2019 was a low-fire season with no major flares. Work was booming. Respect for Groundswell could not have been stronger among grantees and funders alike. The grantees we were funding were doing powerful work. I felt confident that the organization was in a solid place, with a robust donor base, strong reserves, a stellar board, and skilled staff. Our budget and staff were larger than ever—including new positions dedicated to supporting a healthy internal culture. At that point I had been leading the organization for fifteen years. It had been a wild and overwhelmingly positive ride, but I could feel that I was tired and ready to move on. I began talking with my executive coach and board chair about transitioning out of the organization and made preparations for a spring 2020 announcement. In keeping with the best practice for nonprofits of our size and complexity, I planned to give one year's notice to allow a full twelve months for a robust national search for a new executive director. Then Covid hit and threw everything for a loop. I decided to hold off, not wanting to leave the organization in the lurch during a time of such uncertainty.

In an attempt to be responsive to staff concerns about sustainability, we had staffed up quickly during the prior year. As Covid set in, building trust and alignment over Zoom with a diverse team of thirty people, half of whom were new, was proving impossible. There were more and more rumblings of dissatisfaction with the ways people's differences in identity and culture were beginning to rub against one another. Accusations of antisemitism, anti-Asian sentiment, xenophobia, anti-Blackness, transphobia, and sizeism began to fly around at an alarming rate both horizontally between staff and vertically between staff and their supervisors. Sometimes an accusation was a righteous call to correct actual harms, but often it was fear projected on the wrong targets, or a cudgel used to hammer others into submission on whatever the accuser wanted.

Staff also clamored for more and more from the organization, but the complaints and demands felt mainly symbolic. They wanted "More decision-making power!" And also, less time spent in meetings arriving at decisions. "Less hierarchy!" And also, less responsibility. "More clarity about who makes which decisions!" Even though this had been spelled out in detail, multiple times. "More vacation days!" Even though the average staffer was substantially underusing the vacation they already had.

The HR department was wrung out. I remember the day one of their peppiest members showed up to a call with the organization's leadership team completely deflated, saying, "It just seems like it's never enough. It's like they want more and more and they don't even know what more is." It was a few years before the breakthrough article "The Death of 'Deliverism'" by Deepak Bhargava and others would expose how people in the United States were experiencing rising levels of unhappiness due to social disconnection, increased stress about climate crises, and other pressures that even substantial material improvements (such as a whopping 46 percent reduction in childhood poverty) were proving insufficient to solving.[7] Material conditions were improving and yet polls showed people rating themselves as unhappier than before the improvements. This was happening within movement organizations as well, with salaries and benefits up and workloads down in many places but morale declining nonetheless.

In spring 2021, when things seemed somewhat steadier externally, with vaccines available and no major economic meltdown in sight, I finally announced my transition. It was a full year later than my original plan. In an effort to allow enough time for a national search for a new ED, while also being real about my exhaustion, I set my departure date for the end of February, 2022, roughly eight months out. Soon after I announced my transition, the staff conflicts, which had been simmering higher than usual but still felt manageable, boiled over. I found myself trying to address them from a state of utter exhaustion and, as an "outgoing ED," from a position of very little leverage.

During one stretch of time, a small group of staff set their minds to assailing me and other WOC organizational leaders. While many other staff didn't agree with what was occurring and said as much to me and the other leaders in one-on-one conversations, they weren't willing to stick their necks out to disrupt it.

One by one, my senior leaders—including Black, Latina, and Asian women who had dedicated most of their lives to movement work—quit. These were not weak people; they had been through hell and back in their own lives and come out the other side. But what was happening was breaking them. One noted that being in leadership was like "wearing a scarlet letter," and that the attack was so intense it reminded her of gang violence in the neighborhood she grew up in. Another departed citing suicidal ideation. We had lived our entire careers having to be four times as good as our white and male counterparts, with a narrow margin of error. We knew it wasn't just the psychological cuts of people's words that would hurt us, but the real and present danger to our material well-being that could easily follow if our reputations were ruined.

It wasn't any more than two or three people leveling threats—individuals who were either mad about the normal level of supervisorial feedback they were receiving, on a power trip, or both. But the combination of people crusading on their behalf without much discernment, and the number of people willing to be passive bystanders, was a perfect storm. We all knew that being dragged online for being anti-Asian or anti-Black or ableist or ageist or top-down or retaliatory, or any number of baseless accusations that were being tossed our way, could potentially put us out of work. Having been a union organizer who defended working people, I was intensely sensitive to abuses of power and bad bosses and I would not allow them. In the past I had confronted and transitioned managers who misused their power. But I can honestly say that during this period, not even one of the leaders being attacked was of this ilk. They were humble. They genuinely cared about staff. They worked hard to support their teams. What was happening was unfounded and unfair.

Many of us had families to support—not that this should matter—but it was an added stress. Truth, due process, evidence—none of it seemed to matter much in a public square that made little distinction between justified accountability for proven wrongdoing and petty cancellation based on unsubstantiated gossip. Notably, everyone involved in the aggression was a person of color, and nearly all were WOC. This wasn't white people doing something to us. This was what we were doing to ourselves. This was us blocking one another from belonging. One day, alone in my home office, the dam broke and I sobbed in raw grief. I was flooded with the sheer exhaustion of it all as I thought of my movement elders and mentors, my peers working shoulder to shoulder with me, my own sweat and sacrifice for twenty years, to leave the violence of so many white institutions and build something by and for us where we could belong. To see us rip one another to shreds was beyond heartbreaking. The pain of it was excruciating, even with the stalwart support of my board, which was mercifully steady throughout. Eventually, at the advice of my doctor and therapist, who were concerned for my health, I moved my exit date up by two months. No one asked me to do this, but I knew that I was too badly battered to be effective and that the stress was only serving to further damage my health.

I share this experience not to disparage or single out Groundswell. What ripped through our organization was the same wildfire that was ripping through countless other movement organizations at the time and it was hitting women of color leaders hard. I saw several peers going through the same or worse, some without the support of their boards, which was doubly horrendous. Some organizations would not survive. Some leaders were pushed out and would tap out of movement for good. Eventually, thankfully, Groundswell would come through it. When you are a founder, an organization is like your baby—down to the sleepless nights and incredible workload in the early years. What you create, you have to continue to evolve to its best place, collectively. It becomes something that the community owns. Knowing when to lean in and when to step back in guiding and accompanying that collective evolution is a real art, especially when fires flare. In many ways it is the art of community gardening. It is the wisdom to know that keeping the ecosystem healthy and verdant, and thus resistant to fires, is far better than putting out the blazes that will inevitably catch in dry grass. I wish I had known then what I know now, but it's my hope that these pages help other leaders know more, earlier on in their journeys.

Looking Inward and Outward

Although my experience was painful, it was, mercifully, an invaluable and powerful teacher about belonging and the leadership praxis required to prevent dry grass and keep things verdant and thriving. Part of the lesson requires a look inward, to change something in ourselves. Part of it requires looking outward to demand better from those around us.

As the African proverb goes, "If there is no enemy within, the enemy outside cannot harm us." And as Audre Lorde reminds us, "Nothing I accept about myself can be used against me to diminish me." The inward look forced me into a deep reckoning. The reason I was so affected by the othering I experienced from staff was that despite my external success and confidence as a leader, inside I was in many ways still that little Brown girl at sea, grasping to hold on to the acceptance and validation of others.

My enemy within was a deep-seated subconscious belief that I was unworthy of love and acceptance. And that if I didn't prove myself and fit in enough to win people's acceptance, I would drown. Drowning meant being cast out. It meant shame, humiliation, and crushing isolation—all things I felt as a child who was so often shamed and excluded because she was different. While everyone's inner enemy is different, many of the WOC leaders I spoke with talked about their battle with internal narratives that encourage them to people-please and dissuade them from drawing boundaries with abusive treatment from staff, colleagues, donors, and others in movement.

Looking externally, the experience also forced me to understand what the gaps had been in my efforts to create a culture of belonging for others. It was not enough to inspire people into a sense of collective purpose. It was insufficient to give them a lot of creative control over their lines of work, a good share of decision-making power. It was inadequate to provide strong pay and benefit packages and be responsive to additional requests for support. What was needed as my organization scaled up was clear and explicit communication from me as the leader (echoed and reinforced by other leaders flanking me) of how I expected people to behave in relationship with one another, with me, and with the organization—expectations made meaningful by kindly and firmly setting limits and boundaries. This doesn't preclude a co-design of organizational culture, but it does acknowledge the power and responsibility of the leader to set the tone and to hold certain parameters.

In her book *The Art of Gathering*, facilitator Priya Parker wrote, "A ubiquitous strain of twenty-first-century culture is infecting our gatherings: being chill." Noting that many gatherings are ruined when rogue guests monopolize the conversations or otherwise misbehave without any intervention from the host, she urged hosts to "lift a hand to the wheel," detailing how "many people who go to the serious trouble of hosting aspire to host as minimally as possible. But who wants to sail on a skipperless ship?" She concluded, "Often chill is you caring about *you* masquerading as you caring about *them*."[8]

I had to face the fact that in the acrobatics of people-pleasing and fitting in that I was doing to find acceptance and belonging, I had abdicated my responsibility to make the brave interventions and draw the unpopular boundaries that were sorely needed to protect an environment of kindness and belonging for the entire team. I was greatly encouraged in that abdication both by the culture of left movements that I had come up in—which stigmatized anything that could be read as "top-down" and "punitive," and overly romanticized notions like "collective wisdom"—and by the stigmas placed on WOC, such as "If you say no or are assertive in drawing a boundary, you are a bitch." This was reinforced by the adamant advice to not draw stronger boundaries by members of my leadership team—who were also people pleasers or conflict avoidant or both—and organizational development consultants who were supposed to be the experts on management.

Boundaries would have looked like setting clear expectations and norms around principled critique, naming certain behaviors for what they were: abusive and inappropriate. It would have also meant disciplining or firing toxic staff members—the equivalent of rogue guests—who were out of line in attacking colleagues and punching holes in the bottom of the organizational ship that we were all in. In order for kindhearted and constructive people to belong, toxic individuals have to be moved out quickly.

Denise Perry, director and co-founder of Black Organizing for Leadership and Dignity (BOLD), reinforced Parker's point, reminding us that leaders often "don't have the edge for the fight." To transform a high-conflict environment in which belonging is being decimated, she said, "We need to learn *how* to fight, not how to avoid a fight."

MINI MASTER CLASS
Andrea Mercado

Sitting next to me during the bumpy van ride to visit a community project in rural Puerto Rico, Andrea Mercado, executive director of statewide grassroots political organization Florida Rising, talked to me about finding the edge for the fight to keep an organization on mission. "It's the balance of compassion and accountability," she said. "Our organizations do not exist to serve the staff, they exist to show up with excellence for Black and Brown communities. [In 2019] we had a staff member who was attacking Biden on social media. We made a policy that you don't have to publicly support, but you need to refrain from attacking. They decided to continue the attacks and carved F JOE BIDEN into their haircut. We had choices—put them on leave or let them go. We decided that because of other things related to their performance, we would let them go. Staff freaked out. It was the best decision. We can't be afraid to hold people accountable and make decisions that serve the organization."

In hindsight, I can see the errors I made in trying to cultivate belonging that made a challenging situation worse. I can also see the structural elements that stack the deck against WOC leaders' attempts to create environments of belonging. Leaders can't transform these elements alone—they need enough people at the organization who are willing to intervene. The deeply unprincipled and violent behavior of some staff toward organizational leaders within my organization was something that they felt entitled to carry out because the culture and systems of movement send a clear message that it is wholly permissible to treat WOC leaders in this way. That cultural kryptonite needs to be removed from an organization in order for belonging to stand a chance. Thankfully, Groundswell, which was caught in the riptide of conflict that engulfed so many movement shops between 2020 and 2022, got its feet under itself again eventually, sometime after I transitioned out, with the support of a stellar board, a few principled staff members, and a seasoned new ED. I was relieved that an organization that I love so dearly had made it through and would have the chance to continue resourcing grassroots work that delivers real change for the most vulnerable communities.

5

Barriers to Bring Down

If 360-degree vision is about seeing the full picture and becoming more whole in ourselves and in our relationships with one another, then barriers are about the forces that fracture and obscure our full field of vision. Here are a few of the barriers to belonging that movements must bring down to succeed. It's worth noting that while many of these are affecting people of all races and genders working in movements, for WOC leaders dealing with fear and mistrust compounded by racism and misogyny, the impact is worse.

Projection and scapegoating: When external forces of oppression feel too daunting to challenge and closer targets become a proxy. Projection and scapegoating can happen consciously or subconsciously.

One leader, who asked to remain anonymous, shared a story with me about how projection and scapegoating can take hold in a movement. "There was one young leader who I poured so much into. But soon, she wanted me on call all of the time, like, 'I want ten minutes with you, and it doesn't matter what your schedule is.' I said, 'I can't just drop everything and tend to you.' She told me she was in therapy and said, 'You are triggering my childhood wounds because my parents weren't available the way that I needed them to be.' Then she quit. On social media, she said I was this big villain who was an abusive gaslighter who was creating a toxic environment. She made a lot of accusations that the whole team felt this way. I requested an internal investigation with the board. None of the accusations panned out. At the end, I think this person just had mental health issues. And I can't publicly say those things. I never defended myself. I just let it be. It was so painful and hurtful. My intention was only to support and uplift her. I had to dig really deep and really rely on my spirituality to get through that. I relied on prayer, cleansing. I took some time off. I went to the ocean and felt its healing power. It doesn't hurt anymore, but it's still out there, and it feels unfair that this is like a stain on my leadership in the local community. It feels like I somehow got a maximum sentence. And I had no jury."

WOC are subject to particularly intense projection and scapegoating because, whether or not we invite it, we are often perceived as mother figures. Therefore, when we draw boundaries, it can feel like rejection. Our people have a lot of pain. We all have a responsibility to not off-load our pain on people who didn't cause it. And we have a responsibility to draw healthy boundaries with those who do.

Empathy without discernment: When an individual expresses pain and levels an accusation—and people crusade on their behalf without examining whether the accusation is founded.

Zen Buddhist teacher Norma Wong once used the phrase "empathy without discernment" on a large Zoom call she was leading. When she spoke, I saw a sea of heads nodding across my Zoom screen. She had struck a chord. Empathy without discernment is a major trend and destructive force in movement organizations.

Loretta Ross described it this way: "A lot of people tell stories through the lens of their trauma that are as real as can be to them. That doesn't make it the objective truth. While you want to hold that story for that person, you have to be very, very careful what you do with it. Because you have to have other evidence—something to back it up, other than their feelings."[1] She added, "Why you're hurting may have nothing to do with the person standing in front of you, but from restimulated past pain that just got triggered, but you dump on the person accessible to you because you can't get at the past hurt that's inaccessible."

Ash-Lee Woodard Henderson reflected that empathy without discernment "might also live in the generational shift" of younger people seeking to change the more callous movement culture of old. "Of course," she said, "if the [starting point] that is being responded to is no feelings, then the overcorrection we are getting is all feelings." She added, "We need to be thinking strategically about what tactics we might utilize to stop the pendulum from swinging and get it leveled out. It's been beautiful to see BIPOC women sharing personnel policies, especially during Covid, when everyone was having to make up new shit to take care of really fucked-up humans. What is our responsibility as the leaders of twenty-first-century movements, particularly those of us who have a revolutionary praxis but are also trying to be fully human? Let us be the generation that stops the overcorrection." I agree wholeheartedly with Ash's assessment and call to action.

Empathy without discernment is especially potent when the

accused party has, or is perceived to have, more positional power or privilege than the alleged victim. Jon Ronson, author of the excellent book about social media takedowns, *So You've Been Publicly Shamed,* wrote, "The phrase 'misuse of privilege' is becoming a free pass to tear apart pretty much anybody we choose to. It's becoming a devalued term and is making us lose our capacity and empathy for distinguishing between serious and unserious transgressions."[2]

The trouble is, we are living in an era that is anti-information, anti-facts, and pro–reductive reasoning. It's not just a movement issue; it's part of the larger zeitgeist. In his final monologue on *The Daily Show,* Trevor Noah spoke about the importance of context. "We process everything in bites. We have a lot of information, but we don't have the context to process that information. It may slow you down in making a decision, but maybe that's a good thing." We live in an age where social media has shortened our attention spans. Complex problems and ideas are flattened into two-dimensional memes that lend themselves to snap judgments.

The result is an iceberg effect: When taking in a situation, people look only at the tip of the iceberg visible above the waterline, without any awareness and, perhaps most disturbingly, without any apparent interest in the great mass that lies beneath. Staff may rally to the defense of a colleague who was fired without considering that the community members the organization is supposed to serve have long been complaining about that person's performance—and they have been given multiple chances and supports to improve. Similarly, staff may rally to the defense of a colleague who asks for expanded pay or benefits without considering how their current package compares with industry standards or even the internal compensation bands that protect the organization's wage parity.

As I will discuss in greater depth in chapter 15, the misogynist characterization of WOC leaders as "aggressive," "a bitch," or "corporate" whenever we disagree with staff increases the level of difficulty when asking that staff to slow down and consider data, facts, or the larger part of the iceberg. It's a narrowing that is the antithesis of 360-degree vision.

Emotional contagion: Described by *Psychology Today* as "the phenomenon in which a person unconsciously mirrors or mimics the emotions of those around them."[3]

The history of emotional contagion is strongly gendered and raced, with witch trials and public lynchings being two examples. There are, quite simply, fewer emergency brakes in the cultural norms to slow the momentum of a runaway train when emotional contagion targets people of color and women. There is an assumption of guilt for both groups, and WOC lack the benefit of the doubt doubly. Negative emotional contagion spreads fast when a current of fear is running high in the society at large. In Arthur Miller's *The Crucible*, set during the Salem witch trials, the character Abigail catches the contagious fear of witches that has engulfed the town, confessing her own sins and then, in a desperate effort to align herself with the pack and divert their negative attention away from herself, begins accusing other women of witchcraft, announcing, "I saw Sarah Good with the Devil! I saw Goody Osburn with the Devil! I saw Bridget Bishop with the Devil!" The era of Trump and Covid is another time of heightened fear in our society. Trump's call to white people to scapegoat immigrants and people of color for their suffering has led to a surge in membership of white supremacist groups, and a dramatic uptick in hate crimes.

In movement, emotional contagion often shows up as an inability to empathize with another person's pain while maintaining one's own boundaries and perspective. It's what occurs when empathy without discernment spreads through a group of people, fueling baseless conspiracy theories and uncritical groupthink. Emotional contagion depends on a willingness to go with the crowd. Since Covid, scores of movement organizations have seen their work grind to a halt following a pattern that is now so often repeated it is almost cliché: One or two employees accuse a higher-up, or the organization as a whole, of a misuse of power—usually in the form of the mistreatment of workers or identity-based discrimination. Sometimes, these accusations are founded. But many times, they are not. Despite the lack of evidence to substantiate the claims, staff feel deep empathy with the accusers before rallying others and dragging the accused individuals and the organization internally and sometimes in front of the external public as well. While some of this is performative, some is genuinely felt as empathy.

There is a fundamental difference between standing in principled solidarity with someone based on sound judgment, grounded in clarity of facts, evidence, and reason, and being swept up by emotional contagion into a mob that attacks people and organizations indiscriminately. While calling out toxic behavior is important, we have to engage in discernment and critical thinking at all times in this work. Without it, everyone and the movement suffers.

Trauma bonding: Achieving a sense of closeness and safety through a disproportionate focus on shared experiences of suffering and victimization, and on common enemies.

Talking about shared pain and trauma is an essential part of healing, but when it becomes the primary way that a group of people builds closeness, it quickly becomes destructive. It grounds the group in victimhood and fear rather than empowerment, and it crowds out the space needed to bond around radical imagination about the world we seek to create. It also creates an insatiable appetite for more pain and harm and a hypervigilant tendency to scan every room for common enemies to unify against—more often than not causing us to target and attack our own. In essence, it's a gross distortion of the way that survivors respond to trauma by bonding together to find strength and unity to heal and dream of a better life.

Case Study

On March 16, 2021, a white man walked into three greater Atlanta spas and opened fire, killing eight people, including six Asian women. Many WOC movement leaders had a keen understanding of the brand of racism, misogyny, and control that is often directed at Asian women and that was behind these killings. Asian communities across the United States were reeling, as this was the latest in a rash of horrendous violent crimes against East Asian people who were being scapegoated for the coronavirus. Asian elders were being targeted disproportionately, being beaten and even killed. Many were afraid to leave their homes. So too were younger Asian people, including some working in movement.

A week after the Georgia attack, an Asian woman on my team broke down in tears during a Zoom meeting of her department. Her grief was palpable. She had recently expressed fear of leaving her home in a predominately white neighborhood. She also noted that days had passed since the killings and that Groundswell had yet to put out a public statement about them. Clearly, she reasoned, this was because Groundswell did not care about Asian people. The other staff members on the call, including two members of the senior management team, rightly expressed their empathy and concern, but then, to show their solidarity, set about crusading on her behalf (empathy without discernment, emotional contagion). Instead of getting curious and supporting their team by not jumping to conclusions until there was more information, the managers showed up to the next leadership meeting and confronted other colleagues about failing in their duties and not showing up for Asian people.

It quickly became apparent that three out of the four people responsible for issuing a public statement on the killings were themselves Asian women, one of whom was a former sex worker who had been managing her own trauma response to the events in Atlanta and two who had been juggling major family challenges, including deaths of multiple family members during Covid. Despite all of this, there was, as it turned out, a public statement that had been drafted and edited and was almost ready for release. The woman who cast the blame truly believed our organization had failed to act, but that was not entirely true. She deserved care and empathy, like any of us, and she also deserved to be steered clear of hasty conclusions and false assumptions.

The Asian women leaders reacted with frustration and anger to their colleagues' accusations. The senior team members who had brought the accusations backpedaled and eventually relayed to the staff what had happened. People made apologies but by the end of it, multiple people on the team, already exhausted by the pandemic, felt wrung out by the fiasco. Energy was in short supply, and it had been sapped. Trust and relationships that were key to our collective work had been strained. It was all avoidable.

I would witness this cycle play out so often in my organization and others that it became almost formulaic. One person experiences a painful trigger. They react by blaming a colleague or the organization. As if caught in a riptide of emotional contagion, the people bearing witness go into a fight-or-flight reaction. Engaging little to no curiosity or discernment, they rally behind the triggered person and crusade on their behalf against the object of their blame. The more the accused happens to hold positional power, the less willing the group is to listen to their perspective, examine the facts, or look at the lack of supporting evidence. In the end, it becomes a mob mentality.

Performative wokeness: To expose, shame, and humiliate others for presumed ignorance or error as a means of elevating one's own visibility, position, or legitimacy.

The right-wing media has distorted the meaning of the expression "wokeness" as a way of dismissing any voice raised against injustice and harm as whining and performative. Real wokeness simply denotes being aware or "awake" as opposed to asleep to injustice. It indicates a willingness to be of service to others and the greater good by disrupting rather than being a bystander to oppression. This kind of wokeness is a very good thing.

Performative wokeness is something else entirely. It's about the egotistical thrill of one-upping people. It's about optics and window dressing rather than actual change. A non-Native person who offers a compulsory land acknowledgment at the top of a Zoom call but does nothing for actual Native American communities is given more credit than the person who bungles the acknowledgment but actually gives their time and resources to support Native communities. A light-skinned Latina previously accused of colorism goes out of her way to level the same accusation at others to throw the focus off of herself. A cisgender person publicly upbraids an elderly African American guest speaker who used the wrong pronoun for a team member they had just met, refusing to accept the elder's apology. Performative wokeness terrorizes people, creating an environment in which everyone is walking on eggshells for fear of making a mistake, being called out and humiliated next. It is corrosive to authentic belonging. Professor Nicolaus Mills of Sarah Lawrence College described the time we are in as having "a culture of humiliation."[4]

Shame and humiliation are tricky in movement. Many of the most successful tactics in social change are ones that shine a bright light on injustice, forcing the broader public to face the problem and the bad actors to answer for themselves. Whether it was Cesar Chavez and Dolores Huerta using the grape boycott to expose the abuses of agribusiness, Ella Baker organizing marches and Fannie Lou Hamer speaking to Congress to lay bare the violence of whites who upheld Jim Crow, or a local union picketing the house of a bad boss, that light needed to be glaringly bright for change to occur. Seeing television coverage of the police putting fire hoses and dogs on peaceful civil rights protesters shamed the South and awakened many white people to what people of color had been experiencing all along. But there is a profound difference between exposing and punishing. Exposing injustice to hold its perpetrators accountable for stopping bad behavior and making repairs is one thing. Exacting punishment on them through public humiliation is another. One corrects, the other destroys. One draws a boundary, saying no to the weapon of violence. The other simply switches who is wielding it.

My mother believed in self-defense but not in retaliation as a solution. When I was a little girl, she would tell me, "If someone is harming others it is because they are themselves damaged. Hitting them over the head some more is not going to help them stop harming people; it will only damage them more. Protect yourself, but don't seek to harm."

I once raised my hand to speak at a feminist philanthropy conference, and when called on, I said, "The dearth of funding to WOC is shameful." Indeed, a deplorably minuscule 0.06 percent of annual foundation dollars went to WOC. I added that "the people in our sector who were perpetuating this inequity should be ashamed of themselves." Connie Cagampang Heller, my then board chair who was both a donor and a woman of color, and who would later become one of my dearest friends, came up to me at the end of the meeting. She said to me gently, "I don't think shame moves people in a good direction." I was dismissive. "Well, sometimes I think people need to feel ashamed before they will change their behavior." Connie was patient with me over the years while I settled down enough to really take in this perspective. Today, I know from experience that she was right.

In *So You've Been Publicly Shamed,* Jon Ronson interviewed James Gilligan, a psychiatrist who in the 1970s was brought into Massachusetts prisons to help reduce a major uptick in murders among inmates. After working with the most violent incarcerated people, he concluded, "I have yet to see a serious act of violence that was not provoked by the experience of feeling shamed or humiliated, disrespected and ridiculed . . . all violence being a person's attempt to replace shame with self-esteem." Humiliation only leads human beings further into pain and despair.

All of us in movement need to reckon with the question: Are we organizing for the end of domination or for the right to dominate others?

I also took a sobering look at how I, too, have engaged in simply turning the tables. I have added my tweets to a chorus that vilified famous people who made mistakes, feeling the rush of self-righteousness and belonging that comes from calling them out. In 2018, at a repro funders conference, I called out a colleague for marginalizing WOC-led grantees in the design of the site visits. It was effective in cracking open a conversation on race, but in retrospect, the tenor of the process that unfolded was not necessarily the most productive because many of the white people became mired in fear. It might have gone differently if I had expressed my concerns as an invitation to discuss a better process and outcome next time. What is the difference between stepping too timidly in a moment when a stronger disruption is needed to shift calcified norms and blasting people in ways that generate more harm? I recall the advice of my supervisor when I was a young organizer. I was a bulldog in negotiating for workers, but so much so that at times I made bosses feel cornered with no exit. My supervisor said, "You know how to create the pressure, but that's only half of it. You have to give them a path out, where they can meet the reasonable demands of the workers and leave the meeting with their dignity intact."

I fear that in movement, we have too often used the weapons of shame and humiliation on organizing targets. They have been only marginally effective there, and now we have turned them on one another.

Denise Perry, director and co-founder of Black Organizing for Leadership and Dignity, and I discussed how performative wokeness can also reveal sharp class dimensions between younger, paid movement activists from elite colleges and universities and the poor or working-class communities they are meant to support. In her early sixties, Denise—whose journey spans the Black Power era to the present—has accomplished decades of skillful work as a community organizer and somatics practitioner. What I love about Denise is how her deep empathy and compassion for people meet a no-nonsense sensibility. She will go to great lengths to give organizers the resources to do their healing work, but she doesn't suffer fools, entertain bullshit behavior that is destructive to the work, or lose sight of why we are all here to begin with: to serve and empower the people.

The study of theory and terminology has always played an important role in movement, despite class and education differences. When I ask Perry about the difference between the Black Panther Party, which was known for handing "ordinary" people who walked in their office doors books and theories by the likes of Frantz Fanon and Paulo Freire, and the performative wokeness that is occurring today, she was quick to point out the distinction: "The Panthers—they met people in the street and invited them to come study. They used their knowledge to bring people in and not to exclude them."

Performative cheerleading / the withholding of feedback:
Much less prevalent than performative wokeness, but still a major problem for many WOC leaders, is performative cheerleading. This is when people are afraid that if they give a WOC leader the constructive feedback and important information she needs to grow and avoid the problems headed her way, they will be seen and called out as unsupportive or racist. Performative cheerleading (or the withholding of feedback) is most commonly carried out by white people who are mired in white guilt and the fear of being called out as white supremacist, although it can also occur among and between WOC. I've seen it most starkly with Black women leaders, where the fear of being pegged as anti-Black tends to blend with the stereotype of the Black woman as aggressive. That is how many Black women leaders get left in the wind.

Watching a train headed toward a leader and saying nothing to warn her is not support, it's abandonment.

Fragility: Inability to handle reasonable and necessary levels of discomfort in movement work or feedback on one's performance and behavior.

White people aren't the only ones with a fragility problem. Wanting fair and safe working conditions is one thing, but a growing number of people in movement expect their job to deliver to them a utopian experience in which they feel no discomfort—and enjoy a feeling of complete and total safety and belonging. Rajasvini Bhansali ("Vini"), co-author with Akaya Windwood of the excellent book *Leading with Joy: Practices for Uncertain Times,* is an Indian-born Jain, a daily meditator, yoga practitioner, and a former professional kathak dancer. Vini lights up every room with a delightful mix of calm, focus, and charisma. Her home and garden remind me of the magic and wonder of Frida Kahlo's house, an oasis for many a weary organizer. I am among those who have sought a quiet moment sitting amid the lush fruit trees and fragrant flowers planted lovingly by her elderly mother, nursing a cup of hot chai, and feeling my beleaguered spirit settle and come back into my body. Vini is currently the leader of the Solidaire Network, one of the largest and most powerful formations of progressive donors in the United States. The community she has cultivated at Solidaire wields power differently than most of philanthropy, by listening deeply to the grassroots and those most impacted by injustice when moving resources. It's remarkable in philanthropy for its courage. Vini described fragility as straddling this "weird neoliberal and libertarian line when people think all my needs should be met by my organization and if this unit of change meets all my needs, then the world is a better place."

WOC leaders are often punished in harsh ways for not delivering the impossible in this regard.

Fragility is sometimes disguised as a call for sustainability. It's one thing for staff to fight for the right to be excellent in an organization that is fair and sustainable. It's another to fight for the right to be mediocre in an organization that doesn't hold them accountable. We need to look closer to tell the difference.

Fragility can lead to navel-gazing. Norma Wong cautioned against the focus of movement organizations becoming disproportionately internal, "tending to individual/internal organizational hurts until that itself becomes the campaign." Many movement organizations are indeed bleeding unreasonable amounts of time and energy into the internal project of building comfy workplaces and moving away from the external work of securing a just world. The quality of their work is also suffering as managers avoid giving clear and needed feedback out of fear that fragile staff will melt down.

Movement elder Makani Themba said, "I'm concerned about how fragile many folk in the movement are acting. Folk are blowing up whole organizations and engaging in poor judgment because they feel hurt. We need more political maturity to move through challenges with integrity and an eye toward the big picture. It's just heartbreaking." Raised in the Harlem and Washington Heights neighborhoods of New York by a single mother and grandmother who were active in the labor, civil rights, and other movements of the 1960s, Makani Themba is a movement elder whose work as an author, organizer, and strategist has made a major impact on racial, health, and media justice. She continues to play an important role in, among other projects, supporting many of the leaders of the Movement for Black Lives.

This story took the cake: At one conference that Groundswell ran, two Latina staff interrupted an Afro–Puerto Rican woman presenter to make sure the audience didn't feel harmed by a video clip she had shared of Fannie Lou Hamer talking about the retaliation she experienced for daring to vote in the Jim Crow South. Shell-shocked from so many meetings being derailed by someone crying out that they had been harmed by some piece of content or another, these two staffers tried to preempt and protect themselves and the organization from callout. In the process, they undermined the presenter, who was understandably confused. I shared her confusion. The threats to voting rights are no milder today than they were then. This was a conference that people had signed up to attend to learn about voter engagement in these times. What were we shielding them from? How could we instill the seriousness of the situation and prepare people for what they would be facing out in the field if we were tiptoeing around fragility by not talking about it?

It is one thing to retraumatize people unnecessarily by forcing them to watch the video of George Floyd being murdered, or by requiring them to put their own trauma on display at work in the name of team building and organizational bonding. We should reject and avoid this. It's another to expect that movement organizations are going to be non-triggering environments. Our movement ancestors had crosses burned on their lawns, firebombs thrown in their windows, goons waiting to beat them up at the edges of the agricultural fields where they toiled. And yet they stayed focused on the endgame.

At one point I said to my management team, "We are fighting forces that are literally trying to kill our people. We have grantees who have security details outside of their homes and whose families are being threatened. This is not Nordstrom! At some point, people need to take some responsibility for where they have decided to work. I'm not a social worker because I know I don't have the stomach to pull kids out of their homes and bear witness to child abuse. I'm not a firefighter because I don't want to run into burning buildings. Too many people joining movement orgs today are doing the equivalent of signing up to be firefighters and then complaining about having to hold hoses and run into hot buildings. There's a real need for leaders to let people know, 'If this is not for you, that's fine, stop complaining, take responsibility for yourself, and go somewhere that you want to be.'"

Today, there are movement leaders living with the same kind of violent threats faced by civil rights leaders of the twentieth century. The difference is, they are now managing many staff and activists who are ready to pivot meeting after meeting into discussing every pinprick of a comment that may have offended them. My friend Sayra Pinto is a member of the University of Vermont graduate faculty and teaches in the PhD program for Transdisciplinary Leadership and Creativity for Sustainability that engages many WOC leaders. She shared the frustration that many of them feel when dealing with the reactiveness of some staff, saying, "People don't seem to understand the difference anymore between discomfort and harm."

In her essay "Coalition Politics," Dr. Bernice Johnson Reagon spoke clearly to the false expectations of comfort. "Coalition work is to be done in the streets. And it is some of the most dangerous work you can do. And you shouldn't look for comfort. Some people will come into a coalition and they rate the success of the coalition on whether or not they feel good when they get there. They're not looking for a coalition; they're looking for a home! They're looking for a bottle with some milk in it and a nipple, which does not happen in a coalition. . . . In a coalition you have to give, and it is different from your home. You can't stay there all the time. You go to the coalition for a few hours and then you go back and take your bottle wherever it is, and then you go back and coalesce some more."[5]

Fatima Goss Graves, president and CEO of the National Women's Law Center, has spent her career using the law to score wins for equal pay and equal access to education, against sexual harassment and assault, and more. She remembered a leader she admired who gave a speech that stuck with her. "She said, 'Many of you dreamed of being civil rights lawyers. Maybe you wanted to be this since you were a child and you dreamed of being a great civil rights attorney, of being like Thurgood Marshall. What did you think that was going to be like? Did you think that this was just press conferences and going on TV? This work is hard.'"

There are many ways to participate in movement, from donating to volunteering to protesting. Everyone has the right and, I would argue, the responsibility to know their limits and exercise their own agency to participate at the level that is right for them. This logic seems to be lost on many people in movement today.

Fragility also leads to the punishment of others.

Themba pointed out,

There are so many of us calling ourselves abolitionists who seem so ready to punish others. I'm sure it's not because they're bad people. They're just hurt people who bring their pain and vulnerability to the work without adequate tools to facilitate their healing. Quite a few of us think that healing is rest when it really is hard work. Facing people. Revealing things. Figuring out what you're learning and seeking ways to transform, to become better.

I've watched, with so much sadness, people deciding they're too fragile to be in the room with someone that once said something *political* they didn't like. I've seen unfounded and uninvestigated accusations accepted about comrades without question and then used to punish and even exile them. . . . I wonder how much unresolved trauma and unforgivingness are we bringing from our families of origin? I certainly don't have all the answers, but I think that Della Hicks-Wilson's poem offers a clue:

> honey
> do not let your beautiful mind become a battlefield.
> just because someone has shown you their weapons
> does not mean you have to accept the war.

Narcissistic individualism: A single-minded focus on one's own needs and comforts, irrespective of what is best for the collective or the mission of the work.

I once witnessed a staff member blow up an entire meeting when an innocuous comment triggered some unhealed trauma from their past. Months of planning were wasted while the facilitator and leadership spent the better part of the day restabilizing the group. The rise in this type of attitude and emotional immaturity is a sociopolitical phenomenon driven in no small part by the rise of social media and the resulting hyper-commercialization of self. If we don't counterbalance it, it can easily take over and take down organizations.

Victim cloaking: Exaggerating or fabricating harm to gain sympathy and attention, avoid accountability, threaten others, or justify an attack.

Victim cloaking is different from valid claims of discrimination, bias, and abuse that are supported with facts and evidence. It is deep manipulation. The example of victim cloaking that is probably the most recognizable historically is the many white women who lied about rape or harassment to get Black men lynched. Today, it's being used more widely. Right-wing forces want racial diversity and progressive views out of academia. So, they seize on one gaffe in a speech by Harvard University president Claudine Gay to call her antisemitic and terrorize her into leaving her leadership position. A Black staffer at a multiracial organization announces, "Black staff have demanded a flat organizational structure. This organization hasn't delivered, and therefore it is anti-Black!" and threatens to publicly drag the organization on social media if the demand isn't met. A Latinx immigrant staff member doesn't like receiving fair feedback from a Black coworker, so seeks vengeance by spreading rumors that the coworker is xenophobic. A white trans man with a history of serious performance issues derails a meeting to call out his supervisor, declaring the reason he was denied a promotion is because of transphobia.

The motivations for those who use this tactic against WOC leaders range from conservatives who don't want racial diversity or progressive thinkers in positions of power to paid infiltrators and provocateurs, to jealous haters, to grifters seeking a payday from a settlement, to attention seekers, and to disgruntled staff seeking revenge for critical performance feedback or the denial of a promotion.

False claims about violations of worker rights and discrimination are one of the main tools being used to take out WOC leaders. When those who attack WOC leaders wrap their assault in the cloak of feigned victimhood, the attacks go largely unopposed, including by those on the left.

The victim narrative functions as an invisibility cloak for three reasons:

1. It plays directly into tropes about Black and Brown women being "aggressive," "mean," "frauds," and "incompetent."

Thus onlookers accept it without question because, just like stereotypes about Black male criminality or female hysteria, it tracks with the programming the media/society has fed them and that they already believe.

2. It is not recognized as an attack because it is confused with a justifiable defense of a marginalized group against an "abuse or misuse of power" by someone who holds positional power. There is less attention to facts because of the assumption that people in power generally weather things. There is a lack of understanding of what it means to hold power in a micro context (as an organizational leader) while simultaneously being marginalized in the macro context of the societal power structure (as a woman of color living in the United States). A WOC leader doesn't become less vulnerable to attack because she has a powerful position professionally; she becomes more vulnerable to it because she angers traditionalists who want her to get back in her place. And she's much less likely to weather a storm of attack.

3. It's a newer weapon for people of color. We can easily recognize the white woman who falsely accuses a Black male of rape to galvanize a lynch mob because it has happened so many times throughout history. We see that she enjoys not only the rush of power from orchestrating the man's destruction—a power she often lacks in other areas of her life—but also the attention and celebrity for being a victim who is the focus of assistance and protection. We see how the cloak allows the white woman to level her opponent while, within mainstream white cultural norms, staying within the socially acceptable box designed for the "meeker, milder sex" that needs saving

and protecting. We are less likely to recognize lies about various types of victimhood told by members of other groups, because they have been less common historically. Yet, today victim cloaking is widely used by members of other marginalized groups who wrap attacks in false accusations of transphobia, xenophobia, ableism, anti-Blackness, antisemitism, abuse of workers, etc., to take WOC leaders out.

Some WOC use victim cloaking on each other. Just as the white woman cries "I was raped," a toxic woman of color staffer will call "I was harmed," and the mob will descend. Sometimes she will attempt to increase her own status by positioning herself as the brave protector of her co-workers, willing to risk it all to voice what she claims others are too afraid to say. It is deep manipulation. I have observed that in groups of WOC, it is rarely the majority who deliberately cast the woman with power as a monster—it is almost always just one or two people—but the majority will often either join the mob or be silent bystanders to it unless someone intervenes.

Many WOC attempt to defeat or preempt the stereotypes used in victim cloaking by working overtime to put people at ease and prove to them that they are good and fair. White male leaders are rarely required to waste precious time that could be spent moving their organization forward on this level of relational hand-holding to reassure their staff that they are not horrible people. The project of proving one's goodness is a bottomless pit. It saps our time. It tricks us into trying to win over staff who might pose a threat to organizational health, and who we actually have a moral and professional obligation to transition out. The truth is, we cannot counter this alone. We need others, including other WOC, to flank us and actively oppose, disrupt, and block this kind of attack. When accusations of harm arise, we must insist on proper evidence and process and not leave sisters isolated and alone behind baseless or exaggerated claims.

Perpetual deconstructionism: Positioning oneself as better/more knowledgeable by constantly poking holes in the work and thinking of others and engaging from a stance of critique for critique's sake. Consistently complaining and vocalizing what you are against/in disagreement with rather than what you are for/in agreement with. Not to be confused with constructive debate and dialectic to arrive at the best path toward the shared goal of liberation.

A few months before I left my organization, a longtime woman of color colleague also left. We had worked side by side for nearly a decade. In our final check-in meeting, she spoke candidly. "These newer staff have no idea what we went through. What it was like to go into a room full of funders and be the only WOC, the only people talking about organizing before either of those things were seen as credible, and to just have to make a way out of no way, while having low pay and benefits ourselves. Their high salaries, amazing benefits, and allies in the rooms they walk into—we had none of that, and we rolled our sleeves up and figured it out. If we had spent half the time they do complaining, we wouldn't have built shit." She was right. The complaining was incessant, and all the more maddening because our meeting 99 percent of their demands seemed to do nothing to quell it. Meeting their demands only seemed to fuel a culture of whining and dissatisfaction.

The last time I remembered feeling so routinely degraded by others in a work setting was in my early twenties when I worked as a server at a restaurant. There were always one or two awful customers who seemed to delight in complaining in a rude and entitled tone, sending food back to the kitchen, demanding to speak to the manager, and generally treating their servers like dirt.

Caitlin Breedlove, the previous co-director of Southerners on New Ground, wrote about deconstructionist culture during her battle with cancer: "It must be nice, to think you have all the time in the world to cut rather than sew."[6] Grief rose up in me as I thought about "limited time" in the context of a sister leader like Caitlin facing her own mortality, and of human beings as a species (including my own children) facing ours. To watch so many people in movement do nothing but poke holes and tear down as if there were no clock at all is a level of obliviousness that makes me gnash my teeth in frustration.

Others have noted the influence of academic culture on the rise in deconstructionism in movement space. Sandra Bass, executive director and associate dean of the Public Service Center at the University of California at Berkeley, said, "I've spent a fair amount of my time in higher ed, where deconstruction and tearing down ideas and others is often viewed as the height of intellectualism, so I wonder how much these institutions have contributed to this, particularly as movements are often grounded in intellectual frames. We try to address this in my work but it is an uphill struggle."

Deconstructionism is highly gendered. One need only look at the ways in which female political candidates are shredded in comparison to their male counterparts. From Hillary Clinton to Stacey Abrams to Kamala Harris, it is culturally permissible to tear down women who dare to assume positions of power in a more vicious and multidimensional way than it is to tear down men. We know that race adds scrutiny to gender, and so WOC face a higher degree of deconstructionism in the organizations they lead than almost any other group of leaders.

There should always be a healthy amount of space for critical thinking and sharpening our ideas through principled discussion and debate. But constantly tearing everything down—particularly institutions developed by generations of WOC—is neither smart nor strategic.

Othering: Shaming, humiliating, and excluding people for not fitting into accepted sociocultural norms and categorizations.

One of the great ironies of movement is that so many of the people within it talk a good game about the inclusion of those who are marginalized—while meting out the most strident criticism and exclusion of those who do not fit into various cultural boxes. This has been true throughout history. Black women were the engine of the Civil Rights Movement, and a Black gay man, Bayard Rustin, was the lead organizer of the March on Washington, yet none of them were allowed on the mic during that event, and homophobia and sexism pervaded civil rights organizations. While the United Farm Workers boasted more women on its staff than any other union in the United States in the 1960s and '70s, Dolores Huerta was the only woman allowed onto their executive board. WOC were among the crowd who mercilessly booed Sylvia Rivera, a Puerto Rican transgender woman and activist, at New York City's Christopher Street Liberation Day rally in 1973.

In doing this, some people in movements replicate the worst of what they are ostensibly trying to change in the world: the exclusion and othering of people. Scholar john powell, an expert on othering, noted, "When you strip people of their humanity, when you deny people their full participation, when you refuse to see the divine in people—that is called othering. Race is a very powerful way to 'other' in the United States. But there are other forms of othering as well. Around the world, we 'other' people because of religion, language, immigration status, sexual orientation. . . . We are very creative in finding ways to say that someone's not part of the 'we.' "[7]

Even as WOC leaders fight to foster belonging among their staff, they are often left out of the "we" in the organizations they are leading. Leadership is a notoriously lonely place, but it can be particularly desolate for WOC leaders, who often face a more intense form of othering for daring to occupy positions of power.

Today, othering toward and often between WOC is rampant. I have heard from several Black women leaders who were assailed by other Black women who did not debate them on their strategies or tactics but instead questioned their "Blackness." It's worth noting that while some of these women were light-skinned Black women, several of them were not. Being dark brown offered no protection. Long social media threads are filled with comments by Black activists who think Black people who have one white parent have no business ever holding leadership positions in Black movements. Latinx people for whom Spanish was a second language have their authenticity questioned. Trans women often talk about the painful othering and exclusion they experience in predominately cis women spaces, even when the people there are mostly cis WOC.

Bamby Salcedo, executive director of TransLatin@ Coalition, pointed out that the impact is not just emotional wounding, but a material one. "In the Violence Against Women Act, there was no funding to trans-led organizations. There are people [cis women] who have the ability to distribute funds in an equitable way and do not. Trans WOC are part of the human tapestry. Even though we have been part of many movements, our contributions have not been acknowledged. There are conversations that need to happen about who gets to be a woman. In the women's space, we belong."

In our attempt to create environments in which othering cannot thrive, we have to be careful not to overcorrect. Movement elder and author Akaya Windwood, who for eleven years led Rockwood Leadership Institute, a major learning space for social justice leaders, said of movement, "In an effort to be hyper-inclusive, we created space for people to act very badly. If my stack of traumas is higher than your stack of traumas then I get to prevail."

I recall a meeting I once attended where a white transgender man got into a tense discussion with a cis Black woman and a cis Native American woman about who was more oppressed. The Black woman expressed frustration at only just now beginning to be "seen" by the left, and funders, only to feel that transgender people were attempting to step in front of her. The trans man described transphobia experienced from cis WOC at a previous place of employment. The Native woman pointed out that her people suffer greater disparities based on nearly every indicator, from poverty to illness to domestic violence. The conversation wore on and on and derailed the entire meeting because the facilitator was too worried about not including everyone's voice to step in and redirect. Finally, the cis Native American woman intervened with the redirect, saying, "It's not helpful when we play the trauma Olympics." No one could really argue with that, and the debate died down.

6

Two Generational Shifts

There are two generational shifts occurring in movement. The first is the ordinary influx of young people, who, like every generation before them, bring new ways of seeing and engaging the world. The second is the unprecedented shift in the mentality of people of *all* ages that are being attracted to movement jobs at this time in history. Let's start with the first of these shifts.

Every younger generation pushes the older one. That's the way it's always been and the way it should be. Second-wave feminists horrified their parents by pronouncing their right to govern their bodies and express their sexuality and by demanding gender equity in the home and workplace. Young Chicanos, including Cesar Chavez and Dolores Huerta, formed the United Farm Workers union against the cautions of some elders. Many of the Black youth who marched and sat in at lunch counters did so against the will of their parents, who implored them to keep their heads down, collect their college degrees, and move up the socioeconomic ladder. Today, Gen Zers are deepening the work that millennials began, in pushing us to free ourselves from limitations like the gender binary and U.S. norms of martyrdom and overwork that have led to health problems for my and prior generations. They are also challenging a host of other long-held norms in the workplace. Like many Gen Xers, I feel a combination of deep gratitude for most of the push they are bringing (especially around rejecting the gender binary and the martyrdom mindset) and concern about some of it. In an effort to not be a grumpy forty-six-year-old about the latter and to not sugarcoat things either, I sat down to discuss generational shifts with movement elders, Gen Xers, millennials, and Gen Zers to try and understand some of the tensions in the broadest possible context.

While having tea in the home of my mentor Adisa Douglas, her partner Dr. Bernice Johnson Reagon recalled that when she and her peers were college students and joined protests in the South, they were all expelled—even from some Historically Black Colleges and Universities—and many never earned their degrees. Bernice was among forty students expelled from Albany State College in Georgia in 1961 for participating in civil rights protests. This was a huge deal for many of them, who were the first in their families to attend college and on whom the dreams of their parents and communities were riding.

Nearly fifty years later, Everette J. Freeman, the new president of Albany State University, hired someone to find all these former students of what was then called Albany State Junior College and invite them to walk the stage during commencement and receive their degrees. These were not symbolic degrees, but official ones—which Freeman had to negotiate hard with the Board of Regents of the state of Georgia to secure. Bernice, who was the keynote speaker, recalled the sight from her perch onstage, standing behind the lectern. A line of elders, in cap and gown, some pushing walkers, some being pushed in wheelchairs, were making their way toward the stage to collect their diplomas. All wore medallions around their necks engraved with the words 1961 CIVIL RIGHTS SOLDIER. What a sacrifice they had made to let the fire of their youth burn bright—despite the advice and admonishments of so many of their elders—and change the world as profoundly as they did. Ethnic studies, the Civil Rights Act, the end of Jim Crow segregation—my generation owes them so much for being an indelible example of courage. We always need the energy, fire, and radical imagination of the young to push us further along the arc toward justice.

The current generation of young people is no different, and the list of gifts they have already given us is long. The rejection of the gender binary has improved the lives of countless people all along the gender spectrum. A forty-something-year-old friend of mine who has always presented somewhere between mainstream norms of masculine and feminine told me the other day, "I'm a they! I introduced myself to someone that way, and for the first time my gender felt like it fit. It's like I finally have the language that lets me be comfortable in my own skin." With research showing that conventional gender norms create not only inequity in pay and opportunity but differences in rates of disease and death, transgressing these is profoundly good for society.

Young people put up with far fewer injustices in their workplaces than my generation did. Low pay, no benefits, harassment, and discrimination were things that we protested, but not to the same degree. Too often we put our well-being on the back burner to support the cause and the community at any cost. Young people today are pushing many organizations to level up, which is a good thing. "I experience the intensity that millennials bring to work," said Viviana Rennella, executive director of the Windcall Institute, which supports grassroots organizers to rest and reflect to sustain themselves in the work. "They are bringing something with their way of being. Maybe we need to break through old structures. They are bringing the break. We, as leaders, are in the impact zone."

When I hear young people argue for a four-day workweek, I don't disagree (with the caveat that I don't think it is necessarily the right fit for *every* organization). In many ways, it is the unfinished work of the labor movement and would represent a catch-up to other countries where people work far less and have more time to enjoy life with friends, family, and interests outside of a job. When I hear them dream of a world in which AI (if it doesn't annihilate us first) does all the tedious work, freeing people up to not have to work for money at all, and to just spend their time doing whatever their hearts desire, my ears prick up. Imagine if a young artist or scientist, for example, didn't need a day job and could just devote all of their time to deepening their creation and discovery. What an evolutionary leap that would be in the human experience!

While many in my generation are still stuck in issue and identity silos, young people tend to flow much more easily in an intersectional frame, and the notion of differences in sexuality, gender, and race is simply not as big a deal to them—which is beneficial for grassroots organizing and power building. They also pay greater attention to issues like climate change. The energy they are bringing to today's most pressing issues is brave and creative.

The student protest of the genocide in Gaza is one of the most inspiring and hopeful things I have seen lately. I spoke with Layal Srouji (age twenty-five) and Maryam Alwan (age twenty-two), two Palestinian undergraduate students and organizers at Columbia University who helped establish the first of what would be hundreds of Gaza solidarity encampments on college and university campuses around the globe. With WOC at the forefront, student activists at Columbia ran the equivalent of a small village. They had a daily schedule to make sure the one thousand students and community members onsite had access to meals, a medical tent, mental health services, educational programming, and other supplies, and that there was a student press team to address the media each afternoon. They responded nimbly and with great courage and sacrifice to changing conditions. Maryam described: "When we were arrested we had no idea students would jump onto the second lawn and take it over and hold it for so long. It showed me what the real world could look like if people cared for one another. They banned tents, so everyone was sleeping on the ground, in the cold, in the rain. People put tarps over each other. There was a lot of love and community and solidarity. People were interested in learning and in standing in solidarity with Palestinians."

For week after week, students held the space, through inclement weather, the possibility of expulsion, and police brutality. Maryam, who was arrested in the first police raid on the encampment, recalled a second crackdown, "where people occupied offices, one person had his face stomped on and bones broken around his eye. Another person was thrown down stairs and denied access to an EMT. Six people were hospitalized." Despite this brutality, the students persisted.

When I ask Maryam and Layal about the strengths of their generation, they talked about the fearlessness with which young people are willing to confront authority. They also name a savviness in using social media to advance justice. Layal pointed out that students at the encampments have successfully shifted the positions of many key leaders and corporations through online organizing. She said, "Our attention is their currency. They want to advertise to us. Unfollowing them and blocking them—they lose their platform, they lose their value because we give them value. We starve them from the attention economy." She noted that some young creators "are producing content on a level that people would pay millions for. They access a different audience that you would never reach with an on-the-ground protest."

In an age where news media outlets are either drying up altogether or increasingly controlled by corporate and political interests, Maryam sees social media as an important conduit for information, saying it "allows us to tell the truth and the school has to respond. You can live stream, show pictures of what is going on and unravel the narrative spun by our institutions." She also pointed out the way these platforms have shifted the sight line of young people into global events, saying, "This is the first live stream genocide. A lot of my friends and peers are developing relationships where they worry about people [in Gaza] just by watching their videos every day and wondering if they are alive. We are seeing different things completely than what authorities and older people are seeing."

What young people are accomplishing is all the more impressive considering this is a particularly difficult time in history to be young. They grew up amid Covid, looming climate disasters, the erosion of an already fractured democracy, and the decay of empire. The cost of living is rising, minimum wage jobs don't pay enough for rent, and healthcare costs are soaring. Colleges are more difficult to get into and afford. The horrendous events of recent years have had the greatest impact on youth, simply because they have occupied a larger percentage of their lives. Covid left a whole swath of young people more isolated, robbing them of experiences and relationships every prior generation has taken for granted. The cultural impact of four years of Trump—fear, terror, suspicion, fake news—has shaped their views on politics and authority. The increasing frequency of mass shootings at schools, movie theaters, stores, and spaces they are in regularly in their daily lives adds to the declining sense of safety. Social media has shortened all of our attention spans and increased narcissism and obsession with image, making us more divided and less likely to extend grace. And many young people don't know a world without social media.

The leaders of today are also met with less comprehensive supports to prepare them for movement work. The infrastructure that once trained people in grassroots organizing and steeped them in political education has been largely dismantled. "The pipeline, in many ways, has changed," said Jessica Byrd, president of Black Campaign School, co-founder of the Movement for Black Lives' Electoral Justice Project, and former principal with Three Point Strategies. "Our resume pools aren't strong. [The applicants] are met with a set of expectations that they are not prepared for. When I came up at eighteen, nineteen, twenty years old, you went to all these training programs, and they would deploy you different places. A lot of people have decades of that level of grooming for leadership, preparing, doing the same thing over and over again until you are strong at it. That's not the case today."

One of the supports I'm so grateful that I had when I was coming up in movement that many young people lack today is strong guidance from elders. As much as we have always needed the fire of the young, movements have needed loving and grounded elders to guide and temper some of that zeal. When I was a young person, I remember once confronting the legendary organizer Gary Delgado with a talk-to-the-hand gesture. I don't even remember what I was so upset about, only that I was on the verge of tears about some written document we were working on to support welfare moms. But I shudder in embarrassment when thinking of my show of disrespect. I once co-led a delegation of my co-workers into the office of our staff director of an SEIU local where I worked as an organizer. We had a staff union and there was a labor dispute with management, but in hindsight I can see that I took this action without much clarity. The staff director was also my supervisor and someone I liked and respected a great deal and had always been fair with me. I was young and green, and I felt solidarity with my co-workers and had a lot of youthful energy to fight and crusade. While I firmly believe in the right of staff to organize and make fair demands and take direct action if management refuses to negotiate respectfully, I could have started that conversation in a less escalated way.

But each time I showed up this way, an older person pulled me aside and with love and an unwavering firmness told me that what I was doing was not okay and that I needed to cut it out. They talked to me about the difference between healthy critique and debate, and destructive acting out and tearing down. I respected them enough to hear them, sit with what they said, and course correct. I didn't make the same mistake again. My elders taught me about the principal of Sankofa, that you look back and take the wisdom of the past into the future.

"Was I not deferential to some movement elders?" said Cindy Wiesner, executive director of Grassroots Global Justice Alliance. "Yes. But at the same time, there was a practice of grounding and knowing that we had to build bases, build worker power. Our task was building people's organizations. There was a humility to the work, which was important. That's what kept me honest."

The propensity of not all, but many young people today toward unprecedented levels of victim cloaking, performative wokeness, twisting of identity politics, slash-and-burn tactics, and hasty teardown of anyone who holds positional power is playing a significant role in damaging the ability of movement organizations to win. So is the tendency to overfocus on the internal fight within organizations as a proxy for external battles that, for good reason, can feel overwhelming, particularly to young people, who know they will likely live to see even more apocalyptic conditions due to the climate crisis. Said Layal, "You stew in an uncertainty that no one can comfort, so there is the desire to control something." Some of this behavior needs to be challenged, both by elders and by the many young people who are tired of the nonsense and really want to do movement work that wins.

Yet, many older staff are afraid to call in young people. Well-founded fears exist that young people will use social media to light your ass up. What might have once been a disrespectful word or gesture by a young person to a manager in front of a few co-workers has become a callout, viewable by thousands, that can destroy a leader's reputation and seriously damage their career—regardless of whether what is said is true or not. Many leaders are keenly aware that WOC are given no margin for error and easily discarded for perceived mistakes. They have watched other leaders be left alone when their reputations are publicly stoned. They have given everything to the cause and may not have a clear plan B to support themselves or their families if the movement excommunicates them. As a result, many leaders often back off from challenging younger people.

One woman of color colleague put it this way: "Nowadays you really have to stop and think, is it worth destroying my entire career to hold a twenty-four-year-old accountable? To give them the feedback that they need to grow?" More than once, I have regretted backing off from challenging such staffers. We were all movement newbies once, but our size was proportionate to our elders, and our unskilled flailing was manageable. Social media, however, has made young people in movement a hundred feet tall, their outrage often determining the fate of elders and entire organizations.

With so many upsides (many more than I've listed in the previous pages) to what the new generation is bringing, what would elders or peers need to call some young people in about? What are the challenges most frequently named by non-millennials and non-Gen-Zers, and sometimes named by young people themselves about the "younger generation"?

The "just burn it all down" mentality is one. The debate about this isn't just happening between young people and Gen X and older folks, as Layal shared, it's happening among young activists themselves. "There's a lot of 'fuck the school, let's burn it down.' But I find myself repeating that we need to sit down and breathe together and think through what do we build after? What is the alternative that we are building? We all agree that the empire must fall but there needs to be concurrent work around what future we're building to replace it." As my friend Ash-Lee Woodard Henderson said, "Sound bites are not strategies." Ash and others urge us to consider that if you want to burn down the entire government but lack the plan and capacity to build its replacement, conditions are going to get a lot worse for the most marginalized communities. That is neither strategic nor responsible.

It can be particularly excruciating for staff who remember how little movement infrastructure existed when we were young, and saw how much sweat our and prior generations put into building what we have, to see organizations torched in such a cavalier manner. "We as Black people don't have a lot of institutions in this country," said Gina Clayton-Johnson, executive director of Essie Justice Group. "It was not that long ago where there was none of this, and you had to be very careful and very loving with the heart product of all of this work because it is fragile and needs to be nurtured." A Harvard Law School graduate who has dedicated her life work to empowering her community, Gina named her organization for her great-grandmother Essie Bailey, a share-cropper who fled the racism, sexism, and poverty of the Jim Crow

South, only to find, and have to work to change, similar conditions in California. It's Essie's story and the social change work of every generation in her family since that informs Gina's perspective on what it takes to build movement infrastructure.

There is a similar feeling about the knee-jerk takedown of leaders, when it has taken many generations of women of color to pry open the door for people like us to lead at all. One leader who wanted to remain anonymous said, "Now many orgs are led by WOC. We got them there as a community. We put these people in positions of power. And now younger people are tearing them down. Why are you tearing these women down? What is your vision, then?"

A related issue is the tendency to flare and flame out quickly, or hewing toward one-off mobilization vs. long-term organizing. As Layal described, "There is a rage and an anger in all of us, we want to yell and protest and confront something that will feel like confronting the problem. It's very cathartic and necessary at times but it's also very dangerous when you're functioning on just rage, thinking that fervor is going to sustain the revolution and bring us to liberation. It's not. It's the first stepping stone of liberation. There is very unglamorous and monotonous work that needs to be done: organizing and process and systems and coordination."

What Layal described in terms of the lack of appetite for the less glamorous, long-term work is a challenge that can be seen with all of the major uprisings and mobilizations over the past twenty years, from Occupy Wall Street to the massive immigrant rights marches, to Black Lives Matter, to the Women's March on the nation's capital, to the 2020 summer of uprisings. It has proven exceedingly difficult in recent years to convert the energy of these massive mobilizations (all fueled in some part by the galvanizing power of social media) into the long-term work of organizing and base building that is needed to deliver and defend policy and systems change and ultimately material improvements that people feel in their daily lives.

Sometimes it's not rage but fragility that causes people to burn things down, or just melt down themselves, and while fragility is showing up more among all age groups, it is one of the most prominent challenges that people will name about young people. Many older people perceive the younger generation as being incapable of taking in even the most basic levels of feedback that any- and everyone needs to learn a job and advance in their field.

Jessica Byrd is president of the Black Campaign School, was on *Time* magazine's list of one hundred "emerging leaders shaping the future," and served as deputy director for both of Stacey Abrams's gubernatorial campaigns. Byrd and her two siblings lived through homelessness as children, and their loving bond was the inspiration for the name of the first organization she founded, Three Point Strategies, which helped scores of Black women run for elected office and trained Black people in a wide spectrum of electoral work. To watch Byrd facilitate a strategy meeting is like watching a great conductor whose remarkable ear can pick up even the most distant note. Calm, present, unflappable, and brilliant, she can help to harmonize the most disparate group of people. "I got my ass kicked," she said. "My campaign managers, my boss at EMILY's List—they were tough. They got their work done. They showed up as killers every day, and they made me a killer. I look back at those bosses, and they really did want me to be great. They wanted me to be strong. These kids today wouldn't have hacked them, they wouldn't have made it at all."

Dara Cooper, co-founder and former ED of the National Black Food and Justice Alliance, explained how she sees feedback. "That is literally my love language to people: If I believe in your leadership, I'm going to give you some critical feedback, and I want you to do the same to me. But people were falling apart."

Silvia Henriquez, former executive director of the National Latina Institute for Reproductive Justice and the abortion justice organization All* Above All, shared a similar sentiment. "Now, building a bench is much harder," she said. "My definition of bringing people along is being able to have a direct conversation about what's working and what's not working and how their leadership needs to evolve. I don't feel like that's a conversation I can have with folks anymore. That's why I decided to step out of leadership. It is really hard to give feedback, to mentor." The daughter of immigrants, Silvia rebuilt the United States' only national Latinx reproductive justice organization from the ground up through grit and hard work, making it one of the highest-impact RJ organizations in the country before taking the helm at All* and scoring major wins for abortion access—wins that are enabling pregnant people in many states to weather the repeal of *Roe* better than they otherwise would have.

Fragility kicks into overdrive when someone is terminated. "One of the biggest things I hear is, 'We don't throw people away,'" said Dara Cooper. "In the movements I come from, if you are derelict in your responsibility, there is accountability, and you are removed from your post. That is not throwing someone away, that is holding someone accountable."

"This new generation is pushing the edges around gender, sexuality, the praxis of care," said one leader who wished to remain anonymous. "I'm excited about that, and I know there is a way to move with a level of care at the core and not be so fragile and vulnerable that you fall apart at the seams at any sneeze or offense."

This becomes particularly destructive in the context of movement work that requires people to work across differences of race, class, and gender. This work is necessary, and it is difficult and uncomfortable. Young people with a lot of fragility, who carry unreasonable expectations of comfort, can torch an organization in frustration when they feel discomfort.

Entitlement is another issue, which is often paired with a misuse of identity politics in ways that harm organizations. It's common for Gen X or older managers to trade stories about a young person coming into their office and demanding a promotion after only a short time (from a few months to a few days) on the job—and then declaring how unvalued their labor is when they don't get it. Most organizers my age expected to spend at least two or three years learning the craft and proving themselves before being considered for a promotion. I observed a staffer in her twenties, with no leadership or management experience, announcing at an all-staff meeting of a multimillion-dollar organization that she and other staffers didn't need an ED, a board, or even senior management because "We are people of color, we are queer, and we could run this organization tomorrow!" Fellow younger staffers congratulated her for being "so brave." *This,* I thought, *is an SNL skit.* It would be funnier if it weren't playing out and causing serious conflict and damage in scores of organizations across movement. My objection is not to young people leading—many iconic movement leaders throughout history have been young—anywhere from teenagers to early thirties. But they didn't show up riding on just identity and entitlement. Whether it was a young Rosa Parks starting out as a secretary at the NAACP and training at the Highlander Center, or Cesar Chavez and Dolores Huerta studying and practicing organizing with Fred Ross, or a young Dr. King spending years learning nonviolence in India and theology in seminary and honing his craft as a preacher, they put in the work and they demonstrated skill.

There is also an incredibly strong anti-leader and anti-hierarchy streak among young people. This is understandable, given their disillusionment that was fed by four years of Trump, but that doesn't make it constructive. It is often paired with the notion that all hierarchy is white supremacist and that authentic people of color–led formations should be flat. Chrissie Castro is the network weaver of the Native Voice Network (thirty-five-plus Native-led organizations that mobilize through Indigenous cultural values), the co-founder of Advance Native Political Leadership (the premier organization helping Native people run for political office), and the California Native Vote Project. She often reminds Native youth that "Many of our traditional communities as Native peoples had structure and hierarchy" and that "All power is not unearned power."

There is a disconcerting level of ignorance about the differences in organizational structures and how governance works. This is, I think, due to the greater difficulty accessing comprehensive political education about movement history, structures, strategies, etc., which was more readily available to Gen X. One Gen X leader was surprised when a younger staffer who had led and won a unionization drive was disappointed to discover that the organizational chart would not automatically be flattened. She was unaware that unions don't end hierarchy; they in fact reify it, while mitigating its worst effects by enabling the bargaining unit to negotiate with management.

Dara Cooper also challenged the uncritical thinking that abounds about flat organizations, saying, "People don't want to meet a lot, they don't want to work a lot, but they want democratic consensus in thirty minutes with fifty people making decisions. If that isn't the definition of insanity, I don't know what is. You want impossible things. I've been to Colombia and South Africa, all over the world, where I've seen people work to build democratic processes and consensus. We start at nine in the morning, and that shit goes to midnight. So if y'all want democratic process, I'm down for it, but what y'all are talking about is not that."

One area in which there is an interesting dialectic about challenges is the topic of work ethic. On the one hand, there is an opinion—prevalent among many in the Gen X-and-up age set— that young people have overcorrected way past a reasonable work-life balance into the absence of a healthy work ethic. This is in the zeitgeist broadly. A version of this is reflected in a 2022 *New York Times* article by Noreen Malone called "The Age of Anti-Ambition." Comedian Amy Poehler has a bit about it in the show she is currently touring with fellow comic Tina Fey that kills with huge audiences of mostly middle-agers. I think there are some really legitimate issues behind "quiet quitting" that leaders need to attend to, in terms of clarifying core responsibilities along with what is "extra" and when (within reason vs. all the time) "extra" is needed. Still, it is hard to easily dismiss the volume of complaints about young people being late to work, missing deadlines, and doing the bare minimum. One leader was incredulous that she had to explain to several Gen Zers who had signed up to work at an electoral organization that they could not expect to clock out at 5:00 P.M. during a major election week. This had never happened before.

One thing that seems to be getting lost in the overcorrection away from martyrdom is the positive idea of expressing one's agency and passion through work. Work doesn't have to be drudgery, done to benefit someone else in exchange for a paycheck—it can be fun and an avenue through which to express your full and empowered self. Movement workers are not making widgets or mining coal, we are doing something that is deeply meaningful to the well-being of our communities.

Layal and Maryam pushed back hard on my critique around Gen Z's work ethic in some helpful ways. Said Layal, "There is no shortage of work ethic. What I saw on the lawn was only able to happen and maintain itself because people saw a need and filled it. They saw where their power and energy would be most impactful and executed it to a degree that was needed to sustain a community. People sacrificed, didn't sleep. They produced programming, entertainment, education, meals, a people's library, day in and day out." I felt more hopeful after my conversations with them than I had in a long while. My main takeaway is that while there is something in the zeitgeist that is lowering work ethic among some, there is also something that is making it strong in many others.

I think there is more to explore here. As the child of a single working mother, I am a staunch advocate of work-life balance. In fact, I left the labor movement so that I could have more time with my kids than my mom had with me. For those who want to shine and express their talents in a career, it isn't all-or-nothing. There can be balance that also leaves room for surge capacity in moments of key opportunity. There's a happy medium here somewhere between the extremes and I hope we'll land there. I think there are many people in movement, of all ages, who are already there and thriving.

Ultimately, there are places where older folks in movement need to honor the wisdom of young people and follow their lead. There are places where older generations need to find a way to reach out to guide and challenge young people, just as our elders found a way to do so for us. The young people who are not adrift—who have kept their eye on the North Star of liberation—they also need to serve as leaders to their peers, and at times, to their elders as well. Their help will guide us all.

The second generational shift in movement is in the mentality of people, *of all ages,* who are being attracted to work at movement organizations. The analogy I'd offer is this: Imagine you have a crew of firefighters. They are fighting the hottest fire season on record. Half of them signed up for the job because they wanted to fight fires. They are exhausted, they have outdated equipment and insufficient training. If given adequate rest, better equipment, and training, they will be effective at their jobs. The other half signed up because they wanted to ring the siren on the fire truck and be pictured in the calendar. They never had any intention of fighting fires. No amount of four-day workweeks, training, or healing justice is going to make them want to do a job they never signed up to do. They will continue to complain and act out, endangering themselves and their colleagues, along with the masses of people who stand to lose their homes and lives if the fires are not controlled.

This is what is happening in movement. As LaTosha Brown noted, "A lot of people coming into movement now are instant activists. They are there for different motivations—to boost themselves, not to build movement."

Individualism is on steroids with social media–selfie culture. "There is a deep individualist approach to people's politics that is disturbing," said Dara Cooper, co-founder and former ED of the National Black Food and Justice Alliance. Dara is the daughter of Black liberation activists and has spent most of her life in movement. She offers wisdom about what movements should take from the past and how they should move differently, including cultivating joy and wellness—she is a DJ and yoga practitioner—while also building durable infrastructure, including coaching and strategy building for Black and Brown food and land justice organizations to restore self-determination and right relationship to the earth. Dara noted, "The 'There is something that I want, and if it doesn't go my way then I'm going to take down this whole org' stance—I'm seeing that a lot. It's pretty heartbreaking what people are willing to do to entire organizations and ecosystems for the sake of their own self-interest."

Why are people with this mindset flocking to movement organizations? When I came into movement in the late 1990s, the low pay, few to no benefits, long hours, and tough working conditions of most jobs were a deterrent to all but the most dedicated. At the time, most community organizers worked sixty-plus hours a week (often more like eighty) and earned less than $25,000 per year. Many organizations were on such a shoestring budget that they would periodically run out of funds and have to lay off the entire staff, and people would go on unemployment but keep working for the organization without pay to keep key campaigns going. It was a labor of love. Very few people entered with a stance of pure self-interest and ego, and if they did, they generally didn't last long. Those who stayed were mostly people whose primary orientation was one of service and commitment to the communities they were working to empower.

Like most of my peers at the time, when I became a community organizer, my motivation wasn't profit or fame or followers or likes—social media was only just barely beginning. It was a passion for changing the world and improving the material conditions of the most marginalized in our society. If there was any self-interest at all, it was that having experienced and witnessed firsthand the pain, both material and psychological, that exclusion from belonging had visited upon me and those I loved, I wanted to be a part of creating a world where people—including myself—didn't suffer more of the same.

The leaders of my generation dedicated the past two to three decades of our lives to build up movement organizations to be better places to work, to offer good pay and benefits and hours that enabled more work-life balance, often with the encouragement of younger people on our staff teams. The improvements are a good thing and should continue. What we didn't anticipate was that with the deterrent of the shitty job removed, and the advent of Trump inspiring more activism, a wider range of applicants flocked to movement organizations, including scores of people who were less values aligned and whose level of fragility, individualism, narcissism, and penchant for barrier building made them capable of derailing entire organizations.

I once had a staff member who said, "Why do we keep talking about our external mission to queer people and people of color? We *are* those people!" This person, a middle-class, college-educated staffer earning a large salary at a foundation, genuinely saw herself as no different from the grassroots leaders we were supporting—the frontline organizers receiving death threats from white militia members, or the trans sex workers of color fighting for their most basic rights, not knowing where they would get their next meal, or if they had a place to sleep that night. I was dumbstruck. I had been raised by my movement elders with the credo that Toni Morrison so powerfully conveyed in the 1979 commencement speech she delivered to Barnard College: "The function of freedom is to free someone else."[1] This kind of thinking came up constantly. On one call, I tried to reason with staff, saying, "We don't remember Harriet Tubman because she ran north to freedom and chilled in a phat crib up north—we remember her because she went back! Because she sacrificed her own comfort to free others who were worse off."

Ten or fifteen years ago, you didn't see people announcing in interviews that they needed position titles to change "because my life coach said it's better for my brand." You didn't see people in their supervisor's office demanding a promotion after just a few weeks on the job, or declaring themselves qualified for choice positions solely based on their race or gender or some other identity marker. It would have been unthinkable for a worker at an electoral organization to suggest clocking out at 5:00 P.M. close to an election. You rarely saw someone become triggered on an important group call and derail the meeting to have the entire group process, at length, what had just offended them. It would have been odd to hear someone at an organization with generous salaries suggest that there is no difference between them and the marginalized communities the organization is working to serve. Yet today, all of these are commonplace, and they are coming from people of all ages.

One of the hard facts that few people in movement talk openly about is this: In the past decade, movement organizations have been overrun by these types of people: the Karens of movement. Though many lovely people named Karen don't fit the stereotype, "Karen" is typically used to describe white women who call a manager or the police on people of color for doing regular activities—BBQ Becky in Oakland, or Amy Cooper, who called the cops on a bird-watcher in New York. Movement organizations have equal-opportunity Karens. They come in every race, color, and gender. They are distraught that fighting the rising forces of authoritarianism is not more comfy, and they would like to speak with a manager. They would also like more credit (and pay) for building something amazing, despite having built nothing but a pile of complaints. A person who has a learning curve around pronouns or racial justice but is fundamentally passionate about the liberation of oppressed people is usually someone a leader can shift and work with. A Karen, you cannot. The proliferation of Karens in movement organizations has occurred for two reasons: We keep letting them in and we won't kick them out. There are many things enabling the problem, but two stand out:

1. Outdated intake filters. My generation updated the quality of the jobs but not the rigor of the intake filters. Most movement organizations are still asking the same set of questions when vetting and interviewing candidates that they used twenty-five years ago. The focus remains fixed on finding out two things about candidates: Do they have the skills for the job they are applying for, and is their articulation of their worldview values aligned, broadly speaking, with the organization on things like economic, environmental, racial, and gender justice? While this was sufficient a generation ago, it falls far short of what should be required today. We need stronger vetting to get at political alignment at greater depth, as well as motivation and character.

Linda Burnham reflected that previous generations of movement were clearer and more precise about their politics and the absence of that today leads to confusion. "Clarify your politics and we can talk from there. We're not clear what we're asking people to sign on to, so they are signing on to a narrow mission statement, and whatever broader politics are under that are unspoken. So you end up with all kinds of different perspectives and you don't have a measuring rod to say this is in, this is out. In the nonprofit world, people often have not thought their politics through. What is the character of the change that we believe can be made given the circumstances in a particular time frame? What is the relationship between this analysis, the work of this organization, and the long-term vision? We don't engage these questions in a systematic way. Not having engaged them, you can't hold people to account to a set of politics, because it hasn't been articulated. Then all organizations have to go on is a general sense that people are in the same ballpark."

At the end of the day, there is no work-around to the fact that we must reduce the number of Karens and misguided firefighters in movement organizations. We must face the inconvenient truth that no organization will effectively advance social justice unless it brings down the barriers that are keeping the righteous-but-regular people out, and sets the boundaries that keep the Karens from getting and staying in.

Said Rajasvini Bhansali, "We are defaulting into hiring people with nice résumés but no frontline experience. We are increasingly privileging upper-class people for social justice roles in a way that undermines our work overall. The high performers are all people who don't take this work for granted, who believe this role is one of privilege."

Lack of clear boundaries has landed us in the unfettered crisis of infighting and navel-gazing that now plagues movement. "Some organizations can't function because of the internal struggles that are often related to the variety of personal needs people have that need to be addressed for them to be able to engage in the community's struggles. We are working to transform society and that may require transforming ourselves. The challenge is how this can or can't be held by the organization," said Denise Perry, co-director of BOLD. She reflected, "Some of the paralyzed struggles that people have is because they are having internal questions about 'is this what I want to do?' How is our onboarding ensuring that people really understand what they are agreeing to do from the beginning?"

2. Organizational development malpractice. This influx of Karens is being met with a set of organizational leaders who are diligently following the bad advice of a highly unregulated field of organizational development (OD) firms and consultants who are committing massive levels of malpractice. These experts are telling leaders that the best way to deal with the Karens is to give them more decision-making power and create more space and structures for them to express their discontent—which is really just more room to break everything in the organizational house. Doing this, the experts insist, makes you a cutting-edge, collaborative leader, whereas clear boundary setting makes you top-down, i.e., authoritarian, and maybe even white supremacist. At a time when organizational leaders need an Olivia Pope in their corner, they are getting Dr. Oz and some snake oil. Some of this is just incompetence. Some of it is highway robbery, since creating more process and structure requires much larger consultant contracts. WOC are given a double dose, laced with white supremacist and patriarchal notions that we must mother and mammy and that any boundary setting makes us mean. This bad advice combined with inadequate HR and legal support and the fear many managers have of being dragged and canceled online by staff who they know will be angered by any boundary, has deterred many organizational leaders from exercising sound management. As a result, many once-effective organizations have seen their work grind to a halt or have even closed altogether. There are some key bridges we need to build to address the barriers and the generational shifts.

7

Bridges to Build

In reckoning with the barriers that block 360-degree vision and wholeness in movement due to pain, trauma, and generational shifts, how do we bring them down and build bridges in their place? In these tumultuous times, it is not easy and there are no one-size-fits-all solutions. My reflections on solutions are a mix of what has worked for me as a leader and, when it comes to the barriers I have failed at bringing down, what I have learned from others about what has worked for them. I've grouped these reflections into three categories:

1. Upgrade the intake filters. It would be irresponsible for a fire department to hire firefighters who faint at the sight of flames. It's just as irresponsible for movement organizations working in this tough political climate to hire people who fall apart, or tear things apart, at the sight of someone being triggered, or who think the main purpose of their job is their own comfort. Job interviews and reference checks can no longer just test for skills and the ability to glibly parrot back the organization's core values or party line; they need to screen diligently—including with real-time simulations for capacities like emotional maturity and regulation, critical thinking, backbone, ability to receive feedback, capacity to navigate conflict, and an ability to stay focused on the social justice purpose of the organization. They need to test for the comfort applicants have with power and authority: their own power and that held by their manager and organizational leaders, as well as the power to govern in society. People who have significant discomfort with power will often tear down those who have it. They will frequently sabotage their own success along with the success and scale of the organization to keep the work small, unthreatening, and within their comfort zone.

These are difficult things to screen for and no interview is foolproof, but a rigorous screening process should provide strong insight into the character of a candidate. Interviews and screening protocols can be designed in a way that requires applicants to think on their feet and to share real-life examples of how they have dealt with conflict, disagreement, and tough dynamics historically, and to demonstrate how they deal with these in real time. Do they respond to conflict by getting curious and examining the facts, or by stirring the pot and reveling in the drama? When they feel threatened, do they stay principled or do they become panicked and desperate, throwing everyone around them under the bus to save themselves? In a tough moment, are they more likely to do the right and principled thing even when it's hard, or the wrong and unprincipled thing because it's easy? Do they approach gaining power by tearing down those who have it and using their co-workers as stepping stones, or by excelling in their work and teaming well with others? Do they exercise both empathy and discernment when in the presence of a triggered team member, or do they get swept up in emotional contagion and crusade without evidence? Do they have a general mistrust of power and authority that puts them in an oppositional stance to those in leadership positions? Are they comfortable with success and scale—their own, others', and that of the organization? Do they expect the organization to have a structure (like a flat collective) that it doesn't have or plan to have? Will they risk something to stand up for what they believe is right, even when it means disagreeing with their peers? It's a tall order to sleuth out all of this before offering someone a position, yet many organizations are learning how to use simulations, role-plays, and scenarios in interviews along with in-depth reference checks to discern more about candidates.

2. Inoculate and educate. When I was a union organizer, we used the term "inoculate" to mean warning workers in advance about the resistance or retaliation they could anticipate from the boss so that they wouldn't be surprised or rattled when they encountered it. Likewise, inoculating and educating the staff of movement organizations requires explicitly naming the barriers that are not permitted at the organization. This includes common biases in the treatment of women of color leaders (such as the expectation that they mother and mammy). It can be made clear to staff that these are unacceptable at the organization, and that it is their responsibility to disrupt them when they arise. Managers should know it is absolutely part of their job description to disrupt them. Managers at all levels should be invested in training, mentorship, coaching, and communicating a clear sense of what expectations staff must meet to rise in title and salary, and have a clear view of the various paths available for them to advance their careers within the organization and sector.

Teams can be inoculated on why academic norms of imbalanced deconstructionism are harmful within movements and how we understand the difference between healthy and rigorous debate and critique (which is helpful) and performative deconstructionism and victim chic (which is not). Expectations around comfort, family, political home, and utopia can be managed on the front end with inoculation that makes it clear what people can and cannot expect from an employer.

Inoculation begins with the hiring process and it continues with orientation and ongoing staff training and political education. One of the best tools I've seen a few organizations use with success is a written agreement on organizational culture and values that candidates sign prior to being hired. A signed agreement serves as a touchstone for both the potential hire and management to go back to in tough moments to remember what everyone committed to. Decide one year into employment that you want to work for a flat organization? The agreement is a reminder that you were aware it was hierarchical and agreed to that when you came on board. Ready to blow someone up on social media? The agreement jogs your memory that you agreed to a specific protocol of direct and principled communication in the event of a conflict. Core expectations should be reflected repeatedly in the primary internal organizational materials (HR manuals, organizational values and principles, guidelines, etc.). Orientation is also a great opportunity to mandate that all staff read and discuss foundational texts that propel the work through continued political education, like Dr. Bernice Johnson Reagon's article "Coalition Politics."

3. Intervene early. When a staff member perpetuates the barriers, it's critical to address it right away. One of the things that is killing movement organizations is hesitation in setting clear boundaries early. People are being given too little guidance and too much time and space to damage the work and morale of an organization. These individuals must be given feedback and an opportunity to course correct immediately. For example, if there is a fragility about reasonable feedback from peers or supervisors, a conversation must be had with the individual sooner rather than later about what the expectations and norms are around this and, if there is significant pushback, a request made that they think seriously about whether this is the right job for them. The first offer should be generous support to improve. If they don't take that opportunity, progressive discipline should begin, and if this fails, they should be transitioned out of the organization quickly. The most successful leaders—from the winningest coaches of women's team sports to nonprofit and corporate leaders—will tell you that bad behavior spreads faster than good, and toxic people who are not moved out swiftly can in short order cause irreparable damage to the morale and momentum of the entire group.

Establish a small group of high-performing nonmanagement staff who are committed to bringing down the barriers. These are not lackeys doing the bidding of management. They are individuals with a high level of maturity, integrity, commitment to the organizational mission, positive rapport with the larger team, and a willingness to notice and intervene in destructive behavior to help steer the organization back onto the rails of mission, purpose, and values. It only takes two or three people to pull an entire organization off track. Most organizations derail not because the majority agrees with the actions of a few people who are derailing, but because too many people are frozen in fear due to a lack of skills and no sense of permission or responsibility to intervene. It only takes two or three peers intervening with kindness and clarity to put things back on track.

When outside leadership coaching or organizational development support is needed to bring down the barriers, be extremely careful when hiring practitioners. Be aware that the OD sector is filled with practitioners who talk an excellent game but are themselves emotionally unregulated and confused about what is a wall and what is a bridge. Work only with OD providers with a track record of success among those you trust. Hire only executive coaches who have actual experience running organizations successfully. As Akaya Windwood said, "If you have not run an organization, you should not be advising people who are running organizations. If you haven't done the work, don't consult on it."

Developing Core Strength

Have you ever been in a crowded train car where you cannot reach a handrail and have to rely on a wide and grounded stance and your own core strength to prevent yourself from being flung around? It's the same with movements today. We are living in a volatile sociopolitical environment where the zeitgeist frequently jars us from one extreme to the other. The United States went through the Great Depression and the Great Migration, and now it's undergoing what could be called the Great Overcorrection. I first heard the term "overcorrection" used to describe some of the dynamics in movement organizations from my friend Ash-Lee Woodard Henderson. It's the perfect articulation of what is occurring. We have swung from one extreme to another, neither of which is good for movements or the communities we serve.

Now in her seventies, author and beloved movement elder Linda Burnham is an intellectual, organizer, and yoga practitioner who supports some of the most influential women of color movement leaders on strategy and, for the few who take her yoga class, on their warrior pose. Through her lifetime of movement work, Linda has carried on the legacy of her parents, who fought for Black liberation and economic justice in the 1930s and '40s. She served on Angela Davis's defense committee and founded and ran the Women of Color Resource Center of Oakland, California, for eighteen years, among other accomplishments. She is in a class of organizers who were teenagers during the Civil Rights years, in their twenties during Black Power, and who despite COINTELPRO, the Reagan years, and everything since, have stayed active in movement. Talking to me from the dappled sunlight of her porch, while on vacation with her 104-year-old mother, Linda Burnham likened core strength in movement to strengthening the abdominal muscles of the body. When you have strong abdominal muscles, you feel different when you walk down the street. When you have core strength in movement, you feel different when you move through strategy, conflict, and everything else.

We've gone from movement organizations overfocusing on the external and allowing inhumane working conditions to flourish within their own walls to navel-gazing in a quest for total comfort and utopia in the workplace while the external mission of the organization atrophies. We've gone from sweeping blatant racism, xenophobia, transphobia, and other forms of discrimination under the carpet to allowing false accusations of discrimination to become a cheap and easy tool with which to carry out vendettas and destroy people and organizations. From lacking even basic health benefits to employees holding their workplace wholly responsible for healing their trauma.

The solution to the overcorrection is developing core strength.

Four major elements enable core strength. Most in my generation received these, to one degree or another, from our movement elders, but many of us have become disconnected from them and not passed them on. In our focus on building institutions that could take movement work to greater scale and sustainability, we took our hand off the wheel on all four. There is no work-around to putting our hand back on the wheel by making these once again widely available to everyone in movement.

1. Clear values: Core strength holds us in alignment through a set of high-integrity values, such as due process (careful examination of facts and evidence to separate fact from fiction), rigor (courageous accountability, healthy boundaries, and course correction when problematic practices are found to exist), nondominance (a refusal to allow identity labels to be used as tools of domination), and most of all, impeccable accountability to the frontline communities whose rights and well-being we purport to uplift. These values are indelible. They apply equally to all people. The clear and public identification of and calling in to these values is critical in this moment.

2. Long-arc vision and strategy (which is now being reintroduced to a new generation by movement elder Norma Wong). Long-arc vision is the juicy and irresistible vision of what the world will look and feel like after we win the long game. Many Indigenous people refer to this as thinking ahead seven generations.

How I think of long-arc visions: Imagine a world where differences in human diversity—race, gender, sexual orientation, ability, language, religion—exerted no more limiting force on our lives than wearing a green versus blue shirt. Imagine if we saw and appreciated these just as we would the different shapes and colors among the flowers and trees, without a feeling of fear or judgment. Imagine if consuming in a way that supported the health of our bodies and the planet were the easiest and most affordable option. We would look back in disbelief at today's world, where one had to pay more money to get fruit and vegetables that hadn't been sprayed with poison, or household products not made with carcinogens. Imagine if our society ensured that everyone had a home, medical care, and enough to eat. It may seem daunting from our vantage point in the United States, but many Indigenous societies in the past, and some societies today, have achieved either this or something very close to it. Imagine a world where the human operating system has upgraded past the factory settings of greed and dominance, into an ethos of sharing and mutuality. If our vision is for humans as a species to evolve out of greed and dominance, for example, then we don't just seek to win at the existing game (women dominating men, people of color dominating white people), we seek to change the rules of the game (no one dominates anybody).

The road map for fifty years, twenty years, ten years, and even for the next election changes when it is calibrated to a long-arc vision that is brave and bold. The strategy—the way to reach that vision, which includes the short- and medium-term work along the way—is also a sorely undeveloped muscle among movement organizations today. Leaders like Wong and organizations like the Grassroots Power Project are helping movement workers understand strategy in more comprehensive ways.

When we lose the long-arc vision, we waste time debating myopic things that regular people couldn't care less about—like the time I watched a reproductive justice organization rebuff an ally group that offered to bring its sizable membership base to help win better reproductive health access in the south. The reason: The ally organization didn't have the words "reproductive justice" in its official name so was seen as an interloper. When we lose the long arc and the strategy thread that guides us from here to there, we lose the point of the work.

.   .   .

3. Political education: Linda Burnham believes that values and principles are important but insufficient to building powerful movements. "We're not grounded. Our organizations are so vulnerable because we're not good at articulating the relationship between broad social justice values, what we are doing in a given campaign or project, and our longer-term vision and goals. You don't need provocateurs. Anyone with any bullshit can roll through our organizations and throw everything out of whack."

Political education clarifies the specific theory of change, structure, ideology, and worldview that the organization subscribes to. Some diversity in thinking is critical, but too much divergence sets the stage for unhealthy conflict and gridlock. I have seen many organizations hire staff who sign onto a glib, high-level mission statement, only to realize that the team they have assembled is a hodgepodge of Black nationalists and integrationists, hardline communists and raging capitalists, people who are busting the gender binary and others who are throwing gender-reveal parties, those who are fine with hierarchy and those who believe the only fair structures are flat ones. This is a setup for disputes, but we can hardly fault staff for not aligning with things that they were never told about before they were hired.

Political education should also help everyone level up around a sophisticated understanding of race, class, gender, ability, and other identities. I have yet to meet a human being who has not needed to deepen their empathy and deprogram themselves from some set of dominant society messages about another group to show up well with other humans who have different lived experiences. This is lifelong work for all of us. When we deepen our empathy, increase our awareness, we are less likely to exclude people and advance strategies that leave anyone behind.

Helping an entire staff team level up their understanding of movement history, what movements are currently up against, and the collective goal of the organization is important. Linda Burnham said, "I don't think we as a progressive movement do a good job of conveying to people how big and complex and diverse the country is. It leaves many activists with a version of social change that is far too simplistic for the problems we are facing. How do we deepen people's sense of where we are living historically and today so that people have a realistic handle on the extent of the problems and understand that, while substantial progress can be made, you may not fix this in your lifetime."

Political education can also include norms about how staff are expected to conduct themselves with one another. Staff and managers must be oriented to the fact that it is part of their core job duties to notice and bring down the barriers where they occur. They can be supported with training on skills like emotional regulation, for example, understanding how to recognize the signs that they or someone else is triggered, and to implement techniques like box breathing and taking the necessary time and space to move from a triggered emotional state to homeostasis to respond rather than react. They can learn how to hold space for staff to talk about what is hard and painful but not allow people to become stuck in a quagmire of trauma bonding, instead moving the conversation toward shared goals of liberation and how we get there. They can be equipped to disrupt toxicity and not allow people to drag an entire group or meeting down a rabbit hole of performative wokeness. They can learn the practice of principled struggle through excellent resources like Adrienne Maree Brown's books *Holding Change* and *We Will Not Cancel Us* (which includes N'Tanya Lee's essay on this topic), and Loretta Ross's recently published book *Calling In,* along with many articles and talks on YouTube on the same topic.

One colleague of mine, who has been very successful in stabilizing a large organization, told me about dealing with managers who attempt to stay on the good side of unprincipled staff by pandering to nonsense. "I called all my managers into a meeting and let them know it is your job to protect a culture of healthy leadership at this organization. It is not acceptable for you to ingratiate yourself to staff by throwing other organizational leaders under the bus." The directive was clear, they got it, and the dynamics improved.

4. Grassroots organizing is when people gain the skills to use collective power to transform the policies and systems that impact their lives. Organizer, consultant, and political strategist Ejeris Dixon and I came up as community organizers at the same moment in time, but in very different sectors and geographies. They went on to found Vision Change Win and Ejerie Labs, two organizations that support movement organizations to function effectively and strategically and have been helping many shops navigate the conflict and churning that has racked the sector. In a sea of Dr. Ozes, Ejeris and their team are Olivia Popes. Ejeris is also the author of the excellent book *Beyond Survival* on these same topics. As we spoke, I lamented the withering of the robust organizing training programs that had raised us as movement youngsters. Then Ejeris offered a take that rang so true. "When you learn grassroots organizing, you don't just learn a skill, you learn a culture and a worldview. When you touch into organizing," said Ejeris, who has mediated scores of conflicts between people in movement, "you touch something real and sometimes the petty conflicts fall away." This made so much sense to me.

Without strong organizing training, what does the new generation miss out on? Good organizers value listening (80 percent listening and 20 percent talking is the rule of thumb in any good house visit or one-on-one with a worker or community member) and picking up on nuances. They adopt a stance of humility, defining success not by their own egotistical shine but by how many leaders they develop, and ultimately by making those leaders so successful that they put themselves out of a job. They have a credo of primary accountability to the community they serve, supporting its members to determine their top priorities and demands and measuring effectiveness by changes to their material conditions. They learn to stay focused on the North Star of a collective goal, rather than their individualistic objectives. People with solid organizing training and experience receive one of the most powerful antidotes to so much of what ails movements today.

There is no work-around to putting strong values, long-arc visioning, political education, and organizing training back into the praxis of movement organizations. We cannot build adequate core strength without these core elements.

What does core strength look like in action? One example today is around the unionization wave that is sweeping movement organizations. I was once a union organizer and am very pro-union. I think anyone who wants a union has the right to have one. Effective unions bring helpful structure to the labor-management relationship, mitigating the sharp edges of power differentials and giving people a voice on the job. Luckily there are more and more resources popping up to enable this. One of them is Beyond Neutrality, an organization that "supports organizations to respond to unionization in a way that is pro-union, anti-racist, and mission-driven," and that has made a wealth of resources, including an excellent report, widely available.

I believe there are unionization efforts occurring at movement organizations today that are important and necessary to achieve fair and just working conditions. I also observe that there are more than a few that have very little to do with working conditions at all. What I've found interesting is that the demands being made in many unionization campaigns within movement organizations are not around typical issues such as wages and benefits; they are over-whelmingly about a desire to "feel" a sense of agency, often through the right to govern and make high-level decisions about how an organization is run. They are examples of an overcorrection.

Surina Khan, former CEO of the Women's Foundation California, was known for offering one of the best employment packages in the sector. When I was an executive director, Surina was who I would routinely call whenever I needed advice about upgrading the benefits at my organization. So I was surprised when I heard her staff had unionized, and even more fascinated by her story of how it all unfolded. She recalled, "It wasn't that they wanted any-thing in particular. They didn't want higher wages or more time off. We already had a four-day workweek, four to five weeks of vacation, we closed for two weeks at the end of the year, had a flexible schedule so moms can take care of their children or peo-ple can take care of their elderly family and community members. We were at the forefront of progressive feminist organizational practices. When the negotiations started, staff kept asking for things that were already in the employee handbook. Finally, I asked our attorney, 'Can we just ratify the entire handbook?' Be-cause going through each one by one is costing us a lot in legal fees—close to one hundred thousand dollars, which is money that could have gone out in support of our community partners." Two years of process, and in the end the only thing they asked for that they didn't already have was one floating holiday, and of course we said yes. If they had asked for it *before* we would have said yes. In addition, they wanted formal documentation about supervi-sory processes and access to the board. The entire thing was about a *feeling* of agency. Now it's as if staff are not even part of the union. We've rarely heard from the union since bargaining."

The advice she offers to other leaders is this: "I had to change my point of view. Try to look at whatever it is that is a big challenge through another lens, from a different optic, and see if you can learn something." For her, it was shifting from feeling confused and defensive about why staff would want a union when the package was already so good to understanding their need for a feeling of agency and just accepting that they would need to move through the process.

Certainly, not every unionization effort is like this one. At some movement organizations material changes are needed and overdue, but Surina's story is more common than not.

On the other side of the country, in New York City, Teresa Younger took the helm as CEO of the Ms. Foundation for Women in the middle of a unionization drive. She shared, "We got the CBA [union contract]," which she said contained nothing that she wouldn't have easily agreed to without such a formal process, "but then staff would come to me with [requests]. I told them, you've set up a structure where you cannot be in that type of relationship to ask for a particular Friday off, etc. We gave a 3 percent raise to everyone. Those in the union had to give 2 percent of that to the union in dues." After a two-year process to unionize and secure a contract, the staff ultimately decided the union was not useful and voted to decertify [leave] the union.

Then there are the simultaneous demands for unions and flat structures. The movement hills are alive with the sounds of magical thinking. People want "collectives" but they also want four-day workweeks, to clock out at 5:00 P.M. and not spend a second more in meetings dealing with annoying things like consensus building and governance. They want all of the power but none of the responsibility. They want "flat structures" where they are calling the shots but they also want a union, which codifies hierarchy: You sit across the bargaining table from management. They want professional organizations where the trains (and especially their paychecks) run on time, but feel entitled to be promoted into top positions without the skill or experience required to keep things running. None of it makes any sense.

The core strength in this case comes from re-grounding organizational culture and norms in a crystal clear set of values and expectations. We do this by communicating and engaging these early and often and rigorously. There should be no question about the elements outlined in the previous section on inoculation: organization mission, structure, protocol for conflict resolution, etc. There should be no confusion about the details of what people can expect from their workplace: (industry standard for) fair pay, good benefits, adequate time off, reasonable work hours, rigorous proactive and responsive steps to address discrimination, fair and clear progressive discipline, and a fair grievance process.

There should be absolute clarity about what employees cannot expect from their workplace: guarantees of individual healing, the absence of any discomfort, guaranteed employment or promotion (particularly when not doing the job one was hired to do), power to make or influence every decision, entitlement to dictate what the structure of the organization should be, and pay and benefits beyond the budget capacity of the organization. It should be abundantly clear what is expected of all staff, including management: timeliness, professionalism, excellence in work produced, respectful treatment of all colleagues irrespective of where they fall in a hierarchy, and positive contributions to the culture and morale of the team. If there's a union, there should be strong education about what a union shop is and how it functions. It should be known that the organization will honor the contract and workers' right to organize and participate with good faith in future collective bargaining processes and that workers and management will honor the agreed-upon window for negotiating any major new changes. Political education should also convey how unions work.

PART THREE

Staying Well Within the Work

8

Burnout

In October 2014, at the age of thirty-six, I herniated a disk in my lower back. Unable to sit, I spent the better part of eight months either standing up or lying down. It felt like someone had driven a knife into my lower spine and left it there. The pain I experienced was excruciating and ever-present, often radiating down my leg and into other parts of my body. It gave me the sweats and the chills. Most nights I couldn't sleep but would pace around my house and then roll around on the floor on ice or heat, stretching and maneuvering, trying anything to find relief. I was terrified of back surgery and so tried everything from physical therapy, cortisone shots, painkillers, yoga, Pilates, and an anti-inflammatory diet to obscure healing methods to avoid an invasive procedure. Nothing worked.

I've always been sensitive to prescription drugs, and the painkillers made it impossible for me to write and think clearly, which I needed to do for my job. So most of the time I skipped my meds, gritted my teeth, and worked through the pain. As the months drew on, my strategies to find relief grew increasingly desperate.

At one point I ordered one of those contraptions that hangs you upside down to stretch out your spine. It took up an entire corner of our tiny condo. Being incapacitated for such a long period of time was new for me. Growing up I was a multi-sport athlete and a modern dancer. Other than the occasional sports injury that healed quickly, I was used to my body feeling strong and invincible. Since I could not drive or lift things, Tricia had to work overtime to pick up the slack in caring for our kid and home. Friends dropped off meals occasionally and stepped in to help drive me to appointments. As the holidays neared, my toddler earnestly asked Santa to "please make Mommy's back better so that she can carry me again." I burst into tears.

My friends would all ask me, What happened? Why do you have back problems at thirty-six? The truth was, my back problems were a direct result of years of overwork. It was years of sitting. First as a union organizer who put an average of fifty thousand miles on my car each year going the forty miles each way between my home in Oakland, California, and the union hall in San Jose and the various worksites and worker homes in my "turf," which stretched the seventy-five miles between Daly City and Gilroy. Then all that time sitting at my computer as I launched an organization. If I dug deeper and was honest, I knew that toll was also in large part due to the enormous pressure I felt as a woman of color to be four times as good as my white counterparts. I, like so many WOC, have felt the sting of a white colleague's eyes widening in surprise as they realize I'm the head of the organization rather than an assistant, or the keynote speaker rather than hotel service staff.

Being underestimated comes with the territory, as does the exhausting work of claiming your space and establishing your expertise every time you enter a new space. For many years I felt that what I produced had to be flawless to be taken seriously. I lived with the fear that any mistake or a fumble could cost me my entire career or professional reputation.

In my quiet moments, when I allowed myself to slow down, I realized I was terrified about what my injury could mean. I had a wife and a four-year-old daughter who depended on me as the primary breadwinner for our family. Neither my wife nor I had family who was financially able to support us if my income failed. What if I couldn't work and provide? What if, after so many years of building an organization, I had to quit and give up my dream, just as we were finally landing major grants and taking off? What if the pain never ended?

I did what I had always done, I kept going. I facilitated portions of my organization's annual board retreat from the floor while lying on my back. I continued to travel for meetings and speaking gigs, using my organizing skills to charm the flight attendants so they would let me stand up at the back of the plane for most of the flight. I corseted myself in a back brace and stood against walls for hours during conferences and fundraiser house parties. I RSVP'd yes to dinner meetings at restaurants with donors, awkwardly standing behind my chair and leaning over to hear them. I was invited to speak at the Democracy Alliance for the first time, a notoriously white male crowd of some of the largest "progressive" electoral donors in the country—resources WOC had yet to really tap into. How could I pass this up?

When I arrived, it was a panel and everyone else was seated behind a long table. I stood the entire time. "I used to be a community and labor organizer," I said at the top of my remarks, "always telling people to stand up for their rights. No one told me that if you stand up too much, one day you may never be able to sit down." I cracked jokes to make things seem less awkward and people laughed graciously. At one particularly low point, again laid out on my back and struggling to type a grant proposal on a laptop that was propped on my stomach, I instructed my executive assistant to pass me a nearby extension cord so that I could wrap it around the center of the laptop and the back of my knees, securing it there. I found I could eke at least two hours of typing out of this position before collapsing in agony.

My board chair and executive coach finally intervened. They demanded I reduce my work schedule and focus on regaining my health. When I finally had the surgery, the surgeon told me it was the largest herniation he had ever seen. He also warned me that because I had waited so long to have the operation, I may have sustained irreparable damage to the surrounding nerves. It meant that even after removing the herniated tissue, the pain might continue. He couldn't promise me relief. None of the other doctors had warned me of this possibility. I was livid, and terrified. I underwent the surgery and began a two-year road to recovery. I was forced to change my relationship to work, health, and over-efforting. As the Buddhist quote goes, "A stumble may prevent a fall."

A year after my surgery I maintained a healthier anti-inflammatory diet, had reduced my hours to thirty-five to forty hours a week, and would immediately back off and give my body the rest it needed if I started experiencing pain. I also started walking and swimming religiously. In the dead of winter, I found myself standing in the dark at 6:00 A.M., at the edge of the outdoor pool at Mills College, watching steam come off the water before plunging in to begin a set of laps. I had never been a swimmer, in part because I can't stand the cold, but it made my back feel like new, so it was worth it. I began to take care of my health like my life depended on it, which of course it does.

Maintaining 360-degree vision is about the ability to be whole—in society and within ourselves. We cannot be whole without our health. And so many WOC movement leaders, caught in the expectation that we mother or mammy others, and the adage that we must be twice as good to get half as far, sacrifice our health for the work. So much is internalized patriarchy about the requirement that we please others. Brené Brown said, "Perfectionism is not striving to be your best, it's about an orientation to what other people think."

At some point in my recovery, I reflected that I always tell my daughters, "If you did your best and you failed, you can let it go with no regrets and feel proud of yourself." In my own life, I often did the opposite. I over-efforted in an attempt to be perfect and then beat myself up thinking about what would happen if I failed, or if things didn't go as I hoped.

The Culture of Overwork

The more I shared my story with other women in leadership, the more I heard the same story back. Alexis McGill Johnson, the CEO of Planned Parenthood, explained it this way: "It's a marathon," she said, "but we are running at a sprinter's pace." Common conditions leaders I spoke with struggled with and that they directly attributed to running movement organizations included: teeth grinding, insomnia, panic attacks, back pain, skin rashes, hair loss, migraines, anxiety, depression, suicidal thoughts, short-term memory loss, ulcers, and worse. These dynamics are weathering us, they are shortening our lives.

One of the most poignant stories I heard was from Amisha Patel, former executive director of Grassroots Collaborative in Chicago. She shared, "My first round of cancer I worked through chemo and radiation. I took days off, but I didn't go on leave for the six months I was in treatment. I was in a New York City bathroom [outside] a meeting when my hair started falling out. I knew it would be the time my hair would fall out but I went anyway because I felt I could handle it. Could my organization have stopped me? I don't know. I'm stubborn as fuck. My wife tried to stop me. She came with me on the trip so at least I wasn't alone, sobbing by myself in the bathroom. There is something really not right with how we are doing this work and the whole extractive setup of the funding world, of relationships with each other, how much we have internalized from the oppressive systems we are trying to break down. I don't know if I was not ED, would the cancer be back like it is? Would I be facing the current fight I'm facing? I do know the amount of stress that this job entailed and how much of my full self, including my body, I put into the work. Living in tension and stress for years on end with very little break wasn't good. We talk about how we center love in organizing. The reality is that so much of what gets centered is not love. What is the impact of that on our minds and bodies?"

When I asked her if anything could have helped her to slow down and take the time she needed to heal, she replied, "There's probably only a handful of people that I would have listened to. The people outside of the movement who were telling me to take a break I dismissed and was like, 'Fuck off. You live a comfortable life. You don't know.' The people I would have listened to were all the same way that I was. What is at stake in the world takes precedence over what is at stake in my own body. There isn't capacity for people to say 'You need some time to do this.' There was no one."

She's one of so many WOC who continue working through terrible health challenges. Describing the lead-up to the Women's March convention that she, Tamika Mallory, and others organized, Linda Sarsour talked to me through the Zoom screen wearing her usual crisply folded hijab. "The week before that convention I was in the hospital for three days," she said. "I had kidney stones and was dehydrated. We were working from six o'clock in the morning to two o'clock in the morning. We had to work overtime to prove ourselves to our own movement people. Tamika was down to 108 pounds." Sarsour also noted the double standard she sees in the field, as well as the mentality that WOC need to shed. "Why is it that WOC believe they have to work themselves to the bone? It doesn't even occur to many white women to think twice about saying 'I'm going off of social media for four months to go on sabbatical or to live in Bali.' Why do WOC not think we can do that? Why do we feel we have to work every single day? You have WOC not going on vacation for three years straight. That mentality we have about how much we have to prove ourselves in the movement is something I've struggled with."

There is also the acute sense that if you don't demand the rest you need, no one else is likely to offer it. Elle Moxley, founder and executive director of the Marsha P. Johnson Institute, which defends the rights of Black transgender people, and co-founder of the Black Lives Matter Network said, "Knowing when to say enough is enough is important. If you need a break, a sabbatical, there will be no greater advocate than yourself."

MINI MASTER CLASS

Bamby Salcedo

It's October in Los Angeles and I'm walking down the halls of the TransLatin@ Coalition with executive director Bamby Salcedo. It's a typical nondescript L.A. office building, but her team makes it buzz with warmth and care. At the entrance there is a large painting of a Black trans angel with a raised fist and wings so long they almost touch the floor. In an arc above her head are the words TRANS POWER, and at her feet a cream-colored sash adorned with red hearts and the words TRANS IS BEAUTIFUL. In the hallway there are large collages with photos of dozens of trans women who have been involved with the organization, many of whom, Bamby explains, had their lives cut short far too young. We stop in the modest kitchen. There is a smallish sink and no real stove, but with ingenuity and a few hotplates, each day staff find a way to prepare lunch for scores of people who stop in needing a warm meal. There's a clinic where people can get tested and receive mental health services and other care.

Bamby knows firsthand what it's like to need these supports. She fled Mexico at thirteen years old, making the harrowing border crossing on her own and supporting herself as an exploited minor migrant up and down California, and then as a sex worker in Los Angeles. As a young trans woman, she survived beatings, sexual assault, prison, addiction, and innumerable other threats on her life but rose like a phoenix to get sober, earn a master's degree, found an organization, and help thousands of other trans women to find shelter, safety, and their power to organize.

Bamby has an easy and positive rapport with her team members. Some she has known for decades and helped get off the streets. Her vision is a powerful one, and together her team is well on their way to realizing it, having already secured the land for a thirty-million-dollar state-of-the-art center for trans people in Los Angeles. As we sit down together and she takes me through the blueprints, I'm struck by the joy of the place. It's not just expanded clinics and meals and services, it includes runways and sound systems for the celebrations that so embody the indomitable spirit of the trans community.

Says Bamby, "We as trans women have the right to be well. We are often not able to be healthy people because of the constructs of society and lack of opportunities. Addressing those social conditions that have placed us where we are within our society—as the most poor populations in the United States, that have placed trans WOC with the highest rate of HIV infection in the United States and globally, to be homeless, engaged in the street economy in order to survive. All of those things have put us in the position of not being healthy people in mind, body, and spirit. Many of us walk this earth with broken spirits. For us as an organization and as leaders within the community, our task is to develop a strategy to ensure that our community continues to exist in the next hundred years. To get to that place we need to become healthy, to build a healthy community. That is going to happen when we build our political and economic power, our academic power."

Some of the stories of overwork that WOC leaders engaged in without a word from anyone around them are astounding.

Gloria Walton began her activist career in her late teens as an organizer in South Central Los Angeles. "I didn't take vacation for thirteen years. The most I took was Christmas Eve and Christmas Day and New Year's Eve and New Year's Day. I didn't celebrate any other holidays. I didn't celebrate my birthday. I was young and full of energy—consumed with the needs of my community and not necessarily connected to my own needs. I felt like I had the energy to keep going, and I did—until my body told me

I didn't, and I had to sit down." One day, in the middle of a meeting, Gloria felt sharp pains in her chest, which led her to hyperventilate. She thought she was having a heart attack. "I went into the hospital with severe chest pains," she recalled. "It turned out to be a panic attack" from stress and too much cortisol built up in her system. "I never feel like a victim," emphasizes Gloria. "My priority and focus are on the work—the world I want to transform. But organizing isn't easy, nor is witnessing poverty conditions day in and day out. I was pushing a lot down so I could keep going. That's when I started to reconnect to my body, to understand that authentic leadership—embodied leadership—requires you to go beyond the intellect, to root into your heart, to let your soul lead, to trust yourself, your intuition, your experiential wisdom, and to take care of the body because it is the vessel that is holding it all together."

Gloria's story is not an uncommon one for WOC who enter movement young as organizers. The question I have when listening to stories like these is, where were the elders and comrades to say: "Sister, you are doing too much. You have got to take time off." To warn her, "There is a dangerous expectation that Black women exhibit superhuman strength and never feel their pain. You have a human right to reject this to protect your health!" This is an important way that people in movement can support WOC leaders, by being aware of the systemic forces that lead to over-efforting and self-sacrifice, and lovingly intervene to disrupt it.

There were members of my team at Groundswell who did this for me, in particular Alexandra DelValle, my right hand for many years, who often offered to take work off my plate or encouraged me to take on less. I'm also reminded of a practice that I began doing well into my tenure there that I wish I had implemented earlier in my career: By the end of January of each year, I would block out dates on my calendar and put my request in for my major vacations for the year—using roughly 90 percent or more of my vacation time for the year. Occasionally if a major work event came up, I would shift, but I found changing the dates was easier than starting from scratch. This helped me to use my vacation time rather than looking up from a busy year in December, only to realize I had forgotten to take my time.

Letting Go of Overpreparing

One of the most important things that WOC in leadership must learn to do is to set a standard of excellence for ourselves that we can feel proud of but that also allows space for our health and well-being. This means learning to say no, and letting some things be good enough. Society tells us that we aren't worth much, that we should be ecstatic at the chance to sit at the table of someone else's design and prove ourselves every day of our lives. We must reject this way of living and working and choose another way: to value our time and health as precious and to be judicious in where, how, and to whom we give it.

The majority of us have been socialized to overwork and play every role possible. Silvia Henriquez explained, "I was raised to understand that you need to work twice as hard to get half the credit that your white counterparts will get. That was what my parents told me and that's what my mentor told me. Is that true now? That's a generational conversation on how people feel about that, but that was absolutely true when I was coming up in movement. I had to be the most articulate person in the room to be heard. And there is the expectation that you are indestructible and vulnerable; that particularly as a woman of color leader, you have to be all these things at all moments."

She said she tells newer WOC leaders, "It's okay to slow down, not everything needs a sense of urgency, things will be there the next day." She also advises them to take their parental leave, recalling, "I cut both of mine really short. I never realized what I was giving up. I'll never get that back."

Gloria spoke poignantly about finally letting go of the impulse to over-effort and what it feels like to trust yourself enough to know that with a reasonable amount of preparation, your wisdom and experience are enough. "WOC are held to a completely different standard. You don't have room or space to fail, let alone have a hiccup . . . this is exhausting. After twenty years, I finally give myself permission to not be overprepared. To trust myself. To know the work is in me. I am the work. In any room, my presence transforms the space."

Purvi Shah, executive director of Movement Law Lab, is one of the foremost legal minds shaping how the law and those who practice it support movement formations such as the Movement for Black Lives. Some of the bravest freedom fighters will tell you that in critical moments of direct action or tense policy fights, Purvi is who they call. Purvi and I grew up together as twenty-somethings in movement, though her path took her through law school and mine through community and union organizing. She offered this reflection about being present to the reason she over-prepares: "We are all trying to find a way to feel safe. What is animating the preparation? Is it my fear of failure or the clarity of the goal in front of me? If you get stuck in the drive to achieve to soothe your own sense of self-worth then it isn't productive. I had to get to the point where it wasn't about me. If we can stay inside a real sense of purpose that is driven by something bigger than ego and achievement, then you start to be in the flow with excellence."

I resonate with Purvi's reflection on purpose and flow. We need to come away from the extremes. For those of us in our forties in movement, we know what it was to work at organizations in our twenties that ground us to dust. Hard work can be draining and soul killing if you are motivated by fear, codependence, or martyrdom. It can also be energizing, life-giving, and deeply gratifying if you are motivated by love, excitement, and a genuine curiosity and interest in what you are doing. As my wise friend Connie Cagampang Heller pointed out, if something is your passion, it may not feel like work at all, it may mainly feel like fun!

Dolores Huerta, whose movement work has sustained its energy and vibrance into her nineties, has similar advice on thriving over the long haul: "Women have to learn to build up their inner courage. The courage comes from the purpose. We all have to have a purpose in life. That keeps us going, keeps us alive, keeps us young."

There is a natural learning curve that tracks with longer periods of time spent preparing or producing in areas where you are only beginning to build your skills. But if we are not careful, the overpreparation that may have been needed for the first year of public speaking becomes a habit for all future ones. Getting free of this requires decentering ego and self-doubt, and recentering purpose for the community you are serving and trust in yourself.

Overwork has serious implications for the trajectories of people's lives, not just in terms of their health, but in the experiences they give up. Thinking back on nearly thirty years in movement, Cindy Wiesner said wistfully, "We make a lot of sacrifices. I didn't have a family. I didn't end up having kids. It wasn't until my fifties that I finally bought a house. It wasn't until five years ago, at forty-six, that I started saving money and investing and thinking about myself in not such a self-sacrificial way. I took care of a lot of people and organizations and channeled that mothering sentiment. People joke that I'm a movement doula. I've birthed a lot of things—movement organizations and institutions—and I did that at a personal sacrifice. I remember Linda Burnham told me one day, you don't want to be fifty and turn around and have regrets. I turned fifty and I do have that one regret of not being able to have kids." I have many beloved colleagues who feel the same way Cindy does.

There's not a single leader I have ever met that hasn't wanted better for the next generation of leaders coming up. We universally want them to hear the lessons we wish we had known from the start so that they don't have to learn them the hard way. Water all of the gardens that are important to you—friendship, family, hobbies. Look after your health. Take care of your financial future.

"People who are drawn to social justice work are people who care and the need to care seems endless," explained Viviana Rennella. "As women of color we are both more intrinsically acculturated to do that and we have less resources to fall on. A white woman might work a lot but she will inherit certain things to safeguard her. For a lot of WOC, there is a real danger of ending up alone at the end of life with very little. I have seen leaders as they became elders—movement comrades had to rally to take care of them. They did not have inherited property. They may not even have retirement savings."

We must draw healthy boundaries with what we take on—not just in terms of projects, but in terms of battles and messes that need cleaning up. I'm reminded of the Serenity Prayer used widely in many twelve-step programs: "God, grant me the serenity to accept the things I cannot change, the courage to change the things I can, and the wisdom to know the difference." Ai-jen Poo, author, founder of the National Domestic Workers Alliance, and MacArthur Foundation "genius grant" recipient, reminds us to pick our battles and expend our energy with discernment. "Don't try to make everything better. There are some things that you can't fix." Ai-jen knows something about how to focus her time and attention for impact. She has built the largest membership-based WOC-led organization in the country, whose victories in the care economy have impacted tens of thousands of domestic workers and the families they support.

Structural Changes

The answer isn't just to fix our outlook and propensity to over-effort. We also must fix the structures of movement organizations. The single-executive-director model—where one person is responsible for holding the bulk of strategy, board management, donor relationships, the public face of the organization, and major decisions on organization structure—is completely unsustainable. It's a relic of a time when these positions were held almost exclusively by cis white men who could count on the labor of cis white women at home to enable long hours. Today, while men still predominate at the helm of the largest organizations, 62 percent of all nonprofit CEOs are women.[1] With some exceptions, women still disproportionately hold the double shift of an intense job and care for our children, elders, and home life generally. More and more organizations are experimenting with co-director models, more robust leadership teams, and ways of spreading the ED responsibilities to make the load more manageable.

Amid my back saga I instituted an org-wide sabbatical policy for all staff at my organization. Everyone could access a three-month sabbatical after every five years of service. The biggest epiphany that came to me after I took my first sabbatical was the image of a stew. I realized that cultivating social justice in the world is like cooking a stew that has to nourish and sustain people. If you make a stew filled with pesticide-laden vegetables, hormone-filled meat, and artificial colors and flavors, among other toxic ingredients, it might be edible, it might fill bellies, but it will not be nourishing. By the same token, if what we put into the stew that we are offering to movement is stress, overwork, burnout, and sacrifice of our own health and well-being, we might be showing up, but we're not serving the people from our best selves. Our movements are only as good as what we put into them, and that includes love, care, and kindness to ourselves and to others.

Sadly, we don't have great models for this. Historically, a lot of movement leaders have worked burnout schedules their entire careers. Long hours coupled with the stress of knowing their very lives were in danger aged people prematurely. Dr. King's autopsy report indicated the body of a much older man when he died. I worked under elders in the labor movement whose bodies were breaking down after years of working seventy-to-eighty-hour weeks, rarely seeing their families, eating Cup Noodles on the go, and drinking and smoking heavily. We can celebrate and honor what these past leaders won, but I worry that theirs is our only model. Beyond the direct effect of this kind of workaholism and unhealthy lifestyle on leaders, it also drove many people out of the movement. After the 1960s, a large swath of people dropped out of social change movements, like those against the Vietnam War or for civil rights, and checked into ashrams and divinity schools. Taking a spiritual bypass away from the messy and exhausting collective work of structural change, they sought world peace through the individual work of meditation, prayer, and spiritual awakening. The truth is, we need both structural change and healing at the individual and collective levels.

The good news is that many movement organizations are trying out new, more humane models. WOC are at the forefront of much of this work.

Underneath burnout is both the need for structural change in movement organizations and the deep work that most WOC must do to truly love, value, and trust ourselves in a society that does not. This work is not easy, but it pays dividends in our ability to cherish and protect our precious time and energy, focusing it exactly where we think it should go, and drawing clear and healthy boundaries with the rest. One critical boundary to draw is with the call to mother and mammy.

9

Rejecting the Call to Mother and Mammy

No question was more of a lightning rod or generated more responses in my interviews with WOC movement leaders than this one: "Is there an outsize expectation that WOC mother and mammy their staff?" Fatima Goss Graves's response conveyed the prevailing answer: "Yes, and Covid accelerated it."

Throughout history, WOC have felt overwhelmed by expectations from staff, including other WOC, that we caretake at a level never expected of white men, white women, or men of color. Nearly everyone I interviewed shared stories of being held to wholly unsustainable and inappropriate standards of nurturing, vulnerability, and friendship, and being subject to a punishing reaction from colleagues when they failed to meet them. This long-standing dynamic has been intensified by two new demands that are trending in movement: the first, that movement workplaces should deliver "healing" to their employees through everything from group therapy to onsite bodywork to unlimited paid leave for those who have stress and anxiety; and second, that leaders must pause or dial way back on any external work until they can fully "heal" whatever ails the organization internally. This puts WOC leaders, who are always under more intense scrutiny from donors and allies around external impact, in an incredibly difficult position.

When a request or demand is made of a woman of color leader, the expectation is that she will say yes. When she says no, she is often stereotyped as "difficult," "corporate," or "mean" and then punished through relational aggression, which seeks to publicly vilify, shame, shun, or humiliate her (more on relational aggression in chapter 16). Most described feeling utterly exhausted and demoralized by their efforts to meet people's endless and seemingly insatiable needs.

Many WOC bring a leadership praxis that is relational rather than transactional, and that is grounded in care, vulnerability, and collaboration. This sets them apart from many other leaders in positive ways. It is a superpower. WOC are willing to roll up our sleeves and do the full spectrum of work that needs to be done, with humility. This "willingness to do the hard, uncomfortable, and tedious work that has to be done as part of our organizing," said Miya Yoshitani, co-director of the Movement Innovation Collaborative, has been the engine that has powered movements throughout history.

This is true from the sisters who ran carpools during the bus boycotts in the South to the leaders like Ella Baker, Dolores Huerta, and Yuri Kochiyama, who spent less time in the limelight and more time doing the unglamorous work of patiently talking to and developing the leadership skills of youth, poor farmers, and community members. However, many leaders I spoke with felt that instead of being valued for this superpower, the movement takes advantage of it, sucking them dry and then taking their contributions for granted.

There is also the sheer workload that WOC are expected to carry, often without receiving credit. Said Oakland city council-member Nikki Fortunato Bas, "I'm a workhorse. I work my ass off. I carry a lot of legislation. I've led the last two budget pro-cesses. My chief of staff was pushing others to share the work. It's hard to get other people to step up and carry the legislative work. And I don't put out a press release for everything I'm doing, which means I don't always get the credit." I can attest to Nikki's work ethic, which I saw firsthand as a board member of the East Bay Alliance for a Sustainable Economy, where, as executive director, she improved wages, air quality, and affordable housing opportu-nities for workers and people of color across the city.

For many, beneath the pain and frustration of it all, was the low hum of rage—the type of rage that arises when one is put in the tight box of a stereotype or a cultural norm that is difficult to escape. Leaders talked about what the box felt like and some de-scribed how they had successfully Houdinied their way out of it.

I could relate to all of it, viscerally. Including the rage, which still rises in my chest when I think of how often in my own leader-ship journey I encountered people who felt entitled to consume all of me and how long it took me to value myself enough to re-fuse to be swallowed whole. The expectation that I give and give until I had nothing left, while remaining cheerful in the face of those who took pleasure not in fair and constructive criticism, but in pointing out as an act of public humiliation how what I gave was never enough. This treatment of WOC leaders is abusive and it needs to stop.

The frustration and pain I heard from leaders about this dy-namic was like a volcano.

"The mammification particularly of Black women, the extractive nature that people treat us with, the expectation to coddle, is rooted in misogynoir," said Dara Cooper, co-founder of the National Black Food and Justice Alliance. "I lead with a lot of tenderness and care, but that is a choice, it shouldn't be an expectation." Cooper described how Black women leaders are "attacked and shut down" and cast as "a hard-ass, cold, callous machine" for simply trying to hold staff accountable.

Purvi Shah recalled, "I once supervised someone who was violent, combative, and uncooperative beyond any level of decorum. My boss said to me, 'Well, I think you are just not being nurturing to them.' There was no accountability for their behavior."

The demand for nurturing and mothering can force WOC to expend more energy getting their teams to put in work. Andrea Mercado, ED of Florida Rising, reflected, "It's important for me to model 'I'm taking a day off, I'm leaving early for my daughter's track meet' to create permission for others. Sometimes there is such a glorification of overwork that we are still just pushing against. At the same time I believe in rigor and accountability. I'm balancing wanting to take care of our staff and giving them excellent benefits and all this time off, and when it's election season everybody gotta show up and bring their A game and there are going to be late nights and long days."

Many spoke directly to the newly trending expectation that organizations somehow deliver healing and well-being to their staff at a level that is beyond what most workplaces have the capacity to meet.

Denise Perry reflected the sentiments of many leaders whose frustration on this count is boiling over, saying, "I'm not responsible for all of your well-being, that is not the mission of this organization or its capacity."

Amisha Patel, who is now in her second battle with cancer, explained, "It has been critical to me to show up with generosity of love and care with the people I work with. That's who I am. But, as a whole, the amount of emotional labor that as an ED and a woman of color that I've done for fifteen years was really exhausting, often not visible, taken for granted, expected, and sometimes manipulated. I've had to do a lot of work outside of movement space to repair the damage that this has done to me so that I could continue to show up and lead."

It's not that the WOC leaders I spoke with were against healing. Many of them devote significant time outside of work to therapy, somatics, and spiritual practices for their own personal healing. Some of them led groundbreaking work to bring these modalities into movement organizations years before this was popular. They agree with encouraging staff to use their health benefits to access healing support outside of work, and that organizations should offer some tools within the workplace to help staff learn how to move through their triggers without harming others, lead and engage with vulnerability, and deal constructively with conflict. What they are objecting to are demands that are unsustainable for both organizational time and resources and their emotional labor as leaders.

Like so many leaders, Patel struggled to draw boundaries with staff demands in part because of the gendered social conditioning she received as a girl in her family of origin and home community. Unlearning these norms has been part of her personal healing work. She described, "My mother was a factory worker. She grabbed as much overtime as she could, came home, cooked and cleaned for everyone. The model I saw of a South Asian woman was that you just handle shit and you do it on your own. I have strong solo functioning patterns. I spent many years feeling like all the burden, responsibility, was mine. It left me very isolated, stressed out. It hooks in with this early messaging that I wasn't enough so then when it's all on you and it feels overwhelming and unbearable, then it's like, right, because I'm not enough."

Mothering and mammying rob us of the time to vision and dream. We bleed energy keeping people happy enough so that they do not come for us and derail the work we need to do. Alexis McGill Johnson, CEO of Planned Parenthood, said, "The problem when you are a woman of color thrown into a caretaking position is you're not allowed to dream, to think big picture and resource the strategy. It's 'Did you fix the finance system? Did you bring that donor back?' I sometimes describe my job as waking up in the morning and someone is mad at me and if I don't nip it in the bud it will come back to haunt me. It's waking up to fight versus 'Today we're going to crush this week and it's going to move us that much further toward liberation.'"

Vulnerability

The expectation for superhuman amounts of output and nurturing exists alongside a demand for a certain type of vulnerability. Vulnerability is en vogue with the work of thinkers like Brené Brown, who have popularized it as a positive leadership trait. I respect and take a lot of value from Brown's work generally, including her invitation to think of vulnerability as a strength. As Katherine Grainger, principal at Civitas Public Affairs Group, put it, "I interpret vulnerability as the ability to show up as your true self. Not just having to cry or be soft. But bringing all parts of you into leadership." I agree it is important for leaders to cultivate this capacity. Brown has more recently nuanced her analysis to better reflect the challenges that WOC face with vulnerability and the importance and necessity of armor in some situations.

WOC often have people gunning for us. There are times when we need our armor. There are times when vulnerability is blood in the water. There can also be something patriarchal in the demand that WOC leaders perform vulnerability by exposing their pain and trauma, to a degree that is never demanded of men. Sometimes it feels like a command to take your clothes off and get emotionally naked.

Silvia Henriquez, who recently left a frontline position at the abortion rights organization All* Above All for a position at the Ford Foundation, reflected, "I feel ultimately that ask of me in the last two years really did me in. Vulnerability was consistently my low score on evaluations. The comments were, 'Silvia is so good, she's so direct, her vision is so clear, she fundraises really well, but she is never vulnerable, she never cries.' It's been a struggle for me. I don't think of movement work as my healing space. We all come with our baggage, I do too. I deal with that outside of work and come to work with the privilege of getting paid to do this work. My job was to keep our doors open and get everyone paid and make sure everybody else could take care of their families through Covid. When was I going to break down and say 'I need to also teach third-grade math but I don't know how'?"

Henriquez ultimately concluded, "I can't be that leader so maybe it's time for me to find a different path." But she also wondered, "I don't know if men are held to this standard."

Vulnerability can be a strength, and as leaders we have a right to express it. At the same time, for WOC leaders, it is not a panacea. Those who have a deeply patriarchal discomfort with seeing a woman of color in her power—whether it is because they are jealous, intimidated, or just bent on enforcing the status quo—will often disguise an attack on her by imploring her to "be vulnerable." This is also often communicated as a demand that she be more "approachable" or "accessible" or "less intimidating."

What they are essentially saying is "Who do you think you are? You better act like you know your place!" Sometimes being vulnerable is a capitulation to a patriarchal appetite to see us broken, crying, questioning ourselves, never sure or resolute. Vulnerable is not good when it's all we are allowed to be. And the truth I learned the hard way is that you can comply and show your tender underbelly and people will still, and sometimes especially, attempt to gut you or turn and write you off as weak or incompetent.

While staff knowing one another as people and not just job titles is important to a healthy culture, I know from what I have witnessed that the sharing of struggles and vulnerabilities does not make employees less likely to drag and cancel one another. There are times to be vulnerable and there are times to keep your armor up and it's critical to follow your best instincts on this rather than the demands of others.

Jessica Byrd explained, "It becomes performative to reveal something of yourself to put people at ease. Women of color have done it to be seen as more human, to be given more grace, to relate, to demonstrate that leadership doesn't just have to be so top-down, but then the pendulum, I think, has swung too far."

It's important for WOC leaders to ask ourselves: What would it mean to carry myself with a steady confidence, without engaging in artificial vulnerability, victimhood, or smallness to make others comfortable or less threatened by my presence?

Caretaking

The mother/mammy expectation can also take a more literal bent. An alarming number of leaders related experiences with staff members who projected the image of their own mothers onto them and then proceeded to work out their unresolved anger, frustration, and abandonment issues on the leader in wholly dysfunctional and often damaging ways. Oftentimes these were people who the leader had lifted and mentored before the staffer began to relate to them as a mother figure and then turned on them. Leaders have to be careful to avoid this dynamic.

Bamby Salcedo shared, "There was a young person who I knew and supported when she started her transition as a teen. I had seen her grow through her struggles. I knew her parents. I had talked to them to get them to come around. When she was twenty-one or twenty-two, she just completely turned on me. That was painful, really painful. I told her, 'I understand that you have pain, and I'm here for you and we are here as an organization when you need us.' She left the organization and made a claim that I was abusive. There was a whole HR investigation but it didn't go anywhere because she didn't have any basis to her claims. There were some young people who think I'm this horrible monster because of what she said."

Another leader shared the story of a young woman staffer who lost her mother. She poured support and staff development resources into this person only to have their expectations mushroom into something completely unrealistic. Enraged that her boss could not always be on call for her, the young woman quit and then dragged her on social media for being "abusive."

Cleaning Up After Others

Another way the mothering and mammying expectation shows up is inviting WOC in to lead organizations as the cleanup crew when they are falling apart or on the most difficult projects that no one else wants to do. I've lost count of the number of stories from leaders who discovered a few weeks into the job—and it is nearly always a surprise—that the organization is out of money. Sarah Audelo is the former executive director of Alliance for Youth Action, the largest youth voter-engagement operation in the country. She shared, "I started in March of 2017, at the beginning of the Trump administration. I then learned we were months from dipping into our reserves, which was awful as the first WOC ED. It was like, 'Welcome! Surprise!'"

It was a similar story for Surina Khan when she replaced a white leader and took the helm as CEO of the Women's Foundation California. "Within the first few weeks, the controller said, 'We need a cash infusion.' There was only sixty thousand dollars in the bank. It wasn't enough to make payroll. They had drawn down the line of credit. Vendors weren't getting paid, grants weren't getting paid. No one had told me about the situation before I took the job."

Teresa Younger is the CEO of the Ms. Foundation for Women. She grew up one of the only Black kids in a predominately white area of North Dakota, and her parents (who are Black) also adopted other children of other races. Teresa is a nationally recognized champion for the rights of women, a relentless advocate for WOC, and a good friend to many other WOC leaders. She is one of the warmest people you will meet in movement. "How did I walk into a board that was disconnected, a deficit budget, a staff that was traumatized?" she reflected, before sharing the feeling so many leaders have. "My fear in reaching for help was that it would be a critique of me."

In all three of these cases, through grit and ingenuity, Sarah, Surina, and Teresa turned their organizations around. Sarah led hers to help drive the highest youth voter turnout in the history of the country in 2020—up 16 percent from 2016—which defeated Trump. Her organization's national team and affiliates made twenty-five million contacts with young voters and registered 1.5 million people to vote on 121 college campuses across the country. Surina grew her struggling organization into an $11 million annual budget with $14 million in cash reserves, and huge success with programs like the Solis Policy Institute (formerly the Women's Policy Institute), which has trained more than six hundred women and gender-expansive people (the majority WOC) and resulted in fifty-one bills being signed into law—including expanded access to the abortion pill, renewable energy for low-income communities, and a statewide domestic worker bill of rights. Teresa tripled the annual budget, doubled the staff, rebuilt a national board, and built up the endowment by 2.5 times at the Ms. Foundation for Women. She has transformed a fifty-year-legacy institution into a place with a fully aligned race and gender lens in every aspect of its work, from investments to grantmaking to communication and internal policy.

A close cousin of the fixer-upper organization is the difficult project that no one wants to do. WOC leaders are often chosen to lead such projects and then sidelined once they succeed. Ashindi Maxton, co-founder of the Donors of Color Network, New Media Ventures, Emergent Fund, Reflective Democracy, and the Youth Engagement Fund, has worked behind the scenes in philanthropy to move millions to groups whose potential she was able to see before anyone else, groups that have now shaped the direction of the country. She shared a story from years ago, at the Democracy Alliance (one of the largest U.S. networks of high-net-worth liberal and progressive electoral donors): "The first project I built in philanthropy was the Election Administration Fund at the Democracy Alliance. The board was worried about voter suppression in the 2008 elections. Many of the staff were not convinced at the time that voter suppression was a real threat. Back in 2007, it was still seen as conspiracy theory stuff. I took on leadership of what they thought would be maybe a five-hundred-thousand-dollar funding project. It turned out that voter suppression *was* a very real thing, and funders were looking for places to put money and a strategy around it, particularly with Obama running. So it became a six-million-dollar project. As soon as there was that much money there, the number of people angling to have control of the project grew. After the election, at the point that there was nothing left to do but tell the story of the project, I was taken off of it. The advisory board hired a white man to write the evaluation of the work who made sure to tell me on our first call, 'I don't have to answer to you.'"

So how do we resist these unrealistic and destructive expectations? How can we set boundaries so we aren't mothering our organizations and our staff?

- *Say no to mothering and "family" relationships at work explicitly.* Bamby Salcedo, with TransLatin@ Coalition, shared, "There are young people who I've known since they were twelve, before their transition, and they are now thirty and they call me Mom, and I say, 'No, I'm your sister. We are here to do this work and you need to get with it.' Otherwise, people can confuse the love I give with motherly love."

  Gina Clayton-Johnson, executive director of Essie Justice Group, is emphatic. "I'm very clear with our team that 'You are not friends, you are colleagues. We are not friends, we are colleagues,' and that this is a variety of relationship that is loving and supportive but distinct from a parental and family relationship and friendship. I explain what are the contours of colleagueship."

- *Don't be afraid of a fight.* As leaders we have to pick our battles judiciously. Denise Perry thinks the battle for healthy boundaries cannot be avoided. "[They're] like, 'We demand this, that, and the other,' and we give it to them because we don't have the edge for the fight and our avoiding all of the fights validates their position. Transforming conflict doesn't say we avoid the conflict, it means we get in the conflict. We need to learn how to fight, not how to avoid a fight."

This is one of the most valuable pieces of advice I took from these interviews as my tendency to people-please often compelled me to avoid the fight and respond to demands by giving more. I also made the mistake of surrounding myself with people on my leadership team who had the same issues I did, so whenever my instincts did kick in to set a boundary, I was strongly opposed by people who advocated just to give more. In retrospect, there were many more fights that I should have picked.

- *Disabuse people (and yourself!) of the notion that WOC are here to "save" them.* Miya Yoshitani said, "The white-led orgs are going back and forth between understanding the importance of BIPOC women leadership and a harmful fantasy that we are all coming to save them. We need to be assured of our own worth and the power and importance of our leadership while at the same time not feeling responsible for saving everybody."

- *Set and reset expectations to be sustainable for the leader given the size of the org.* Bamby Salcedo noted, "Our organization is rapidly growing. It makes it harder for me to engage with people the way I engaged when there were only three to four of us. Everyone was so used to 'I want to talk to Bamby,' and I would make myself available, but now I can't, there is so much work I have to do. Thirty minutes to spend with someone and hear their complaints is not productive. I have to set that boundary for my own sanity." Manage people's expectations and let them know that all you are juggling limits your capacity to be present for everyone.

- *De-link your self-worth from pleasing others.* Congratulate yourself when you hold a boundary you know is healthy even when it disappoints others. Yoshitani said, "Being able to disappoint people and still hold on to your feelings of self-worth and dignity is important. Everyone's expectations of you doesn't mean you have to expect those things of yourself."

- *Don't assume people understand the demands of leadership. Tell them.* Several leaders I spoke with noticed staff shift out of demanding mothering once they sat them down and explained in detail all that they were holding to make sure the paychecks and benefits—the very things the staff depended on—were consistent. They also explained that if something went wrong, they, as the leader, would be the one who donors, board members, and the public would blame.

- *Remind people that leaders are human beings who continue to show up to work while managing ups and downs in our personal lives.* Staff should hear that just as they are juggling work with health issues, caretaking responsibilities, and major life changes like divorce or the loss of a parent, so are their leaders. We are human. We are not machines. We too deserve empathy and grace.

- *Be diligent in maintaining the right ratio of internal to external focus.* As WOC help their organizations strike the right balance between this internal work (on organizational health) and the external work in our communities (helping communities improve their material conditions), important decisions have to be made about where to expend time and energy. If all the energy is expended externally, the internal house will be a mess and it will eventually impact the quality of the external work. If all the energy is expended internally, the external work will grind to a standstill and the organization will succumb to navel-gazing, without much accountability to its larger mission and the communities it serves. There is no one-size-fits-all formula. Some seasons of organizational growth and development may require a more intensive internal focus on structure, systems, and culture, and others more of an external focus. But leaders need to be aware that particularly in these times, and particularly with WOC leaders, staff can rarely be trusted to set ratios that are not warped by problematic and stereotypical expectations of mothering and nurturing. Leaders need to exercise some authority here.

Educate and inoculate staff about how the mothering and mammying dynamic shows up and let them know that it will not be tolerated. Let this be part of the beautiful legacy that we leave to the next generation.

10

Setting Boundaries

O ne of the most difficult aspects of leadership today is balancing compassionate and vulnerable leadership with the clear and healthy boundary setting that is needed to protect both the mission of an organization and the well-being of the people working within it. This is especially challenging today because of the level of pain, anxiety, and malaise that exists in this era of political and cultural divisions and heightened awareness of climate catastrophe. Most leaders take this into account and empathize with the suffering of their staff members. And yet, they must set limits.

Leaders have a responsibility to not allow anyone to treat the organization as a whipping post or a place to off-load their pain onto others. Boundaries to protect against destructive behavior within our ranks should be drawn just as diligently as they are drawn against outside attacks. Many of the problems we now have in movement organizations are a result of poor boundaries. Whole swaths of people have conflated decision-making and boundary setting with abuse and authoritarianism. It's past time to put the mission of organizations back at the center of gravity.

"Boundaries are the distance at which I can love you and me simultaneously," said Prentis Hemphill, author of the excellent book *What It Takes to Heal* and founder of The Embodiment Institute. In the movement context, I would extend this to the distance at which I can love you, me, and the mission of the organization.

I once mused dryly to myself that if I didn't make a change, the inscription on my headstone would read HERE LIES SHE WHO SUFFERED FOOLS. Boundary setting was one of my hardest-learned lessons as a leader. I emerged from my childhood as a hard-core people pleaser who deeply feared rejection and isolation. I knew the pain of intense loneliness and I never wanted to feel it ever again. As Hemphill reminds us, "It's the places where your shame persists that your boundaries are hardest to hold." As a child, I felt great shame about my racial identity. As I've written, growing up a Sri Lankan and white kid who was too brown to be accepted into the white community, and without any Sri Lankans around to accept me into theirs, I never enjoyed the feeling of a people who claimed me as their own. By the time I was well into adulthood, I was deep into codependency. I had great capacity to love others and far less to love myself.

Even though I had strong friendships and a chosen family outside of work—and didn't depend on work for friendships, as many in movement do—I relied heavily on external validation. This fueled a powerful work ethic, attentiveness to the needs of others, and a lot of professional success. It also made me a sitting duck as a leader. People could easily mess with me.

Whenever people showed an unwillingness to carry their load, I would happily volunteer to put it on my back instead of holding them accountable. Many of the leaders I spoke with echoed this tendency, particularly when they talked about their early days holding positions of leadership. "In my younger days, I didn't understand how not to be a doormat," said Cindy Wiesner. "For many WOC, queer folks, working-class folks, there is a way in which this society—our families, religion—trains us to defer or be in service." Amisha Patel said, "I caught so many balls that then allowed people to say, 'Well, Amisha will handle it, so I don't need to have ultimate responsibility for a thing.'"

When people made sloppy mistakes on the job, I would think of the hardships in their lives and double down on support and encouragement instead of offering clear and constructive feedback or transitioning them out. When they spread rumors about me, instead of confronting them and standing up for myself, I'd work harder to win their trust. Like most codependents, I got between people and the consequences of their actions, robbing them of the opportunity to fail, be accountable, learn, and grow. This disempowered them. It also left me, the organization, and everyone else in it at risk because I had left enough room for toxic or incompetent people to throw their weight around.

Miya Yoshitani got feedback from her team on exactly this. "There was a staff person who was in a position they couldn't handle and who I should have fired," she said. "It was my responsibility. Not doing it and taking on more of their work definitely fit into a pattern of me not being able to fully hold someone else accountable, and letting my compassion, concern, and tendency to take care of people get in the way of the decision that needed to be made. After I finally did let this person go, I received feedback about the impact that my indecisiveness had on the rest of the team."

Weak boundaries create more work. Like most codependents, I was burning myself out with all the work to please. I was consistently teaching people how to treat me badly. When a staff member did something awful, it was as if two tiny women appeared—one on each of my shoulders—and started talking directly into my ears. The first woman would say, "Empathize with the pain that this behavior is coming from and try to help them! They've been through so much in their life." The second woman, who looked like she had been through some shit, would suck her teeth and clap back, "Been through a lot in their life, huh? Yeah, well so had that lady who killed Selena. Girl, you better armor up and protect yourself!" Faced with this binary, I'd usually make my next move based on the advice of that first tiny woman, with less than great results. Today, I follow a third woman, a wiser one, who values compassion and firmness and says, "Treat everyone involved with kindness and empathy, but draw clear and healthy boundaries that are needed to protect you and the organization."

Hailey Magee, a codependency recovery coach, wrote:

> To break the people-pleasing pattern, we must learn how to sit with discomfort instead of reacting to it. We must also live with:
>
> - The discomfort of others being unhappy with us
>
> - The discomfort of letting others handle their own problems instead of rushing to fix them
>
> - The discomfort of having difficult conversations and setting tough boundaries
>
> - The discomfort that comes when we realize others' happiness isn't our responsibility, but our *own* happiness is.[1]

One of the first things my mentor Adisa Douglas warned me about was to be careful of people demanding my time, energy, and presence. She urged me to not fall into the trap that many

WOC fall into: feeling overly grateful to be asked to take a position or to be on a stage, running themselves ragged. Hearing this from her empowered me to begin to say no early, saving me from a world of problems.

Finding Your No

Getting to a clear no can be a journey for many WOC leaders. Dara Cooper said, "I got this request to give a talk. I thought I said no. I was so upset because they came back [with details]. I thought I said no, numerous times! I went back and reread my emails, and my no was porous as hell. I learned about porous boundaries from Nedra Tawwab's excellent book *Set Boundaries, Find Peace.*"

Once you can deliver a clear no, the next step is being "willing to hold a no despite people's reactions," which Cooper pointed out is often not immediately accepted when it is a woman of color delivering the no. They "will make you feel bad, they will push back as much as they can, but that's not your bag to hold, that's theirs." We have to learn to hold our boundary anyway. Author Melissa Urban reminds us that when we set a boundary and allow others to violate it, we are teaching ourselves that we can't trust ourselves.

Saying no isn't only necessary when it comes to direct requests or invitations. It also extends to those to whom you give your energy. "There will be moments when people hit below the belt, or throw you up against the ropes," said Cindy Wiesner. "In that scenario it is like, 'Okay, Cindy, you can help facilitate this. I'm skilled at walking through the fire. But do I have to go through the fire? No.'"

As one begins to draw boundaries, it's important to check that we are doing so in a healthy way. Early in my career, when a problem arose, I would delay, letting the embers of a bad situation glow and spark, hoping they would extinguish themselves. Then, when there was a raging fire, I would come in and draw boundaries with a fire hose of anger or irritation. The poet Jaiya John wrote about this in his book *Freedom: Medicine Words for Your Brave Revolution:* "Your boundary need not be an angry electric fence that shocks those who touch it. It can be a consistent light around you that announces: 'I will be treated sacredly.'"

There is, of course, no formula for setting or relaxing boundaries, and a calculation must be made in every situation in order for a leader to have the most strategic response. If you are indiscriminately vulnerable, you may show your tender underbelly and find that people still gut you. If you are indiscriminately fiery, you may be pouring gasoline on a situation that could have easily been resolved with a softer approach.

Many leaders are backing away from drawing healthy boundaries on the advice of misguided organizational development consultants or out of fear that staff will retaliate and drag them on social media. In hindsight, the individuals that created the most havoc in the projects and organizations I have led have nearly always been the most fragile. The least able to receive feedback without becoming defensive or falling apart, the least able to manage their emotional triggers without spinning out or lashing out at others.

MINI MASTER CLASS
Rajasvini Bhansali

"I'm seeing a lot of kowtowing to keep people happy. Building discipline within organizations is critical. We have a culture of rigorous feedback. Staff get hard feedback. They expect it. If they don't get it, they ask for it. Managers are trained in how to deliver it. It's done with a lot of skill, but at the same time not shying away from it. I keep a particular eye out for fragility. If people start being fragile and toxic, I believe it is my role as a leader to help them move on."

There's another challenge that many former-organizers-turned-managers or EDs face. The first job of a good organizer is to see the positive potential in natural leaders, no matter how traumatized they are, and stick with them to develop their skills. You rarely have to kick anyone out of an organizing committee—if that's needed, the other committee members will see to it. The first job of an ED is to protect the organizational mission and the safety and well-being of the entire team. This often means firing people who refuse to stop punching holes in the bottom of the organizational boat that everyone is in. If we don't make this adjustment from organizer to manager, we will give people too much time to sink the ship.

One of the places where leaders have the hardest time drawing boundaries is in moments of conflict. "We need stronger leaders," said Jessica Byrd. "When you are inside a tough moment and your first response is to retreat—I think that's where it gets really tough. We need people who have their chests out a little bit, who are not afraid of confrontation and direct dialogue. I can give feedback because I also get it and am willing to get it."

I agree with Byrd. But I would add that it is difficult, if not impossible, to hold staff through conflict in an environment where the leaders are targeted and abused and not well flanked. This is where boundary setting intersects with building your squad and surrounding yourself with people of backbone and integrity. If you are attempting to navigate conflict and the people around you—your senior team, your managers—are conflict-averse people pleasers who think boundaries are mean, you will fail. You must be flanked by people who are also willing to have the tough conversations, set limits, and take the heat to protect the organization and everyone in it.

To Be Flanked

One Halloween, I was driving my daughter Kwali and her friend to a dance class when I saw that a neighbor down the street from us had hung a mannequin of a decaying corpse from a noose in their front yard as part of their ghoulish holiday display. My stomach turned. This would have affected me on any day, but it was just a few months after the murder of George Floyd, so the specter of a lynching hit me particularly hard. I felt instantly protective of my family, especially my co-parent, Tricia, who I knew felt the least safe of all of us walking in Tacoma as a Black woman.

The year 2020 had been painful enough, I didn't want her to feel the shock of seeing this. Seeing the neighbor in his front yard, I pulled over and rolled down my window. Using my organizing skills, I connected with him first as a neighbor and a fellow parent, telling him how I enjoyed his flowers in the spring each year and seeing his kids—who were close in age to my youngest—playing out front when I walked my dog by his house each day. Then I told him that I imagined he had no idea the impact a lynched corpse would have on his neighbors of color, particularly his Black neighbors, but that given the history of lynching in this country—past and present—it chilled me to my core. I asked him to take it down. He was defensive initially but softened as we talked, and agreed to take it down. The next day, it was gone. The following day, he hung a life-size doll of a zombie child from the noose instead. I didn't know whether he was being dense or defiant, but I knew I didn't want to deal with it. I called up another neighbor, a progressive white woman I sometimes walk with. "All the white folks in this neighborhood with Black Lives Matter signs," I told her, "this is where it goes from a slogan to actually showing up." I asked her to handle it, and she did. Within two days she had worked her network of progressive white folks and they had talked to the neighbor and got him to take down the entire noose display. Several Halloweens later, it has never gone back up. Sometimes, we need people around us to handle it and set the boundaries. The same is true in leadership. We need people around us who will handle it so we don't always have to.

We don't all arrive to leadership as boundary-setting Jedis surrounded by people who will flank and support us, but these are skills and structures that can be learned and built. As Melissa Urban said, "Boundaries make people feel safe." The ability of leaders and those around us to draw clear and healthy boundaries does not strike like lightning. These are muscles that must be strengthened through ongoing practice each and every day. Kind of like the heart is a muscle. "Boundaries," said Brené Brown, "are a function of self-respect and self-love." And the heart of any successful movement should always be love.

11

Healing Ourselves

A few years ago, I was talking with a good friend. At the time, we were both executive directors of major national organizations. We were commiserating about how much time we spent working on ourselves so that we could show up well in the world not only as mothers, partners, and friends, but also as leaders. That included therapy, meditation, support groups, journaling and reflecting, executive coaching, and peer coaching. We calculated that we spent about five hours a week engaged in this kind of work—on top of our regular work and the time we spent parenting young children.

It was a lot, but we agreed that it felt necessary to stay grounded as leaders in the choppy waters of the times. Social justice movements are full of people who still have wounds from childhood, from personal relationships, from previous jobs. As leaders, when we don't do our own work to address and heal our pain and trauma, it can harm others and the organizations that we are trying to lead. And when unrepaired trauma intersects with the enormous stress and pressure of leadership, it can reify old dynamics or become a powder keg, ready to explode on others or implode on us. As movement leader Grace Lee Boggs taught us, "Transform yourself to transform the world."

As an only child and latchkey kid of a single mother, I grew up doing a lot for myself. By age nine, I was packing my lunches for school, doing my laundry, and, when my mom worked late, preparing dinner (mac-and-cheese-from-a-box level of cooking, but still). There was nothing atypical about this for many other kids in the 1980s, but it set a pattern for my mother and me: It was us against the world. We each did things ourselves, and we didn't let many people in. Beneath it all was a feeling that others could not be trusted and that one needed to maintain control to stay safe.

This shaped me into a fiercely independent self-starter. When I was thirteen, I wanted to take more dance classes than my mom could afford. So, I woke up at 5:00 A.M., before sunrise, and took two buses an hour across town to the dance studio to mop the floors. While I mopped, I danced in front of the studio mirrors to Mary J. Blige's album *What's the 411* on my bright yellow Sony Walkman. Paying my own way made me feel powerful. When I wanted something, I knew what to do on my own to make it happen. This would serve me well in many areas of my life, including the start-up phase of my organization—a time when I needed to inspire others to join me. I had no problem accepting responsibility for launching the organization, which made me fully accountable to the mission. I worked hard, kept my word, and always did what I said I was going to do, which instilled confidence in external partners and motivated increased investment from donors.

During the start-up phase, I had a tight team of two other people who were, coincidentally, also latchkey kids and only children of single moms. We had similar working styles. We were comfortable huddling together periodically to strategize and align, then running our individual work areas with a fair amount of autonomy. As the staff grew, and people came on board who were more relational in their working style, the dissonance was apparent. This dawned on me during an icebreaker exercise at one of our staff retreats.

In pairs, we were prompted to share a time that we felt fear about a work task and how we worked through it. The person I partnered with spoke of being nervous when facilitating a large training for the first time and how she immediately called her most trusted confidants and colleagues for support. I talked about how I was once terrified before speaking to a large audience. I handled it by locking myself in a bathroom stall for ten minutes and praying—in part to a higher power and in part over my index card of talking points. Other people looked outward for support. I looked inward.

I recalled my conversation with my mother about how she survived that terrible period of our lives after I told the truth about abuse. "Who was your rock?" I had asked her. "I was my rock," she replied. Years later, I was doing the equivalent at my organization: not delegating enough, overcontrolling my team members, and piling more tasks onto my back when they weren't done exactly to my liking. I was overworking myself and getting in the way of the brilliance and creativity of my staff members. A more versatile mode of leadership was needed to build broader staff engagement and buy-in on everything from big-picture strategy to HR policies—not to mention to make my workload sustainable.

I worked with a therapist to uncover the childhood pain and parental messages that made me hesitant to trust others. I worked with a coach to make a plan around how to delegate and get out of the way, and with an organizational development firm to help me develop new organizational structures (such as an expanded executive team and a cross-departmental staff body to work on certain decisions) and new practices as a leader (such as more delegation and more time devoted to building rapport with staff). The result was a more manageable workload for me, more joyful and creative room for my staff, and a stronger and more innovative organization. Still, I had by no means arrived. Finding the right balance between decisive and collaborative decision-making within a hierarchical organizational structure would be an ongoing challenge and learning process for me. But I had advanced my healing considerably, and it had paid off in my leadership.

On the flip side, I saw how trauma that I left unhealed could, over time, hold back my leadership. In my case, it surfaced in codependence creeping into how I led. Being rejected by my Sri Lankan family, growing up without any other Sri Lankans around, and being treated as an outsider by so many of the people I encountered had left deep wounds. This was only compounded by being gaslit by my mother about the racism I experienced, and by most of my Sri Lankan family about the sexual abuse I had suffered.

I knew the pain of intense othering and loneliness. I had developed adaptive, codependent behaviors—people-pleasing, overwork, lack of boundary setting—to prevent anything from touching these excruciatingly tender places.

The path I was on was no longer viable for me. I was suffering, and the work was suffering. I had to sit myself down and ask some tough questions: To what degree had the gaslighting I had experienced as a child led me to gaslight myself? To second-guess and override smart instincts to draw healthy boundaries and protect myself and the organization from mistreatment and abuse? How had my father's family treating me like a traitor to the race—for "snitching" on my abuser and leaving with my white mother—

led to a subconscious tendency to prove myself trustworthy to many people of color, even those who were incredibly untrustworthy themselves?

Codependent leadership meant I often put myself between people and the consequences of their actions. This meant offering too many chances to people who should have been fired long ago. I hadn't yet learned to do what Sara Bareilles once described as "Allowing someone the dignity of their discomfort." I had not yet read *Codependent No More*, by Melody Beattie—a book that changed my life—and so had not yet learned that failing to draw healthy boundaries is in fact a major way of denying people opportunities to learn and grow.

Having grown up so isolated, with no real group of people shielding me from attack, I also had no concept that as a leader, it was critical to surround myself with high-integrity people who would protect me and have my back.

MINI MASTER CLASS

LaTosha Brown

Some of the best advice I've received during my toughest moments in leadership has come from community organizer and political strategist LaTosha Brown. Hailing from Selma, Alabama, which she described as "the birthplace of the voting rights movement," LaTosha's voice is a force that transforms whatever it touches. I've seen rooms full of uptight New York funders and policy wonks let down their armor and drop into their souls as she cracked open the silence at the top of a meeting with a freedom song and then asked, "When will we give up the idea that our freedom is beholden to white donors giving us something?" I've seen the faces of weary Black voters waiting in three-hour lines to vote in Georgia light up as she gave them an impromptu speech of encouragement through a bullhorn. And I've seen some of the toughest political strategists influenced by the analysis she offered on myriad platforms, ranging from MSNBC to Harvard University.

LaTosha is a person who checks for the sisters around her. She notices when someone has been underwater too long and she dives in to pull them to the surface. In a News-One feature on "Black Joy Blazers," she recalled, "The first time I remember using my voice for activism was in elementary school, and these bullies were messing with this little boy. And the first thought I had was *Aw man, I'm gonna have to scuff up my pretty patent leather shoes.* It didn't matter if they were boys, and I was a little bitty girl. It didn't matter if they could beat me, if they could win or not. Everything in me said something was happening that was wrong, and I needed to act on it."[1] For me, LaTosha embodies the type of backbone we need more of in our movements and in the world: people who are willing to "scuff up their shoes," to risk something to stand up for others and for what is right.

On my journey, LaTosha often showed up out of the blue with messages I needed to hear. One time, after I was on the receiving end of some particularly venomous hate and had posted something on social media in an attempt to defend myself, she called me up. It was late at night and I was distressed, exhausted, and alone in a strange hotel room in one city or another where I was speaking. "Vanessa," she said, "it's clear that this really got to you, but think about whether you really want to give it that much power by posting a response." Then she said something I will never forget: "You

can tell the true leaders because of the arrows in their back."
That was a revelation for me—being targeted wasn't out of
the ordinary. In leadership, it was par for the course. Much
later, after a board meeting in 2017, she came up to me at
the break. "I don't know why I am being guided to say this
to you. I'm not sure I know what it means, but maybe you
will know what it means: stop apologizing. You don't need
to apologize anymore." I knew exactly what she meant. I
wasn't literally apologizing in the meeting but I was doing
so energetically with my body language and mannerisms. It
was precisely the message I needed to hear.

In my mature, adult mind I knew I had nothing to apologize for when it came to my Sri Lankan family's negative
reaction to my truth-telling about abuse. I knew that they
were the ones who owed me an apology for not protecting
me as a child. But my child mind had absorbed their shaming and subconsciously hoped they would someday forgive
me for having the audacity to inconvenience them with
such a truth. In subtle ways, there were times when I was
standing in front of a room full of people of color when my
stance was one of apology, of proving my worth and goodness and convincing people that I wasn't a traitor.

At one point, after responding to some wildly disrespectful behavior from a couple of staff members by offering
them even more of my time and support, I found myself on
the receiving end of another call from LaTosha, who gave
me what I can only describe as the world's best talking-to.
"Vanessa," she told me, "why are you extending yourself
and appealing to people who are trying to hurt you? What is
happening is hurtful and harmful—cut it off! You don't owe
anyone space to tear down your work or character. You
don't need to reward people who are stabbing you in the

back!" I got quiet and took in her words. I was filled with a different kind of shame for not having stood up for myself. But I knew her words were not intended to shame me. She was speaking the truth firmly and from love, and her words snapped me out of the codependent trance I was in.

My executive coach, Helen Kim, often implored me to be more strategic about the people I chose to spend time on. She cautioned against focusing too much on problematic people, trying to win them over or get them to stop doing damaging things. Instead, she told me, I should deepen relationships with the most grounded and high-performing people who had the capacity to stabilize the organization. Intellectually, I got it. Still, it was a struggle for me to heed this advice. Toxic people hit on my pain triggers, and pain had a gravitational pull on my focus and energy.

My dear friend of more than twenty years, Dr. John Scott, is a student of the late, great civil rights hero and historian Dr. Vincent Harding and an expert on diversity, equity, and inclusion and the Theater of the Oppressed as a modality for healing and transformation. He's also my triathlon training buddy. One day during a long bike ride, John said to me about childhood trauma, "We return to the scene of the crime." In other words, we either recreate or attract to ourselves some version of the scenario we were harmed by. For me, my family abandoning me as a child was my core wound. So it stood to reason that until I healed, as a leader, I would continue to surround myself with and waste my time on too many people who lacked the capacity to have my back and were sure to abandon me.

I had many people of integrity around me as well: in my chosen family, among my friends, on my board, among my colleagues, and even a few on my staff team. These were people who cared about me, who had my back, and who would tell me the truth. At times, I didn't invest as much time as I could have with these people, and I let the toxic people too close. It took many hard lessons to sharpen my discernment and focus my energy on the wiser and kinder humans.

My journey to healing around many of these issues has involved weekly therapy; a twelve-step program for codependence; EMDR (Eye Movement Desensitization and Reprocessing) therapy and soul retrieval to move beyond childhood trauma; daily meditation, journaling, psychotherapy; my own version of art therapy through painting, singing, and dancing; swimming; daily mantras; and more self-help books and podcasts than I can count. Healing is never fully done, but I am proud of the progress I've made. And I'm so much more at peace in my life and in my leadership.

Here are the mantras I began to work with daily. They have helped rewire my brain to set healthy boundaries and allow me to honor myself and become a wiser leader. Sitting in front of my altar, I light a candle, say three oms, and meditate. I close my meditation by saying each mantra out loud slowly and deliberately, until I can really *feel* each of them in my body. I also work with a few of the shortest mantras throughout the week while swimming, saying them to myself to the rhythm of my strokes and breaths.

1. My dignity and grace are unshakable.

2. I am disciplined and do not react to nonsense.

3. I deserve love, kindness, and backbone from those around me.

4. I am free from seeking validation from others.

5. I set healthy boundaries clearly and cheerfully without irritation or anger. People's negative reaction to my boundaries is none of my business.

6. I trust my higher power to guide me. I maintain a high vibration so that I can hear its guidance.

7. I understand that safety comes from managing myself rather than controlling the behavior of others.

8. I am free and joyful. Moving toward freedom with courage brings the greatest security and abundance.

9. I am safe, divinely guided, and protected.

10. Even though [insert whatever is difficult], I love and accept myself. (This one is from my elder and friend Dr. Bola Cofield.)

James Baldwin once wrote, "It took many years of vomiting up all the filth I'd been taught about myself, and half-believed, before I was able to walk on the earth as though I had a right to be here."[2] I felt a wail break free in the center of my heart the first time I read these words. Reading Baldwin has always felt like sitting with a timeless prophet who reaches directly into my soul to uproot what I have tried so mightily to ignore, but that must be pulled out for me to be free. It's ongoing work for me, putting my hands in the soil of my own consciousness to pull up the pain, trauma, and rage that don't serve my highest purpose. When the grip of my awareness isn't strong enough, I reach for the shovels and trowels of my mantras, meditation, and other healing modalities, along with the wisdom of those kindred souls whose insights I trust. There is so much I still have to learn, and here are four lessons I gleaned through my own healing that have helped me walk more effectively in life and leadership:

1. *I can trust my instincts.* After certain failures and falls, I agonized about whether I could trust my own instincts about people. It took some time, but I eventually realized that my instincts were not the problem. The problem was that I consistently overrode them. The gaslighting I had been subject to from my family continued with me gaslighting myself—I was repeatedly talking myself out of what my gut told me was true. When I thought back on the people who did harm to me, to other leaders, and to the organization, they were usually people who I dismissed nagging concerns about, telling myself that I was probably paranoid. The solution wasn't adopting new instincts. It was learning to listen to and trust the ones I had. The solution wasn't to stop trusting people. It was, as my wise and wonderful former sister-in-law Tamara once told me, "Trust people, V. And also trust them when they tell you who they are." This came down to being impeccably honest with myself. Too often I wanted to believe people had integrity more than I wanted to face the truth that they did not—and that I would have to take some action, at times uncomfortable, to protect myself and the organization. This included having direct conversations, blocking certain individuals from access to or control over key functions that could damage the organization if handled irresponsibly, documenting disciplinary action to signal clear boundaries, and with some people, firing. There were times I did this effectively, and others where I doubted myself and stepped too far back.

2. *I deserve to be protected.* I was so busy taking care of everyone else and the organization that I failed both to ask for the protection I needed as a leader and to register and

receive the protection that I was offered. My board included some of the most prominent and courageous movement leaders of our time. They had both the capacity and backbone to protect me against unjust attacks. I often waited too long to ask for their help and then focused my entire ask on protection for the organization, feeling it would be selfish to share how vulnerable I felt. When the board protected me anyway, I had a hard time taking in that support and letting it ease my mind. I was triggered and frozen at the scene of the crime—the moment when I was a child and my family turned their backs. Despite all of the evidence to the contrary, I was convinced it was happening again. I had to work hard to register that this situation was different, and to receive the love and support that was being extended to me by these incredible leaders. By the same token, I had trouble taking in how some staff also had my back. Very few of them had the courage to speak out in group settings, which was maddening, but some did take action behind the scenes to protect me and to prevent toxic people from taking the organization off the rails.

3. *Let the mud settle.* When I was in the midst of a particularly anguish-inducing moment of leadership, my coach, Helen Kim, reminded me of a Buddhist concept: "Do you have the patience to let the mud settle, so that you can see clearly what is the right course of action?" This can be challenging, especially when people trigger your own unhealed trauma, thereby kicking up a lot of mud. It is important to allow time for the mud to settle so that you can differentiate between what is yours, what is theirs, and what is the wise and most responsible course of action to take as a

leader in that moment. This can be excruciating. There have been moments where everything in my body screams, "React! Say something!" even though I knew I was too activated to see clearly. At times like those, I have had to exercise the greatest restraint.

In their wonderful book *Leading with Joy*, Akaya Windwood and Rajasvini Bhansali wrote, "Moving toward stillness is somewhat counterintuitive when faced with hostility and possible annihilation. However, in that moment of pause it is possible to take a breath and consider options. And there are always options—never only a single possibility."

4. *Don't be an island.* Generational habits die hard. The "I am my rock" adage from my mother deeply informed how I moved in the world. I realized there was a world of joy, support, and learning that I missed out on for many years by being so nose-to-the-grindstone with the work of leadership that I didn't invest the time in deepening enough friendships with other leaders, especially other WOC EDs. I connected with folks and had good rapport, but I didn't often share the hardest things I grappled with in leadership. When I finally began to share, I was stunned by how much my peers had also been holding in about what they were going through. I've had fantastic executive coaches over the years, but I learned there is something irreplaceable about what you can learn from your peers who are, in real time, navigating many of the same leadership struggles you are. I'm grateful I was finally able to be vulnerable enough to deepen those connections, but saddened about the years I lost and struggled in relative isolation before I was wise enough to do so.

The interplay between our individual healing and our relationship to movement can be a beautiful gift. "I still feel the cold water on my skin sometimes," said Greisa Martínez Rosas as she remembered being a nine-year-old girl, holding hands with her siblings and parents while crossing the Rio Grande.[3] Like so many undocumented families, they lived for years in fear of being found out until tragically, her father was deported after a simple traffic stop revealed that he was driving without a license—which many cities refuse to issue to undocumented immigrants. Greisa began fighting for the rights of undocumented immigrants while still a high school student, leading walkouts and other actions before going on to lead one of the nation's most influential immigrant rights organizations, United We Dream. Then, in another blow, she lost her mother to cancer. Indomitable, Greisa, who is out and proud as queer and an undocumented DACA recipient, has led United We Dream to build a membership of more than four hundred thousand people and an online reach of four million.

Greisa Martínez Rosas reflected, "I have been deeply transformed by this work. I was ashamed and afraid and organizing found me in that place and the community and the connections I built helped me embrace the parts of me that I felt were the most unlovable. I try to understand myself and the trauma that I carry and how it shows up. In the past five years, committing to being in therapy consistently and taking on my spiritual practices have helped me with myself, this movement, my staff, my friends, and my colleagues."

What we learn from healing ourselves can make us better leaders and inspire how we support healing within the organizations and spaces where we lead.

12

Healing Within Organizations

ealing work is critical for leaders, but it is also essential for every person working in movement. We have all seen someone who isn't doing their emotional work blow up a meeting or campaign, or even destroy an organization, because they are triggered or in their feelings. As the saying goes, "If you don't heal what hurts you, you'll bleed on those who didn't cut you."

Linda Burnham described the type of movement that most of us age forty and older will recognize. "I came up in a set of movement organizations that were from the neck up. [It was,] 'We don't give a shit about what else is going on with you, just do the work and if you fall out, oh well, somebody will possibly pick you up, but who knows who.' I found my way to yoga or I wouldn't have been able to stay in this work." Much has changed since then.

WOC have been at the forefront of bringing healing into organizations. Ai-jen Poo brought somatic practitioners in to support her team and the worker leaders at the National Domestic Workers Alliance more than a decade ago. Denise Perry and other founders centered somatics within Black Organizing for Leadership and Dignity and inspired Black organizers across the nation. As Forward Together's leader, Eveline Shen did breakthrough work for the reproductive justice movement in introducing activists to Zen Buddhist practitioner Norma Wong and Forward Stance, a mind-body methodology using tai chi, meditation, and other modalities. There are phenomenal healing practitioners like Gina Breedlove, author of *Vibration of Grace: Sound Healing Rituals for Liberation,* who do powerful, transformative, and effective work with movement groups and individual leaders.

Nonetheless, there is a debate about how much healing work should be done within organizations versus on an individual basis, outside of work. Movement workers are not immune to the decline in mental health and emotional regulation caused by the pandemic. Many leaders know that healing needs to be addressed, even if only to keep mission-related work from derailing. Yet, there are land mines to navigate when bringing healing modalities into workplaces.

Raising expectations that organizations "heal" their staff can feed into inappropriate expectations of mothering from WOC leaders and move the center of gravity of the organization away from the external mission. "I do think as women of color we are asked to hold and handle people's emotional loads that we're not equipped to handle," said Linda Burnham, movement elder and former head of the Women of Color Resource Center. "And people come with huge emotional loads, not surprisingly, and looking for someone to handle them or a place to act out."

"A lot of wounded souls showing up to work brings a lot of drama and mess," explained Gloria Walton, "and therefore a lot of distraction from mission and purpose. I want to figure out how to build a humane organization. We are here for a mission greater than any of us individually and all of us combined."

A few of the leaders I interviewed also flagged just how wrong things can go when staff or consultants without deep skills in healing modalities hold space in ways that harm people.

Ash-Lee Woodard Henderson, formerly of the historic Highlander Research and Education Center, is an adored child of movement. Ash was raised in a small town in the foothills of Tennessee, at the knee of Black Panthers and other Black liberation freedom fighters. Having witnessed the effects of COINTELPRO and state violence, and having had her own organization firebombed by white supremacists, no one would fault her if she were cagey and bitter, but Ash is the opposite. A minister at heart, she brings clear and militant politics together with a huge capacity to love and encourage those around her. The "movement church" spaces she leads with song and testimony are among the most welcoming and nourishing I have participated in. Ash has seen unskilled attempts at healing result in "randomly applied spiritual practices and ideology around mental health and care and compassion and vulnerability with very little study, which is to me very dangerous."

I experienced these dynamics firsthand. After Covid hit, emotional outbursts and conflicts arose at my organization like never before. People became more easily triggered by something someone said and instead of pausing and responding thoughtfully, they reacted from an unregulated emotional place with rage, crying, or sharp accusations. My managers and I spent inordinate amounts of time mediating disputes and helping people repair relationships. My HR department brought in a consultant who had done good work for us before and said they had excellent training on managing triggers that they could run with our team. *Great!* I thought. *This is exactly what we need!* The workshop was a bust. Despite a disclaimer from the facilitator that people could share as much or as little as they wanted, some staff felt pressured to divulge their own history of trauma.

I made it clear after this experience that certain levels of healing should not happen at work. Providing staff with tools that
allow them to recognize when they are triggered and to slow
down enough to respond from a grounded place—great. An invitation to recall and share childhood trauma with co-workers—not
so great.

Another challenge is the notion, increasingly popular among
younger activists, that individual or internal organizational healing must be the primary focus and fully completed before external work can be done. Two WOC leaders I respect, Makani
Themba and Sandra Bass, addressed this in a Facebook thread:

> **Themba:** There is generally less understanding of power
> and how to build it. . . . Of course, there are exceptions but
> I'm concerned about how few people actually organize and
> hold themselves accountable to measures of success in
> terms of what we are changing, transforming.
>
> I do wonder if part of the problem is that a therapeutic
> frame . . . is inherently individualistic and sees self-
> actualization as the primary goal.

> **Bass:** I certainly agree with the importance of care,
> attention to, and consideration of the impact of trauma on
> our mind, heart, and body and how we heal as part of "the
> work," but it, too, can get mired in therapeutic modali-
> ties . . . any framework where pain and problems are
> centered and not where we really want to "be"/what we
> really want to build/create, we tend toward therapy and
> narrow thinking and away from more generative and
> revolutionary work.

Ironically, some of what afflicts movement organizations today
are the individualism and commercialization that buttress the

barriers I've discussed earlier in this book. Veteran organizer Lisa María Castellanos called it "movement influencer syndrome." "It feeds the ego like nothing else," she said. It's an aspect of the digital age that glamorizes activism for activism's sake. The cure? "A dose of humility that comes from talking to everyday folks and listening to the heartbreak of their stories."

For so many organizations, this collective healing must be a return to a primary conversation with—and accountability to— the communities most affected by injustice. Sarah Audelo said it plainly: "At the end of the day, we exist for our base, for the people in our communities. That doesn't mean we should treat staff badly, but how do we keep our base at the center? It is impossible for our jobs to satisfy everything we need."

It can be easy to overreach from generosity and support into a kind of codependence that attempts to relieve people of their own responsibility to do their own healing work. Cindy Wiesner reflected, "We try to make meaning as we get consciousness, of what has happened in our lives, whether you grew up in a fucked-up family dynamic, whether some really horrible shit happened to you, you grew up in poverty, there are ways in which consciousness-raising helps you make meaning and understand it is not just about you. It is systemic and it happens to millions of people and part of then coming into action is when you decide, I want to do something about it—become an activist, an organizer—so it doesn't happen to other people. There is a way in which we come to movement to deal with that deep alienation and pain. I feel like the flip side of that, the codependent side, is then coming to movement or organization asking them to then be responsible for helping you heal."

Dara Cooper named it directly. "What are you doing to work on your shit? Because a lot of folks tend to have a box of shit they want to sit on your lap and for you to own and as I'm getting older, I'm like, 'That ain't my box, I'm not carrying this. That's yours!' What kind of work are you doing to address the childhood wounds and help you be accountable?"

MINI MASTER CLASS
Linda Burnham

Are we asking too much of nonprofit movement organizations? Linda Burnham says yes.

"Partly what we're struggling with," she offered, "is that our organizational forms, primarily 501(c)(3)s/nonprofits, are not capable of doing what we need done, and we're asking of these organizational forms things that they are not designed to do and cannot do well. If you look at mature movements, which ours is not, they have a very developed cultural component that is taking people into a different place where they are not just talking politics, where their hearts are being lifted and their spirits are being lifted. Mature movements understand that whole people need a lot and that you can't pile all of that into the same space. It is very difficult to do the heart and spirit work in the same space where you are figuring out how we're going to make a campaign happen, or how we're going to have this theoretical battle. Our movement has neglected cultural work."

Healing within organizations needs to be rightsized to what is possible and appropriate within a work environment, and balanced with a culture in which people are expected to take responsibility for their own healing outside of their place of employment.

13

We Are Not
a Monolith

WOC who work in movements today range from communists to capitalists, from no-border advocates to xenophobes, from champions of nonviolence to proponents of armed struggle. WOC rise by selflessly lifting others and sometimes by ruthlessly stepping on the necks of our sisters. In my own movement journey, no one has done more to see, lift, and support me than WOC, and no one has tried harder to destroy me. We cannot realize our full potential to evolve, and to work effectively together, and stay well within the work if we do not interrogate these differences between us.

In 1983, the great civil rights activist and culture worker Dr. Bernice Johnson Reagon called uniting a diversity of people to organize "coalition politics" and penned a piece by the same name that still resonates powerfully today and into the future:

> You don't go into coalition because you just like it. The only reason you would consider trying to team up with some-

body who could possibly kill you, is because that's the only way you can figure you can stay alive. . . . Before . . . you had all these little cute villages and the wonderful homogenous societies where everybody looked the same, did things the same, and believed the same things, and if they didn't, you could just kill them and nobody would even ask you about it. . . . We have just finished with that kind of isolating. . . . There is nowhere you can go and only be with people who are like you. It's over. Give it up. . . . It gets hard to stay out in that society all the time. And that's when you find a place, and you try to bar the door and check all the people who come in . . . in that little barred room where you check everybody at the door, you act out community. You pretend that your room is a world. It's almost like a play. . . . It's nurturing, but it is also nationalism. At a certain stage nationalism is crucial to a people if you are going to ever impact as a group in your own interest. Nationalism at another point becomes reactionary because it is totally inadequate for surviving in the world with many peoples.[1]

Groundswell Fund, the organization I founded and ran for seventeen years, was created by cis WOC and evolved into an organization led by cis WOC and trans and gender-nonconforming people of color. Nearly everyone on our team came directly out of grassroots organizing in communities of color. For years, our work to support organizations in dismantling structural racism and all forms of inequality was focused on external action. There was a tacit assumption, on the part of many of us, that an organization like ours, with WOC leadership, didn't need to dismantle structural racism and bias from within. We were wrong.

When George Floyd was murdered in 2020, I was away from the office on a three-month sabbatical. Our communications director (a white trans person) worked with two other organizational leaders (both Asian) to draft a public statement. On the eve of its release, they shared a copy with our full staff. It was met with shock and anger. Black staffers rightly raised objections about the statement, saying that it positioned Groundswell outside the Black community, as if it did not comprise Black staff, board members, and grantee partners. The statement also missed key points that Black people in the organization would have made had they been included in the process. The team reworked the statement, and we set a new policy that said no statement about Black liberation would ever be drafted again without input from Black staff. It was a lesson for us as an organization that we required a systemic change, not just a quick fix. It was clear we needed to make an organizational commitment to ongoing political education and active learning for staff—to address all sorts of bias and oppression.

External forces have created some powerful commonalities among WOC. But just as powerfully, there are major differences in our histories, lived experiences, and strategies for survival. There are fights that are easier or harder to win depending on the affected group. In 2021, President Biden signed the Covid-19 Hate Crimes Act into law to protect Asian Americans from growing attacks, while the George Floyd Justice in Policing Act stalled in Congress. The forces of slavery, colonialism, internment, deportation, incarceration, class, and transphobic violence have shaped each of us differently. There is vast diversity within the categories currently used to label us. For instance, the designation Latinx includes Chicanos with a long history of union organizing, Republican-leaning Cubans who fled after the revolution, Black Dominicans deeply affected by colorism, and non-Spanish-speaking Indigenous people from Guatemala with recent memory of the bloody traumas inflicted by the U.S. military. The category Asian includes wealthy tech executives who hail from bustling cities like New Delhi and Tokyo and have settled in affluent white suburbs, as well as low-income Southeast Asian refugees who live alongside Black and Latinx people in ghettos, working in sweatshops and factories to support their families.

Our differences create obstacles, both internal and external, that WOC must overcome if we are to stand in solidarity. Accordingly, stereotypes in this country often cast East Asian women as passive, Brown women as angry, Black women as aggressive, Native women as stoic, and trans WOC as hypersexual or drama queens. The same comment will often be received differently depending on the perceived race and ethnicity of the woman who delivers it. In interviewing WOC movement leaders for this book, I found that there were pronounced differences in the experience of Black and Brown leaders who contend with stereotypes.

Class differences are also evident. Once, as a young organizer, I was stunned when an older organizer of color who I admired looked at the sign-up list for an action we were planning and exclaimed, "We have researchers and welfare moms. We've got the brains and the brawn!" I was too green to have the nerve to speak up, but I remember thinking, *Why didn't he see the moms as the brains?* I've seen liberal arts graduates form elite, invite-only groups where they discuss Marx and Gramsci and "strategize" about what movements should do, without any way for people of different classes or educational strata to engage, other than as "the masses" who they plan to "organize" to implement their strategies. I was once at a meeting where a working-class cis Black woman was asking questions in a heartfelt attempt to understand how to use trans-respectful language, only to be shamed by a wealthy, white trans person who scolded her in front of everyone about not asking her questions correctly. Classism is real and yet, in an attempt to break out of the many predominately white movement spaces that deal only with class, to the exclusion of race and gender, we often overcorrect away from any conversation about class at all. This kind of snobbery is a problem, in no small part because the majority of people of color in the United States are poor and suffer the worst hits from capitalism.

Some of the best and most dedicated organizers I know grew up in conditions that are similar to those of the communities where they ended up organizing. They have a natural ability to relate to community members as equals rather than treating them paternalistically, like people who need to be saved. They have cultural competency. They build trust quickly. They are deeply invested in victory. That doesn't mean that folks who are from different walks of life can't show up in this way, but there is often more of a learning curve. Ironically, many organizers who grew up poor and have ascended into the middle class can find themselves in movement spaces where everyone else grew up middle-class or upper-class. They describe people not understanding why they are not taking nice vacations, or enjoying the same standard of living as the rest of the team, because they are helping relatives keep their rent paid and electricity on.

Gloria Walton shared, "I am an amalgamation of the communities we organize. Growing up in Mississippi, my mom was getting paid eight dollars an hour working full-time and still having to be on public assistance. I have acquired privilege having gone to college . . . but it's not where I come from nor the reality of where many in my family still are."

Ignorance about class, race, and colonization at once can intensify this even more. There is limited understanding about the different access groups have to certain rights and a poor understanding about how our liberation is bound up together.

Judith LeBlanc, executive director of the Native Organizers Alliance and citizen of the Caddo Nation, said Native women routinely deal with the assumption on the part of others in movement—including other people of color—that "Oh, the poor Indians, they had their land taken away, too bad, but here we are in the twenty-first century, so what?" They don't understand "sovereignty and what it means for people on reservations and Native people in urban areas to be dual citizens." Native women, who overwhelmingly rely on the federally funded Indian Health Services on reservations for their healthcare, were hit the hardest by laws like the 1976 Hyde Amendment, which banned the use of public funds for abortion. "Indian Health Services has very limited OB-GYN services also. Native women have to travel great distances for care. The reproductive rights movement didn't understand this."

Anti-Blackness is rampant in many Brown communities, and xenophobia is widespread in many Black communities. Anti-indigeneity shows up in non-Indigenous people of color. Transphobia is widespread among all groups of color. And each one of us holds, to varying degrees, an internalized version of our oppressor. And if we are not careful, we can reproduce this harm with one another.

As an organizational leader, I have had to coach non-Indigenous staff of color not to discount grant applications from Native leaders whose style of communication can be circular and grounded in storytelling, rather than linear and packed with data. To effectively evaluate grants, we in leadership can find ourselves having to do similar kinds of training with people of color that we do with white people, helping them see beyond a Western, colonial mindset that insists only linear communication equates with clarity and credibility.

I remember mediating a conversation between a Black staff member who wondered aloud why Latinx people didn't just "speak American" and the Latinx staff who heard this comment but couldn't respond because she, believing in the stereotype of the angry Black woman, was afraid to provide her Black colleague with honest and important feedback about how problematic that statement was.

There is so much we are still learning about the dynamics that occur when we come together across different identities. I have led teams of people that included WOC who have organized gender-reveal parties for pregnant friends, and gender-nonconforming people of color who are actively busting the gender binary. And on more than one occasion, I have seen cis WOC who base their position and authority in movement on being part of the "most" marginalized group in America balking at the suggestion that they have more gender privilege than transgender people of color, in almost the same way that some white women balk at the notion that they have racial privilege. We don't often have the tools to navigate tough moments like these in ways that don't create more harm and disconnection.

Viviana Rennella shared her frustration about the failure of some organizers of color in the States to fully account for the experiences of immigrants who fled brutal regimes. "The experience of immigrant women, we are having to learn so many things about the insular world of the United States. My experience of living through a military dictatorship and having a father incarcerated and disappeared. I remember being involved with Critical Resistance early on and they were like, 'We're going to do an action and get arrested.' As a couple of us were holding back, a Nicaraguan woman said, 'Can we have a conversation around the fear that we have of police brutality? Where we come from, when you get arrested, you might not come back.' What we lived through, you lose your sense of possibility for the future, you cannot plan, you are living day-to-day because there is no future in the type of chaos that we came from. It's an instability that is not two years of a pandemic or an economic meltdown like we saw in the United States in 2008. It's an instability of two to three generations: constant coups and government overturns and economic meltdowns and dictatorships. Entire families are living day-to-day."

Teresa Younger reminds us that "You don't know my story. You don't know who my friends are, how I grew up, or who my family is. When I talk about family, people assume I'm talking about Black people, but my sister, who is Korean, doesn't identify as Black and my other sister, who is Japanese and Black, doesn't identify as only Black. Not all Black women are having the same experience. My family did not come up from the south, my father was in the military. Going to the south doesn't make me feel any more comfortable than going to North Dakota. We have to recognize the multiplicities and dynamics of who is at the table."

I relate to Teresa on this point. My racially ambiguous appearance has always sparked questions and assumptions. Growing up in Seattle, I would get "Where are you from?" from white people, and "What are you mixed with?" from Black people. When I worked in the Bay Area as a union organizer, I told one of my shop stewards from Mexico City that my family was from Sri Lanka (pronounced *shree-lanka*), and misunderstanding me, she exclaimed with joy, "Chilanga!" (pronounced *chee-langa*), slang for someone from Mexico City. I've been mistaken for everything from Latina to Hawaiian to Native American to Black. From the time I understood what race I was at nine years old, I have always been honest about my identity—even when it meant being teased and bullied for being different.

I once had a Black woman in movement spend years trashing me to anyone who would listen. She accused me of taking opportunities from Black women. After a speech I gave to a large crowd that was shared widely on social media, she called me on the phone: "You ride so hard for Black women, and a lot of people think you are Black, but every time you take the stage, that is a spot you are taking away from a Black woman." I was confused. In the speech I had named Black women as the vanguard of social change in this country, but I had opened it by telling the audience that I was of Sri Lankan and white descent. People have mistaken me as a Black woman before, but I have never passed for a race that I wasn't or failed to correct anyone who voiced an incorrect assumption. I have never taken an opportunity meant for someone of another race. We are all shaped by the environments we are raised in. Because the main people of color I grew up around were Black people, and because of the outsize role that Black people have had in my life as friends, mentors, family members, and close movement comrades, I have often felt more at home in the Black community than in any other, despite not being a member of it. When you are a Brown girl who is abandoned by the Brown family that had been your entire world into the wilderness of a majority-white city, and the only people who offer you shelter from racism are Black people, that shapes you.

She knew the painful story of my childhood but didn't care because it didn't fit into the neat and tidy boxes that were her limited understanding of how people experience race in America. Most people, especially those who knew me well, dismissed her attacks on me. But a few others treated me with suspicion. Later, I learned that there were several other women leaders she had viciously bullied, all of them non-Black WOC with racially ambiguous appearances. Bigotry comes in all colors.

One of the ways we bridge our differences is to listen with humility and empathy to one another's stories. As I say even to my dearest Black women friends and family members, "As much as I love you, I will never fully know what it was like for you to grow up in America as a Black girl. And, as much as you love me, you will never fully know what it was like for me to grow up in America as a Brown girl in the wilderness. But what we can always do is fully listen to each other's stories, with empathy and open hearts, and the desire to understand each other more over time."

In 2017, I gave a speech to open a major funder briefing that Groundswell was hosting in New York. It marked the public launch of our 501(c)(4) (a type of nonprofit organization that allows some partisan electoral activities), Groundswell Action Fund, whose one-million-dollar annual budget was, at the time, the largest fund centering WOC-led electoral work. Depending on how you looked at it, this was cause to either rejoice or be deeply depressed. It was a million dollars against the backdrop of a multibillion-dollar landscape of "progressive" electoral giving, which spoke to the near-complete shutout that WOC electoral organizations had experienced from electoral donors. It was also the first time that a small set of white male funders with major clout had ever come to one of our events. And it wasn't as if they just happened to show up to an event focused on WOC. Some of them had entire power maps dedicated to them on my office wall that I had used to run organizing strategies that would get them to show up to the meeting. I generally found that if three to four other people who they respected called them about the event, they would RSVP. With some, I had made as many as fifteen calls to finally get to the people who would move them.

At the top of the meeting, I welcomed everyone. Out of more than one hundred attendees, there were six men in the room—four cis electoral donors, and two trans men (a donor and an organizer), whose work was not mainly electoral. I opened the meeting by announcing the launch of our 501(c)(4), pointing out the groundbreaking nature of launching a WOC fund in such a male-dominated electoral arena. And then, inspired to underscore my point, I prepared to thank each of the four electoral guys for coming. Instead, I said, vaguely, "I want to thank our brothers in attendance," and then proceeded to name-check the four electoral donors but not the two trans men. I was oblivious as to what I had done.

After the meeting, one of the trans men confronted me about my erasure of trans men in the space. I was mortified and apologized profusely. I then reached out to the other trans man to make amends with him as well. He told me that my comment had upset him so much that he couldn't follow anything for the first half of the meeting. I apologized again. Graciously, he said that he was sure I had no doubt endured more as a woman of color, and he forgave me. I was humbled. I felt awful for days, embarrassed and ashamed that my actions had hurt people I cared about. I understood that what I had done was not just about hurt feelings but was part of a culture that allowed transphobia in our society, assaulting people's dignity and costing them jobs, housing, and sometimes their lives. I dedicated myself to studying more about trans justice and inclusion, and I vowed never to make the same mistake.

Then, a year later, I did it again. This time, on the last day of a four-day strategic planning gathering, I was facilitating a meeting of Groundswell Action Fund board members about board recruitment. We were all exhausted, but we had a good list of potential board members up on the flip chart, all of them cis and trans women. Then one of my cis women board members posed a question. "Would we ever consider having men on the board?" The group contemplated it for a moment and there was a short discussion about the pros and cons of doing so. A month later, I was approached by one of my board members, a white trans man, who said it had taken him some time to be ready to talk to me about what had happened at the board meeting. I looked at him blankly. I didn't know what he was talking about. He reminded me of the conversation. Then he shared how painful it had been to watch a room full of cis WOC—some of whom had been on the board with him for years—not remember that we already had a man on the board: him. I apologized profusely and after a moment of wanting to melt into the floorboards, I faced the fact that I'd need to up my learning and work on trans inclusion even more.

The truth is, in the United States, we are all swimming in oppressive waters. We all have limits to our awareness. We are going to mess up. When it happens, all we can do is pick ourselves up, take accountability, make amends, and work harder to ensure it doesn't happen again. After the second episode, I renewed my study of trans justice and made a commitment to focus on trans inclusion.

Pressure Cooker Moments

A few years before I left my role as executive director, my organization had an in-person retreat at a beautiful and serene place. The grounds were filled with majestic trees, quiet meadows, scenic hiking trails, and lovely gardens. The country air was fresh and sweet and I could feel my whole body exhaling away from the hubbub of the city. We had closed our physical office and gone virtual two years earlier, and much had happened since then. The organization had quickly grown from a staff of three to fifteen people, most of whom were meeting one another for the first time at this retreat. The most senior program director and I had infants or toddlers at home and were logging long hours, managing a major uptick in travel on little sleep. I'd had my back surgery and was continuing to crisscross the country, standing up during flights, meetings, and speaking gigs.

Anticipating standard organizational growing pains, I had set us on a yearlong process with an external organizational development firm to assess our needs and provide recommendations for smart growth. We were six months into that process when the staff retreat rolled around. The OD consultants joined us for the retreat and presented a PowerPoint of their findings and recommendations. One of their recommendations was that we hire a deputy director who could be more internally focused on infrastructure and culture as I and many others in leadership were being increasingly pulled to represent the organization externally. Excitement rippled through the room about this and their other recommendations. A woman of color staffer raised her hand and asked if the organization would be implementing this recommendation. The presenter turned to a finance staffer, who also happened to be one of only two white people on the entire staff, and said, "That may be a question for you, since you know what is possible in the budget." The finance staffer responded in a flat and matter-of-fact tone, "No, there is no money budgeted for this position currently."

Unfazed, I took it as a fact delivered in the tone that many in accounting tend to communicate about dollars and cents. But I could immediately see the race dynamics ripple through the room of staff who ranked lower than this person in the organizational hierarchy. WOC were dreaming about what they wanted, and a white woman had authoritatively told them that they couldn't have it. "Let's not worry about the budget for now," I said, intervening. "This is our time to just dream together. Let's allow ourselves to play and vision about what we want to do, and then we'll look at the money and figure out a way to make it happen later." The room settled a bit. Then the same woman of color staffer piped up again: "Thank you for saying that, V," she said, adding that she didn't appreciate the white staffer's comment, which she described as "an ouch." Another woman of color, who was forever ready to stir the pot of any conflict, backed her up: "I find it challenging, at a woman of color–led organization, to have a white woman dealing with the money." Our white colleague sat silently. I could see from the expression on her face that this comment stung.

Then, something unsettling dawned on me. I recalled a not-so-distant supervisorial conversation with this white colleague during which I had delivered strong feedback about their failing to tell me and other leaders when we were going over budget—a mistake that had resulted in a budget deficit that I was currently trying to fundraise us out of. She had shared with me her reticence to tell people of color no for fear of being seen as "the mean white lady." I told her that if she was going to support a woman of color–led organization, she needed to get over her white fragility and do her job so that I and the department heads could make informed decisions and keep our budget in the black. She accepted the feedback and agreed to improve. Here she was, doing exactly what I had asked her to do, and the thing she most feared would happen was happening. As more people raised their hands and piled on, I felt like I had set her up.

A tense atmosphere filled the room once more. I didn't want to publicly share a performance issue. However, I also wanted to normalize and create space for finance staff to communicate budget limits. Gingerly, I said, "I appreciate the comments. It's important for us to grapple with these things. And I want to say that as a woman of color organizational leader, I feel supported when finance staff tell me clearly what is and is not in the budget. That is their job, and we need them to do that so that we can stay in budget and so that WOC managing budgets in this organization can make informed decisions." *There,* I thought, exhaling. *We should be good now.* Suddenly, the WOC who had named her "ouch" burst into tears, apparently feeling reprimanded by me. *What is happening?* I thought. I immediately tried to clarify that there was nothing wrong with what she shared and that my comment was intended as a clarification, not a reprimand. But the room was spiraling. We took a break. Confused, I turned to my leadership team and the OD consultants and asked, "Did I do something wrong?" The OD consultant said, "Not technically, but the optics are that you stepped in to protect the white woman." Oh, I could see that. When we resumed the meeting, we shared more about the context of the situation. It turned out the staffer who cried had recently left a job where she felt oppressed by white women superiors. And with the finance staffer's permission, I shared the backstory about the budget deficit and that I consider it supportive when our finance staff tell us what is within and outside of the budget. Things then settled down a bit, but I learned to be more careful. I also learned to pay closer attention to hiring people who were not so fragile that the typical dynamics of multiracial spaces would send them spiraling into a fit of tears or a rage in which they announce that a colleague shouldn't be in their position because of their race.

A year later, three WOC staff members complained to me about white staff members making what they described as "cringy" remarks about race. The gist was "They mean well, but it's grating to be around—can you talk to them about stopping this behavior?" I had noticed comments like this in my one-on-one interactions with these team members but had either addressed them in the moment or ignored them and kept moving to get the work done. My place in the organizational hierarchy meant I wasn't threatened by these people in the slightest. From my perspective, they worked for me, not the other way around, and the other people they were accountable to were a board of directors that was predominately WOC. None of the staff who complained to me suggested disciplinary action, and when I suggested the idea of sending these colleagues to racial justice trainings, they agreed that was a good idea. I mandated this for the white staffers, who were more than willing to comply.

When I checked back with the staff of color, they said things were better. *Great!* I thought. *Problem solved.* Much later, when we finally hired a deputy director, more serious complaints came to my attention. I realized that there was more under the surface that staff had held back from sharing with me. I should have asked more questions and taken additional steps to reassure staff that they could safely tell me the full story about what they were experiencing. By the time the full story had surfaced, some preventable damage had been done.

I upped my work to address microaggressions from white colleagues. Growing up a mixed-race child in white liberal communities, I had become desensitized to some types of microaggressions as a form of survival. They were simply too prolific, and the people committing them were too resistant to feedback. If I had poured all my energy into challenging everyone who behaved in this way, I would never have accomplished what I set out to do. When I became an organizational leader, I had to resensitize myself to see and respond to subtle forms of racism that white staff dished out to me and other staff of color so that I could put a stop to it.

It's past time we stopped whitewashing our differences within social justice organizations. It's time we devote time to learning our respective histories and speak openly and clearly about how our racial, sexual, ethnic, and class differences lead to tension as often as they lead to understanding and commonality. We reject being seen as a monolith by white people, but it's time that we also resist seeing one another through stereotypes and with mistrust. Working in a space with a united organizational mission rooted in social justice also means working on our interracial and interethnic relationships. We all need to better support one another across our different histories and lived experiences.

As Ash-Lee Woodard Henderson put it, "Let difference not be a bad thing. If it harms people—in the true definition of harm, not in the liberal-ass application that's happening a lot—then let's struggle. Otherwise, how are we going to build a multiracial democracy if we can't practice multi-ideology, multi-sector, multinational movement-building relationships? Difference is okay, it's a strong point in building healthy democracies."

Today, tribalism and division are the primary tools being used by those driving societies toward authoritarianism and fascism. The muscles of our minds and spirits must grow stronger to reach for one another, to empathize with our respective experiences, and to discover how to be whole.

PART FOUR

Superpower #2
Boldness

For decades, WOC have been an antidote to the affliction of timidity that has overtaken many progressives in this country. We have often led the way in moving beyond incremental improvements, demanding change that is truly needed for our communities. Wrote Akaya Windwood in her book, *Leading with Joy: Practices for Uncertain Times,* "Lately I've been experimenting with centering my time and attention on the world that so many of us are working hard to create. I imagine it tirelessly. It has become almost a prayer. Imagining is not mere whistling in the dark—it is a potent act of transformation and world building. It is the process by which we locate our North Stars and find our way to liberation." To be bold is to walk in our power. To do this, we must overcome the deep discomfort many WOC have about wielding it, trained by a society that has wanted to hold us down, putting obstacles in our way.

Linda Sarsour

Being bold requires holding a clear note that might not resonate with those around us. Brooklyn-bred Palestinian

American Linda Sarsour is one such leader. Author, organizer, mother, and founder of the grassroots Muslim organization MPower Change, Linda is one of the most electrifying speakers I have ever heard. Whether she is a thousand feet away on a main stage or across the table from me sharing a meal, her presence is a master class that could be titled Don't Ever Apologize for Your Power. In the fifteen years I've known her, as the driver of countless campaigns, as one of the four leaders of the Women's March, and as a devoted mother, she has been undeterred. Undeterred through death threats and doxing, vicious online attacks, and having to walk ten feet in front of her children in public lest they are harmed in a strike aimed at her.

As we walked together through a crush of people in Seattle's bustling Pike Place Market, weaving our way between the booths selling fresh flowers and wild feather hats and the famous fish stand where they throw whole salmon to entertain the crowd, she told me in a calm and steady voice, with an unmistakable Brooklyn accent, "Allah already knows how I will die. I release that, and focus on what I am here to do." A few hours later, sitting in a hard wooden pew in a Seattle church, I watched her speak to a packed audience to thunderous applause. Her words cut through fear like a sword. I consider myself a fairly bold truth teller, but sitting in that church I became aware of some unhelpful timidity like a rope that had been slowly tightening around my chest for months. Her words sliced clean through the air and I felt that rope fall away. I left a bit freer than I had arrived. *That,* I thought, *is the power of a good organizer. They remind you to release the fear that never belonged to you, so you can claim the strength and clarity that does.*

Linda fights with equal fervor for the human rights of her people in Palestine as she does for the lives and freedom of Black people, Jewish people, and immigrants here in the United States, and she does it, as she put it, by "going outside." Of all her profound and quotable phrases, this simple one is by far my favorite. By "going outside," Linda means going to the people—in the neighborhoods, in the streets, in the community centers, which is where she spends most of her time—instead of staying stuck onstage or on the internet.

She recalled that in Brooklyn after 9/11, "even Republican and white women at the local community board were like, 'I know what is happening to the Muslims is not fair.'" But when Sarsour began to speak out about the police profiling Muslims, "all of a sudden white people said they would not align, and because of that, other people of color in my community would pause, thinking, *If the white folks aren't with it I got to think about whether we should be with it.* People calculate whether to align with another oppressed group or a power structure that they think might protect them." To be bold and effective as a woman of color movement leader is to stand in the dissonance and hold your note anyway.

14

Staying
On-Key

One evening, early in my career, I found myself alone in a hotel room, upset. Earlier that day, nine other people and I were in a sterile boardroom. I was one of two people of color there—the other person was new to the group. I had served on the leadership board of this nonprofit organization and supported its efforts to achieve racial and gender equity for more than two years. The board had recently voted to approve a new strategic plan filled with bold values on both fronts. Today, our task was to elect new board members. Looking around the table, I waited for one of the white board members to point out what seemed to be an obvious problem: that all the candidates on the slate before us were white. But no one spoke up. So, as we moved toward the vote, I decided to say something. I chose my words carefully. I began by thanking the (all-white) subcommittee for their work on recruitment, acknowledging that it can be difficult to generate interest to serve from among the larger membership. I then raised the concern about an all-white slate not aligning with the values in our newly minted strategic plan. I reiterated that I wasn't blaming anyone, that I had experienced the challenges of board recruitment myself, and offered to roll up my sleeves at the upcoming general membership meeting, working alongside the subcommittee to take another run at recruiting a more diverse slate from the members of color who had not yet been asked and who would be there. The chair, a white man, said sharply, "Vanessa, what I'm hearing from the committee is that they tried very hard. I think we should respect their work." People looked down, some shuffling their papers. No one challenged him, but they did agree to my request to postpone the vote.

After the meeting, I confronted the chair in the lobby. He called me abrasive. I said, "Let me ask you something and I want you to answer me honestly. Is there any way that I could have raised concerns about electing an all-white slate that would not have felt abrasive to you? Or is the only option to not have raised it at all?" He said nothing. I felt sick to my stomach. I went back to my room knowing in my gut that I was in the right, that I had not been unkind or unfair to my colleagues.

In my hotel room, I collected myself and called two people, a co-worker and Connie Cagampang Heller, a board member from my home organization, where I was executive director. Both are WOC, and I knew they cared about me and would tell me the truth. They listened carefully as I went over what was said, blow by blow. They offered insights, along with words of comfort. They helped me regain my equilibrium. Thanks to their support, I could trust that I held the right note, keeping this group in alignment with its new strategic plan and its accountability to communities of color that sorely needed funding. It was the rest of the room that was off-key.

I love to sing. I have since I was a little girl. To this day, one of my favorite places is in the middle of a choir, surrounded by other voices. Being a woman of color leader in movement often feels like striving to hold a clear-bell note amid other people's discordant misperceptions of me. I often think of the phenomenal congresswoman Barbara Lee, who was the only member of Congress to vote against authorization of military force against Iraq after September 11. Ultimately, we would learn that Iraq had no weapons of mass destruction and had nothing to do with the attacks on the World Trade Center, but in that moment, she had to stand absolutely alone, holding her clear note amid so many who were way off-key.

A woman of color in leadership must be able to discern when we are on-key, even when others are telling us we are not. We make a perfectly reasonable comment in a meeting only to have it be read as aggressive. We set a healthy and reasonable boundary with workload or with repeated poor performance from someone we are supervising and are regarded as "uppity" or "mean." We exercise a normal level of assertiveness and clarity and are seen as domineering. We are friendly with colleagues at work but are regarded as cold and unapproachable for not cultivating friendships with them outside the workplace. We do any number of ordinary things and are viewed as out of line. Yet if a white person or a male person of color had done the same, their actions would be seen as acceptable, even admirable. In so many ways, we are told to know our place and get back in it.

Gloria Walton recalled an instance where this dynamic occurred during a phone call. "Stop attacking me!" a white colleague told her. "Shortly after, they expressed a profuse apology to me verbally and then later sent an email," Gloria said. "They admitted my voice wasn't elevated, that I was actually calm, and they didn't know what they were responding to. It made me remember in a visceral way: This is what institutional racism and bias is. You can't even see or hear me for your bias that has you blinded and projecting. You are that indoctrinated in racism. It's unacceptable, but it happens all the time."

"My partner is male and he ran a nonprofit at the same time that I was running a nonprofit," said Enei Begaye, executive director of Native Movement, based in Alaska. "I have seen how male EDs articulate clear and concise feedback, and people move on and do what's needed to be done. Me giving clear and concise feedback gets interpreted differently. I've checked with my partner, asking him, 'Before I send this email, how does this sound?' He says, 'It's fine, that's exactly how I would say it.' And then when I send it, the response is defensiveness. 'Why are you talking to me in this way?' People aren't used to women talking in a clear and decisive way."

Enei also said she noted the difference when making her case to funders. "Men, their word is just taken, and the doors open for them. Whereas I would say the same thing and have to bring more evidence."

Oakland city councilmember Nikki Fortunato Bas told this story. "Ten days after shelter in place was declared, we worked to pass California's strongest Covid eviction moratorium that [ran] through July of 2023. At a recent city council meeting the landlords went crazy. It was pandemonium. I had to shout to be heard. During the public comment, they were yelling and calling me 'liar' and all sorts of names. They didn't address my male colleagues that way." She also noted that when she was elected president of the city council, she was treated differently than prior male chairs by the mayor, a white woman named Libby Schaff, who refused to address her by her title for months after her election.

There is also the isolation factor of trying to stay on-key amid the dissonance. "It's fucking lonely," said Kim Jackson, a state senator from Georgia. "There are not a lot of us. It's not that I can't find kinship with people who don't look like me, but there are certain conversations that you want to ask another woman of color, 'Did this happen to me because I'm me?' I was in a committee on HHS where they were discussing whether they would let trans children have access to medication, and the bill they brought forward was trash. The statement laying out why the bill is necessary was all fake news. The one thing I can do on a committee as a Dem is ask questions of the presenters and the author. That has been my role, to ask really good, pointed, thoughtful questions, and I was asking 'Help me understand the difference between letting an adolescent receive medication for diabetes and gender dysphoria'—which is the language in the bill. The chairman cut me off and said, 'We all know that diabetes is different and you can't choose that,' and didn't let me ask another question. I'd never been cut off before. I'd never been treated that way. It was so disrespectful. I leaned over to a white woman and asked, 'Is this normal?' and she said no."

Many women shared stories of being told that others found them intimidating or unapproachable. I could relate. This happened to me time and time again, even though I did my utmost to be friendly to those around me. At some point, I realized that some people will always view confident WOC as intimidating and unapproachable—and that the only way to put those people at ease is to appear overly humble and apologetic. And that, of course, doesn't serve anyone.

Ashindi Maxton, co-founder of Donors of Color Network, shared a series of examples that epitomize the micro- and macro aggressions that Black women leaders are often subjected to when they express their power in perfectly normal ways. "When I'd say 'I have fifteen years of experience,' staff would say I was lording it over them. If I expressed disagreement, I was told I was 'having tantrums.' When I asked, 'What does that look like?' they said, 'It's not what you say, it's your body language. You cross your arms.' Once, when I made a mistake, a colleague told me, 'If I would have made a mistake like that, you would have reamed me out.' I said, 'When has that ever happened?' She couldn't give me one example. When a conference director kept bringing me these rainbow-colored programs—not an LGBTQ statement, just rainbows—after I had repeatedly asked her to change the design, I finally said: 'If I've said I want to change something, I don't want to keep seeing it the same way.' A colleague told me [in response], 'You're so abrupt. You make people cry.' I said, 'I shouldn't have to say it four times.' Her response: 'Maybe she [the designer] didn't understand you.' Then she trotted that story out over and over of how I overstepped in using my authority."

Being underestimated is another part of the dissonance. "I spent so many of my younger years feeling I didn't have anything of value to contribute," said Purvi Shah, founder of Movement Law Lab. "I was undefeated as a lawyer largely because I was underestimated by everyone. I would go to the court and people would say, 'You are the intern.' Or I would go to the attorney line and they would say, 'Ma'am, you can't be in this line,' assuming I was not a lawyer."

Andrea Mercado, ED of Florida Rising, one of the premier electoral organizations in the country, shared her experience of being underestimated. "I've had to do a lot of work to get through not feeling smart enough, good enough, even as a woman who got a scholarship to an excellent university and has twenty years of organizing experience under my belt."

The forces that encourage us to doubt ourselves are not coming from just white or male spaces; they are also coming from other people of color, including WOC, who are exerting their own internalized racism, sexism, and transphobia. This often hurts the most because these are often the folks we count on to have our backs. But the truth is, all kinds of people treat WOC leaders in ways that they would never dare to treat white or male leaders.

What happens to us when people see us in a warped way and reflect that false picture back to us over and over again? How does this affect our perception of ourselves and our ability to hold a clear note? If not counteracted, stereotypes can give their subjects a kind of self-perception dysmorphia. If we don't know how to protect ourselves, we will forget who we are. We will doubt ourselves, quiet our voices, and step back from leadership—which is exactly what many people want.

Just as advertising encourages women to be insecure about their physical appearance so that we will spend millions of dollars on products and procedures to "fix" ourselves, workplaces push women to doubt themselves so they are easier to underpay, overwork, and generally treat in a more extractive manner than their male counterparts.

What can we do about it? We can break the silence and name this dissonance in all of its dimensions, calling on people in movement to notice and disrupt it. A prime example of this is when women in the Obama administration made a pact that if a man reiterated the same idea a woman had raised, other women would not stand idly by. Instead they would speak up to give the woman credit.

We can have people to call on who are our tuning forks in disorienting moments. We don't want to be so egotistical that we can't take in critical feedback and adjust when we may in fact be off-key. But neither do we want to be so ungrounded that we take off-base feedback to heart, allowing it to block our brilliance from contributing to movements. "When you are leading an organization, it is hard to get a sense of how you are faring," said Fatima Goss Graves, president and CEO of the National Women's Law Center. "I tend to be hypercritical of myself, and the outside world is too. You're never actually as good as your best headline, but you are never as bad as your harshest critique. I think about that a lot when I encounter flowers and really harmful criticism, and the better thing is to be clear about what I am doing and why."

We can also listen to the tuning fork within. "There's always been this intuitive voice, my highest self, my soul, or goddess," playwright Sarah Jones explained. "This society can really prevent me from listening and cultivating a relationship with that inner knowing. Leaders cultivate this despite that constant drumbeat of 'who do you think you are?' When we are really attuned to that inner knowing it is such a healing balm. When I am in that part of myself, there are profound collective miracles available."

Many leaders talked about devoting time to the things that allow them to hear this inner voice with clarity: meditation, gardening, swimming, listening to music, going to the ocean. They talked about the small ways they have found to attune to it even when they are in public, perhaps by bringing their attention to their breath, putting a hand on their heart, placing two palms on their knees, rocking slightly in their chair, or humming softly. Attuning to this voice is one of the most profound and important ways that we have our own back.

Surina Khan, former CEO of the Women's Foundation California, uses this strategy. "I believe in visualizing what we want. We had a retreat that we self-facilitated. I brought them to our home, we hung out, cooked together, and got to know each other better and we had a conversation about the culture that we want to co-create. We visualized it in detail. We wanted people to be kind, to help each other, to recognize that one person's success is all our success, to greet each other when we arrived at the office. We reported back to the team our vision and invited them to add to it. Slowly you filter out people who are not part of that vision. You can begin to see the red flags in some people that they won't fulfill that vision." When Surina knew in her gut that she needed to restructure the organization for it to thrive, her clarity of vision, now shared by the rest of the leadership team, allowed her to do this. "We shrunk but my theory was it was like pruning a flower bed." Her theory was right; after years at an annual budget of $1 million or less, the organization grew to $8 million.

We can square off and directly challenge mistreatment. We can keep driving forward and win. Boldness is, for many, about the entire arc of leadership, from the courage to step into a key position to what we do with that position once we get there. Kim Jackson, the first out LGBTQ state senator in the state of Georgia, recalled wanting to run for elected office since she was thirteen years old but having to find the boldness to overcome her fear. From a rural part of the state, Kim recalled when "my hometown had just elected their first Black mayor, so there was someone who looked like me sitting on the dais making important decisions for my town. I left that meeting knowing I wanted to be in elected office. Then I came out as queer, became a minister, all of these things made running for office seem much more complicated and harder to do, but I still felt this draw to policy as a means to social change." At the time Kim ran her race, there were two out Black lesbians in the state legislature but none in the senate. What helped her persevere were "conversations with multiple people, validators from different parts of my community, who said, 'Kim, we think you're ready.' Simone Bell was the first Black queer woman elected to a general assembly in the entire country and it meant the world for her to say, 'Kim, you can do this. It will be hard. You will be the only one in the senate. But you can do it.'" In 2020, Kim won her race.

MINI MASTER CLASS

MINI MASTER CLASS
Pramila Jayapal

Congresswoman Pramila Jayapal hasn't changed since taking office. I first met her a decade ago, when she was leading the immigrant rights organization OneAmerica and answered my request to come speak about voter engagement to a group of grassroots women of color leaders. An immigrant herself, and a longtime leader in the grassroots immigrant rights movement, Pramila was seen as one of us—generous, heartfelt, and a tenacious fighter for our communities.

When we sat down more recently to talk about this book, she shared, "It takes all this time to build respect where a white man or a white woman will walk into a room and be accorded a level of respect from the beginning. In my first term in Congress, I was speaking on the floor about an amendment around the predatory hunting of wolves, and I had written the speech and had an amendment to prevent that, and Don Young, who is no longer with us, was leading the discussion on the Republican side and said, 'Well, young lady, you don't know what the hell you are talking about.' This is on the floor of the House! I challenged him. I had no idea what I was doing, but someone during our orientation had said if someone insults you on the floor of the House that you can challenge them by telling them to take down their words. I said, 'I demand that the gentleman take down his words.' It was the only instance in which Don Young offered a public apology, and it was because I demanded it on the floor. The parliamentarian the next day said, 'I've never seen that happen.' There are these remarkable things that happen, even in Congress when you are elected by 150,000 people, you still face these things."

Once in her position, Kim helped pass a bill that enables people who are victims of stalking to move without paying penalties for breaking a lease. "The phone calls I received after it was law were women saying, 'This bill saved my life. I had kids and would not have been able to afford to break my lease. This bill enabled me to get to safety.'"

WOC leaders must begin to feel entitled to a world in which we are not the only ones holding the clear note but where there are other on-key people flanking us. I envision a future in which I no longer have to be the one at a board meeting to raise the issue of racial equity because enough white people have done their work to raise it themselves. And if I did raise it, others would immediately correct toxic attempts to cast me as incompetent, angry, abrasive, or not a "team player" for doing so.

Balancing Top-Down Decision-Making with Collaboration

It's one thing to be on-key and courageously push ahead even when those around you are off-key. It's another thing to be off-key and ignore the wise voices of reason around you. As a leader, how do you know the difference? How do you know when top-down or collaborative decision-making is best?

All the WOC leaders I interviewed for this book said they strive for a collaborative leadership style. They believe that a collaborative approach on everything from crafting strategy to setting org policy is important on two counts: First, it's a way to tap the brilliance of a broader set of people in the process of generating good ideas, shaping them into a plan, then testing them out. Second, unilateral decision-making is risky for leaders who are equally likely to receive all the glory if their decisions pan out, or all the blame if they don't—a liability for any leader, but especially for WOC who are allowed little margin of error.

This embrace of collaboration is reflected in many studies of women (of all races) in leadership and management positions at nonprofits and in corporate America. Collaborative leadership is consistently named as something that sets women apart from their male counterparts—and as a strength that makes us more effective at building and leading teams. This is a departure that women often make from traditional cis white male top-down models of leadership, where the leader often presumes he has all the answers.

Ai-jen Poo, president of the National Domestic Workers Alliance, the largest membership organization of WOC in the United States, said that WOC "tend to do things in teams and communities, and there is an intelligence to that. A subconscious rejection of the idea of rugged individualism, which is a very gendered concept, and that leadership is this sole journey or role. Partly out of survival, maybe out of insecurity, but also out of intelligence, leadership [for us] is a way more collective endeavor. There are more collaborations, more partnerships, more coordination, seeing an ecosystem, an interdependence kind of approach."

For most of the WOC I interviewed, unilateral decisions were rare but also necessary at key moments. One leader spoke anonymously of the tension over a senior team hire. "My staff rebelled over my hire," she said. "Really angry. They had gotten together and voted that they didn't want her, but not for reasons that made sense. I hired her anyway. They made her life terrible the first six months, so I feel terrible about that. Now she is one of the favored members of the leadership team. Now I constantly get emails—'I don't know if everyone appreciates how amazing this person is.' And I'm like, 'Some of y'all literally took a vote against this excellent woman.' "

Striking the right balance between making unpopular top-down decisions and deferring to the will of the group was one of the things I struggled with most as a leader. I tended to err on the side of capitulating to the group when enough people felt strongly about something. Sometimes it worked out fine—the group helped me notice potential pitfalls or opportunities that I had missed and enabled a sounder decision that I and the collective felt good about. Sometimes staff were hell-bent on making a decision that I was certain would fail. If it wasn't about something especially crucial, it sometimes felt more important to demonstrate trust and support for my staff—and give them the opportunity to experience failure—than to overrule them. Other times, the stakes were higher and yet I overrode everything inside of me that screamed *No! Wrong hire! Wrong strategy!* and capitulated to adamant staffers, only to deeply regret it later. Regret because important work didn't get done and because in hierarchical structures, staff are more than willing to take credit for decisions they make that go well, but quick to let the leader take the fall for ones that don't.

Amisha Patel

"In leading a coalition, it is so easy to have the approach of just trying to listen and facilitate, but sometimes you gotta *go*! Sometimes I'm not doing my job by just facilitating; my job is to stand in my power, be decisive, and move. In other moments, we need a more collaborative approach to ensure grassroots leaders are at the center of decision-making. It can be easy to fall back on a staff-driven response. There aren't shortcuts. It can be easy to skip that, but then the work and what we are building is very thin. We might get a couple of wins, but the roots don't run very deep and it's easy for it to be washed away."

The inconvenient truth is that there is no one-size-fits-all. There are moments when top-down decisions are the right ones and others where collaboration is best. The question for WOC leaders is, how do we get clear on which one is right at any given moment? Especially when our instincts can be thrown off by deep programming around race and gender. And for the people who work with us, how can you help create space for leaders to make both kinds of decisions? The fact is, WOC face a greater expectation that we collaborate and secure the approval of the majority on *all things,* and we are subject to harsher punishment when we make a call without that approval.

In her book *Untamed,* Glennon Doyle recounts entering a room where her teenagers and their friends were watching TV. She asked them who was hungry. Without looking up from what they were watching, the boys raised their hands. The girls, on the other hand, looked furtively back and forth at one another. Eventually, one of them answered for the whole group: No, they weren't hungry. When it came to answering a question about how they were individually feeling in their bodies, the boys looked within and the girls looked to one another. As Doyle shows, collaboration isn't always healthy. Sometimes it is less about inclusion and more about how women are conditioned to be "polite" and "nice" and to conform.

I've witnessed the same dynamic in some groups of WOC when a question is posed about strategy or tactics. There are times when, instead of daring to suggest bold and innovative ideas, everyone hesitates, looks at one another, and drives toward agreement, which often means settling for the least original idea. I've seen this type of collaboration create a chilling effect, stifling healthy debate.

Sometimes, fear is at the root of collaboration—fear of the punishment that can come with being perceived as "too much," "too opinionated," "difficult," or "domineering." This can have real and material consequences. As Janet Hubert, the original Aunt Viv on *The Fresh Prince of Bel-Air* told Will Smith when confronting him for bad-mouthing her, "I lost everything. . . . Calling a Black woman difficult in Hollywood is the kiss of death." For WOC, it doesn't take much to be viewed as a threat. In some cases, collaboration in the form of making one's opinions subservient to the will of the collective can be a capitulation to patriarchal norms. It's a deal with the devil to play small in exchange for the sense of safety that comes with being regarded as "nice" and not a threat.

Sometimes collaboration is driven by internalized racism and patriarchy and buying into the mistrust others often direct toward

WOC. This manifests itself as self-doubt and a tendency on the part of many leaders to undervalue their years of experience and expertise and override their gut instincts.

"What does it mean to trust yourself?" asked Cindy Wiesner. "So many of my early years coming up in the movement were riddled with my own self-doubt and not believing that my opinion mattered because it was often undermined or questioned. Later I would come back to my own assessments and my gut and realize, actually, in that scenario, I was right."

"Trust your gut," Enei Begaye said. "You know it. You've lived it! I grew up learning not to trust myself. Always being second-guessed as a Native woman, always that subliminal message that my opinion and thoughts need to be verified, double-checked, said by a man or someone else. We learn not to trust our gut. I've been leading for twenty years! I don't know everything, but I know where to trust my gut in the areas I know."

The expectation that WOC leaders should treat everyone on their teams as if everyone's opinions count equally—irrespective of their skill or experience—is one of the ways that patriarchy shows up. Leaders are effectively told that their decades of experience and track record of success are worth nothing.

Mona Sinha, global executive director of Equality Now, who has led at the highest levels in the corporate, nonprofit, higher education, and philanthropic sectors, said, "A hunch is a powerful tool for leading but often overlooked. I strongly rely on my intuition. It protects you. There is a certain power in knowing that you are your own safety net."

The question to ask is, what is motivating the approach? If it is ego and the focus on self, either the desire to flex to feel larger than others, or the desire to protect a fragile ego by collaborating to please people, then it's the wrong motivation. If the motivation is a sense of service and accountability to ensure the work fully honors and is worthy of the communities we support, then it's the right motivation.

As Gloria Walton put it, "The most important thing is to root in your values so when people don't agree, you are clear on why you felt this was the best thing to do given the context, circumstances, and your position."

Akaya Windwood offered this wisdom: "Don't trust your ego, trust your heart. I've learned to discern. When my ego wakes up it's because some external shiny thing is happening and I feel 'I'm all that.' I say, now that I'm awake, let me filter it through my heart. I've made the mistake of saying 'that sounds shiny and bright and fun,' but my heart isn't feeling it, and it ends up being a mess."

In my own leadership journey, I have made both collaborative and top-down decisions that were wrong calls because they were driven by ego and right calls because they came from deep accountability. There were two top-down calls in particular that I'm proud I made. One, in 2012, was to launch a program to support grantees who wanted to build out their capacity for voter engagement and election turnout. At the time there were no nationwide programs that ran trainings and coaching in this area that were culturally competent around both race and gender and would be well received by our mostly women of color–, queer-, and trans-led grantees. In movement, the further you move toward the structures and funding that enable direct contention for the power to govern 501(c)(3)s with voter engagement capacity, 501(c)(4)s that can engage on candidates, and PACs that can run people for office, the more white, male, and cis it becomes. This is by design. We had been shut out and I wanted to bust open the doors. In a few short years our grantees went from engaging a handful to tens of thousands of voters, winning and implementing exponentially more victories for their communities. Elected officials went from ignoring their calls to calling them to ask them what it would take to get their organization's support. Women of color EDs took the helm at major electoral coalition tables in tough states like Georgia. Some of our grantees saw their staff and members so inspired that they ended up running for and winning elected office. Moving more WOC, queer, and trans people of color toward the power to govern was the right move and an investment that continues to pay off today.

The second came after Donald Trump was elected president in 2016. I knew that the strategy my organization had at the time was insufficient to meet the moment. We were funding only 501(c)(3) organizations, which limited the electoral muscle our grantees could use, and we were exclusively funding in the reproductive justice sector when the strongest grassroots organizing power to protect the communities at the heart of our mission sat with key organizations across a variety of sectors—from climate, economic, and racial justice to immigrant and LGBTQ rights. Maintaining the status quo would have been the equivalent of trying to change the thermostat amid a massive hurricane. We needed to fund the organizations with the power to change the larger weather system.

I knew that to reach the strongest organizations, we would need to bust out of the RJ silo and fund these groups wherever they existed. I also knew we needed to launch a 501(c)(4) that could fund 501(c)(4)s—(c)(4)s can challenge and support specific candidates more directly than 501(c)(3)s, which are required by law to remain nonpartisan. Michelle Tremillo, leader of the Texas Organizing Project, at that point one of the only large-scale (c)(4) nonprofits led by WOC, advised funders that resourcing only (c)(3)s is like asking organizations to fight with one fist. I could see that 501(c)(4)s had more power in the electoral arena, and were the domain of white men. Almost all people of color and WOC-led efforts had been relegated to the (c)(3) lane.

I could see that the visibility we had gained within philanthropy, and the relationships we had built with many women donors who were tired of ceding the political-giving space to their husbands, had put us in a position to recruit (c)(4) dollars that would enable more WOC-led and trans people of color to have a voice in the electoral arena.

I talked with my senior team. Some were enthusiastically supportive. Others expressed concern: Would it mean more work for our team? Did we have the expertise to fund outside of RJ? Would broadening out beyond RJ be mission drift? In turn, I responded to each of the concerns—we would staff up and bring on more expertise to advise grantmaking. But the anxiety persisted, based in a fear of moving from the familiar to the uncomfortable, particularly at a moment of terror about the Trump presidency. I knew I could not cater to this. I went straight to my board, which was made up of some of the boldest and bravest movement leaders of our time. There, I instantly found strong support. In short order we updated the organization's mission statement and established a new (c)(4) and a new (c)(3) fund that would fund the best organizing shops outside of RJ. By year's end, we granted $1 million to the top WOC-led 501(c)(4)s across the United States in time to help them prepare for the critical midterm elections—and, through the Liberation Fund, a similar amount in (c)(3) dollars to the strongest organizing shops. In broadening our approach, we became one of the largest funders in the country of WOC-led and trans people of color–led grassroots organizing, allowing us to be better advocates in more sectors of philanthropy. We positioned ourselves to use our full power and access within philanthropy to unlock resources for grassroots power building. Our work would improve the field, not just in the money we moved, but in the rooms of other funders and donors we would influence to move more resources to WOC-led electoral work in key places like Georgia. Our grants were among the largest received by several 501(c)(4) organizations whose phenomenal voter engagement and turnout in states like Georgia and Arizona was critical to advancing the promise of democracy in 2020.

Had I capitulated to a more collaborative process with staff by creating a process for them to amplify their concerns, none of this would have been possible. I had to stay focused on what our communities needed, and I had to move forward with those who were ready, at the pace that the moment required.

Many top-down calls that I deeply regretted were in hiring. I hired people I had worked with successfully for years in other capacities without a rigorous interview process. The result was insufficient vetting to ensure a good fit and a less-than-welcoming environment since staff viewed them with trepidation. Other times I had a bad feeling about a candidate, but every staff person on the hiring committee was enthusiastic, and so I relented. I overruled what I believed to be the best and most accountable action for the communities we served, and instead acted out of ego, a desire to stay in the good graces of staff and not be perceived as domineering. In the end, the people we hired underperformed and, in the worst cases, tried to tank the organization.

Sometimes, I leaned into collaboration, and the result was positive. The development of two five-year organizational blueprints involved a yearlong strategic planning process that engaged the board, staff, and key stakeholders. The resulting plan was stronger because of the diversity of expertise and perspectives that shaped it, including those of the board members who voted to approve it.

This is the wisdom I took from the leaders I spoke with: Believe in your core values, stay accountable to the grassroots communities you serve, strive for a transparent process that welcomes collaborative input wherever possible, trust your gut, and use the people whose wisdom and clarity you trust as a sounding board— then make your best decision. If that decision fails, it will be a lot easier to live with the failure, knowing you had a thorough process, than if your process was simply to go with your first gut instinct, or to acquiesce to the majority opinion.

Building Your Squad

I have yet to meet an effective woman of color movement leader who didn't experience someone trying to take her out. As I've shared, my friend LaTosha Brown's reminder sticks with me: You can tell the real leaders by the arrows in their back. Every woman of color leader is wise to say to herself "I have a right and responsibility to protect myself," and to regularly ask, "Who is protecting *me*?"

Your squad is a small group of people you can trust without question. First and foremost, they must be people who fundamentally wish you well and want you to succeed, not just in work, but in life. They must be able to celebrate and be genuinely happy for your success, without jealousy or envy. They should not be "yes" people who offer you empty praise no matter what you are doing, but rather those who are willing to be honest with you, even if that means challenging you.

My squad includes my co-parent and best friend, Tricia. We are each other's cheerleaders in life and are just as elated when the other has a win as when we have one ourselves. When I think of Tricia, I think of Oprah's story of buying her first nice car and how Gayle King was even more over the moon about it than she was. That's how we show up for each other. One time when I was struggling to ask others I respected for help, she told me, "V, you are not a burden." It helped me immensely to hear that. My squad also includes my mom. Our worldviews are not always aligned, but we love each other dearly and always want the other to be well and thrive. My elder and mentor, former civil rights activist Adisa Douglas, is also in my squad. My squad includes dear friends and chosen family, too. Connie Cagampang Heller has challenged me more than once when I've fallen into anger and frustration, and she has helped bring out my kinder, better self. Cathy Lerza, another mentor, has never failed to lend an ear and support in hard times. One of my oldest friends from college, Jessica Horn, offers me calm, clear-eyed advice with a global perspective. Longtime movement colleagues Shaw San Liu and Dana Ginn Paredes—who together with their partners and kids have become my chosen family—challenge and help me sharpen my thinking about U.S. movements while wrapping me in love and care, often over delicious meals with plenty of laughter. And Kumi Oya and her husband John Scott, with whom I run or bike most weeks, often conjure the stories and wisdom of civil rights freedom fighters who are now ancestors, reminding me of the concept of Sankofa—to look to the wisdom of the past in order to go forward. My squad includes about ten movement comrades that I have come to know over the years. Each is smart and strategic in distinct ways, operating from love and, most of all, courage. Another person in my squad: Harriet Tubman. My first hero, from the time I wrote my first tiny book report in second grade, she opened my imagination to dedicating one's life to the fight for freedom, and her example of unwavering clarity, courage, and sacrifice has been a North Star.

I didn't always have a great squad. There's a song by musician Jon Batiste called "The Light Shines Brightest in the Dark." I love this as a metaphor for life and movement work. Hard times have clarified who has my back and who will leave me blowing in the wind. When hard times reveal this about people, it's time to move them out of our inner circle.

The insights of other leaders, like Akaya and Vini, have helped me hone what I am looking for in my squad, in terms of people who can hear my unedited thinking, be "in it" with me in the messy part of my processing, and offer warm but unflinching honesty.

Akaya Windwood spoke about the four people she holds close. "I find it's helpful to have a group of women in my corner who will say, 'Girl you need to think again.' Any one of the four of them knows they don't need to ask permission [to tell me that]. They are exquisitely kind and loving and ruthless, and I need that."

Rajasvini Bhansali shared, "I have an amazing coach. An amazing therapist. I have a squad that I rely on. I have friends that I need to call and say the wrong shit to, and be extreme so they say, 'Okay, let's not jump off the ledge.'"

Your squad has wisdom and insight that goes beyond your own, providing fresh perspectives and advice.

Vini continued, "I have surrounded myself increasingly with people with a level of political maturity, not just identity alignment. That is protection for me as a leader but it is also protection for my collective work. I have people around me who I know will disagree with me but will always do it from a place of 'we are in it together.' They are not trying to tear me down, to prove themselves, to steal credit, or those kinds of interpersonal dynamics that break our hearts as leaders."

Minnesota state senator Erin Maye Quade recalled the relief she felt when she finally made the leap from feeling like she had to figure it all out by herself to calling in the help and support she needed. "When I started UnRestrict Minnesota, it was the first time I had led a coalition. It was a new muscle. I was drowning. I stayed in that a little too long before I asked for help. There were other WOC who had experience. I finally got help. I built a new structure. The problem wasn't just mine, it became all of ours. It was a beautiful journey."

Your squad must also be made up of people of courage who will risk protecting you if you are unjustly attacked. And they should be people who move in the world with love, kindness, and integrity. It's no help to be advised or defended by those who lack these traits. Once you have your squad, there is no room you will ever have to enter, no problem you will have to tackle, and no audience you will have to face alone.

"Squad is so important," said Silvia Henriquez. "We need to find our people. There is a group of WOC who I can text. Some are close friends, some are colleagues, people who I came up with in the movement. We have each other's backs."

"There are times when we are in crisis when it is really tough to figure out what support you have," said Purvi Shah. "Not only are the state's crosshairs on you but people within our own movement's crosshairs are on you. The only people who have come to my aid in those moments have been other WOC who have been through an attack. That sense of community is worth everything. Knowing that you can get someone's back and they can have yours, that is invaluable for WOC leaders."

One of the things I learned about building a squad is that it is important to get clear on what you need around you for the path you are walking. We all walk different paths and have different needs. For me, one of the things I need is people who are comfortable with power and success—their own, mine, and others'. This doesn't mean they don't put me in check if I exercise my power in ways that are abrasive or off-key—because my folks surely do, and sometimes I need that! It means that they are not intimidated, threatened, jealous, or scared when others exercise their power to the fullest to make a better world. I also need people who are highly strategic and share my values but have different perspectives on tactics and approaches. Their vantage points bring different knowledge of movement history, a global orientation rather than a U.S. one, experience in other sectors of movement. This helps me kick the tires of my thinking before I act.

Linda Sarsour told me two stories of squad solidarity. "I was in Mexico after the Women's March and the Muslim ban. I had been doxed and was receiving death threats. A friend of mine texted me and said, 'Tamika is outside city hall.' She had organized all these leaders in NYC and held a press conference to say 'Hands off of Linda Sarsour.' She didn't tell people 'I'd like to invite you.' She said, 'I expect you at a press conference at noon outside city hall.' That is the only time in the last twenty years where I've seen an organized response to something that was happening to a woman of color. After that, the Jewish people who came to city hall advocated, and the Jewish community then felt responsible to come out with a letter that spoke against threats to me and my family."

Linda also shows up for her squad. "When Representative Ilhan Omar was under attack—Congressman Zeldin had put forth a resolution that he was going to pass through the House that would condemn her on record—I organized eight hundred progressives across the country to sign a letter to say 'Hands off Ilhan.' We also drafted a resolution to counter Zeldin's resolution. I took a group of people to Nancy Pelosi's office and said, 'Just in case you didn't get my email with all of the signatures on it, here is the printed version. If the Democrats want to win in 2018, these people on this letter are the people who knock on doors when you are trying to run for office, who move immigrant communities, Black communities, young people. If you want to ignore it, that's on you.' They understood the power we were wielding. The House resolution that is now on the record is the one we put together and it affirms a commitment to a country free of Islamophobia, antisemitism, and anti-Black bigotry. Not only did we defend Ilhan but we were also able to produce something to counter the opposition."

It took me years to believe that I deserved to have people around me who loved and respected me, and who had backbone. It took me even longer to have the level of discernment about people's character to not keep trusting people who were untrustworthy. I made mistakes in how I allocated my time, shortchanging my investment in deepening relationships through just connecting and getting to know people rather than through strategizing and accomplishing tasks.

Trust and discernment are essential skills in building your squad. My friend and movement colleague Vini is one of the warmest and least armored people I know and has a strong squad around her. Offering her take on how to mix trust and discernment, she said, "A cultural lesson from growing up in India, Jain, and in a Rajasthani family who are dear to me, is wherever you show up, you belong. The requisite labor to prove that you are part of my world is not part of our ethos. Of course, one has to be discerning and the discernment comes over time for me, with reciprocity, with mutuality, with noticing: Are people just calling me when they need something, or are we connecting from time to time just because we saw something that made us think of the other person? Are we remembering important markers in each other's lives? Being in it for a really long time with people through thick and thin feels important to me. I call on different people for different things. Similarly, different people call on me for different things. I see that as a web of relationships that are truly self-nurturing and that can sustain over time with care but not demanding too much emotional labor."

What I also appreciate about Vini is that she recognizes that her openheartedness comes more easily than it might to others because of life experience: "I want to name my privilege in this. I have been loved more than I have been harmed in my life. If we have been betrayed and harmed more than we have been loved, then that shapes how we look at the world."

Below are the most helpful things people in my squad have said to me over the years, at my absolute lowest moments in leadership. I hope they bring strength and encouragement to those who are experiencing similar challenges.

In the area of self-worth, people told me:

- Your light is yours. It doesn't belong to any organization. You will take it with you wherever you go and create beauty in the world.

- Your being is your real power. It goes beyond race, sexuality, and identity.

- Your immense contributions cannot be erased. They are indelible.

On keeping sight of the big picture, I received this advice:

- Salt in a glass of water tastes terrible. The same amount of salt in a lake is unnoticeable. Widen your perception of this one moment to the lake of your lifetime of experiences and contributions. This will widen your perspective.

- Accept that not everyone will know your heart.

- You can't take what is happening personally. There's a virus going around movement, and almost every organization has caught it.

- Give the mud time to settle so that you can see more clearly the right action to take.

This advice helped me avoid people-pleasing, knee-jerk reactions, and a downward spiral of self-blame and instead slow down, take the blinders off, see the larger terrain, and make more strategic decisions.

On courage I was told:

- Imagine the worst-case scenario and know that you have the strength to survive it. Then you will be free, and people will have no power over you.

- Some of your worries are grounded in fear and your own trauma rather than reality. Don't create a barrier or problem where there is none.

- Get out of the victim space—despite the comfort it may give you.

In one irrational moment, I was convinced that if I failed at a particular leadership challenge in front of me, everything would be ruined, everyone would leave me, and I would be unable to find work. This advice helped me off that cliff, which was just about my childhood trauma of abandonment.

On boundaries:

- Stop trying to please people. Don't appeal to people who are trying to hurt you. You don't need to reward people who have it out for you.

- Don't get between people and the consequences of their actions. They may need to lose a job.

- Don't waste time and energy trying to reason with confused or toxic people. Redirect it toward people who are clear.

Boundaries keep you healthy. They make you efficient. They protect you, those around you who are serious about the work, and the mission of that work.

On solidarity:

- If you are dragged in public for things you didn't do, I will have your back and gather others to have your back in public. We will not leave you alone.

- I've been there. You will get through this. Keep going.

- I see you. I respect you. I know who you are.

I can't overstate how essential it is to hear these things as a leader when you are in the middle of a storm. We all need people who will remind us that we are flanked, seen, and resilient and that we must keep moving forward.

MINI MASTER CLASS
Ai-jen Poo

We must be scrupulous in whom we allow into our inner circle. When I asked Ai-jen Poo what advice she had for her younger self, most of it was about the importance of building your team.

1. Keep your mentors very close.

2. Work with people you trust and who trust you.

3. Look for every chance to lift up other WOC.

4. Trust your big ideas and be as ambitious as you want to be. Never moderate your ambitions because you are afraid of failure or because you're told you're doing too much.

Ai-jen's second piece of advice is incredibly important. Having squad-caliber people both on your board and on your leadership team is a must. If you don't, you may not notice anything amiss when times are good, but in moments of tension or crisis, you will find yourself unprotected.

One of the things I learned the most from my interviews with WOC leaders is that the people who were most successful in steering their organizations through tough waters were the ones who told me some version of the following: "I don't care how technically good somebody is at the position I am hiring for. If they lack the capacity to have empathy for leaders, and the backbone to do the right thing instead of the easy thing, I don't let them anywhere near my leadership team."

The most dangerous kind of people to allow close to you as a leader are those who have excellent technical skills or a magnetic personality but lack courage, maturity, and kindness. These individuals have just enough credibility with those around them to be able to lead people in a damaging direction. They may either undermine you to satisfy their own thirst for power or, when faced with threats, will move from fear and cowardice, not hesitating to throw you and others under the bus.

"It is real, it is not our imaginations," said Andrea Mercado in addressing the plight of WOC leaders. "We are questioned, doubted, left out to dry, attacked. I've seen how WOC are exploited, treated, used, and objectified and sometimes by each other. That is why so many of us feel moved to cultivate radical sisterhood, and for me that has been a real calling."

15

Feminism's Problem with Power

I t was three in the morning, and I was enduring yet another sleepless night. It was the end of 2021, a low point in my leadership journey. I sat in front of my altar in grief. I was part of a generation that had pried open doors that were previously closed to WOC. I had helped pave the way for sisters to assume leadership positions across movement organizations. But now that we were finally seeing the fruit of our labor, I watched as these leaders were being systematically attacked. For more than a year, I witnessed weary leaders join Zoom calls, haggard and often in tears. And the force that was ripping through movement organizations was now hitting my organization. I picked up a pen, in the dark, and wrote this:

• What do you do with a badass sister who is shut out of the room of power?

You clamor for her to get in!

What do you do when she is let into the room but denied a seat at the table?

You demand she have one!

What do you do when she has a seat but is ignored?

You demand that she be heard!

What do you do when her ideas are heard but not acted upon by leadership?

You insist that she be put in leadership!

What do you do when she is put in leadership with no power or resources?

You raise hell until she has both!

What do you do when she is poised to lead with power and resources behind her?

You destroy her.

As bell hooks reminds us, "Sometimes people try to destroy you precisely because they recognize your power—not because they don't see it, but because they see it and they don't want it to exist." Boldness is undercut when we don't deal with this head-on.

The first major turbulence at Groundswell occurred in 2018, when we began to really scale up. I confided in a trusted colleague about my confusion at the destructive behavior I was witnessing from a couple of staff members who were attacking the organization and people in leadership positions and sowing distrust among the team. I was facing an uphill battle in the white world of philanthropy, where I was trying to open hearts and minds and raise money for our communities, and then I would come "home" to my staff—and get kicked in the teeth there too.

WOC with the most decision-making power at Groundswell were increasingly regarded with fear and mistrust, and cast as caricatures of the ruthless bitch. I had been working in movement for twenty years and leading this organization for thirteen. For all that time I had received glowing annual reviews from staff, board, and partners alike. No one had ever described me as being dominating or unkind. Either I had undergone a personality transplant, or the lens through which people were viewing me had shifted. The same was true of other leaders—for years, high marks from staff on annual reviews, but now, mounting complaints.

I was truly puzzled: After a decade of struggling mightily, our organization finally had a large budget, offered pay and benefits that were well above most other organizations in the sector, and we gave program staff a lot of creative control over their areas. In so many ways the organization exemplified a model that many women of color leaders were pushing for, one that consciously departed from conventional top-down models to encourage collaboration, debate, and co-design.

My colleague said in response to my confusion: "Well, you're successful now."

"What do you mean?" I asked, perplexed.

"Think about it," she said. "Did you ever have these problems when you were a small and scrappy organization rubbing two pennies together?"

"No," I admitted.

"Well, there you go. Success scares people. Women of color with power scare people."

In the blueprint of America, WOC were never supposed to have power. When we dare to attain that power, others, even among our own, work to tear us down. The message is clear: Keep your head down and know your place or become a target. It becomes important to stay alert. We must ask ourselves, when is the demand to "check your ego" a helpful reminder, and when is it a basic discomfort with confidence and a message to get back in line? Groundswell pulled out of that tailspin fairly quickly, thanks to quick action by a few of us on the leadership team to clearly and firmly call people in. The choppy waters smoothed out again for a couple of years. Still, it was a lesson for me about the discomfort with power within the left's own ranks.

"I wasn't an ED until Donors of Color," explained Ashindi Maxton, "but I was doing philanthropy for years. I have founded five organizations that move millions of dollars and most of [this work] is not attached to my name. A lot of the work I put in was behind the scenes. Was I behind the scenes because that's where I was most comfortable? Or was it because every time I stood up and anything I built was succeeding, I was shot at?"

"As an organizer I would say yes to anything I thought would help our movement, and I was a workhorse," recalled Elle Moxley. "My persona began to be more popular. I started being called a co-founder of different things. Then there was disdain. I couldn't understand it. All I did was say yes to what y'all asked me to do, and now I'm the bad girl?"

"We organized seven million people across the world," remembered Linda Sarsour. "Every continent had a protest. That hasn't happened in our generation. Women of color bring strategic leadership, but people only want us to have leadership up to a certain level. People set a bar for us and the minute we go a little above the bar, someone is there with a mallet ready to knock us down."

Having worked in predominately male fields, like the labor movement, I was shocked to find that the pressure to conform to behaviors that I considered to be the epitome of patriarchal expectations was often far greater toward leaders in "feminist" spaces where women predominated. (I use "feminist spaces" as a catchall for environments where cis women and gender nonbinary people are in the majority and there is a stated commitment to things like women's rights, reproductive freedom, and gender justice.) Be polite and agreeable, withhold or soften strong opinions, play small—these messages were everywhere. In an ironic twist of "sisters doing it for themselves," we truly didn't need men at all—we policed the hell out of one another! Some of this transcends race. For example, in my observation, white women regularly police one another into gender norms as do women of color. Some of it is highly raced and blends with white fragility to create a particular punitive response from white women toward WOC who assert themselves—for example, the trope of the angry Black or Brown woman. Most of it is rooted in fear.

The Cage

Oppression is a cage. We shout and clamor for freedom. But when the cage door swings open and the power to taste freedom is within our reach, what do we do? Some people seize their chance and fly headlong into their power, embracing freedom and encouraging others to do the same. Others stay in the cage, paralyzed by fear, playing small to avoid being noticed. Still others make an enemy of women who have dared to open the cage door, accusing them of misusing their power simply because they have it. This is because the theater of battle with someone familiar feels safer than fighting the real foes: white supremacy, patriarchy, capitalism. I have seen many WOC who dared use their power to bust open the cage door and fly out be viciously attacked. I have seen WOC stand around silently and watch it happen. I've seen WOC do everything possible to close the cage door, trapping themselves and all their sisters inside.

Many WOC instinctively keep themselves small and away from the cage door to keep from being attacked. I struggled against this instinct mightily during my first ED job, terrified that if I exercised my power people would think that I thought too much of myself.

Gina Clayton-Johnson of Essie Justice Group described "that dynamic, that very specific thing of knowing that I would be more successful in this space if I was just a little less competent, is something that I'm very familiar with as a Black woman and as a woman." She is adamant that "when young Black women come work for me, the first thing I have to work with them on is to say, 'You can leave that—performances of incompetence to make yourself more likable—at the door, because we don't need to do that here.' I have empathy because I did it too! I have been rewarded for presenting as confused and not competent."

In the early part of that first ED job, I spent a full year working with an executive coach who kept telling me to "get in the driver's seat!" and working with me on this, before I finally began to step into my leadership. No sooner had I done so than I began dealing with the crabs-in-a-barrel attitude of competition and jealousy. Several of the leaders I spoke with described this at length.

"Why her, why not me?" said Linda Sarsour, describing this mentality. "A woman of color is making a quarter million a year, and instead of saying, 'That's fair and that's where I want to get to,' another woman of color will say, 'Damn, why is she making that? Why did she get a book deal and not me?' Yes, there are people in the movement who may have sold out or harmed, but a lot of the women I see criticized—nothing that these women have they didn't work their asses off for. There's nothing I didn't sacrifice my family for, my time for, get threatened for—but the movement expects us to prove ourselves in ways they don't expect from anyone else, not even men of color."

Many WOC buy into the scarcity culture. Ai-jen Poo recalled, "When we were coming up twenty years ago, especially in national spaces, you were always the only woman of color in the room, or if there was another you never knew if you'd find solidarity or someone who wanted to be the 'better' woman of color in the room." "As a leader," said New York state assembly member Jessica González-Rojas, "I leaned into abundance and was mindful of lifting our sisters while we climbed. It wasn't always reciprocal."

Georgia state senator Kim Jackson talked about "the notion that you can only have one or two strong Black women in the space, so the feeling among Black women of not wanting me to move up in the caucus or certain opportunities—like they know that only three of us will be invited to the White House. It shows up in petty ways. One of my colleagues got an invitation to the White House and she was in the office [that had previously belonged to] an older woman of color. This older woman said, 'You stole my invitation!' even though it didn't have her name on it." Kim also shared examples of how we can pivot away from this impulse. "This incident called us into a meeting with each other and we made a pledge that if something comes across our desk that is an honor for us that we will tell the other people so we can check inboxes in case anyone missed theirs and to recommend each other for opportunities. We've pooled our money to get staff for incoming women of color elected, paid her caucus dues."

Fear of success is broader than WOC and speaks to a larger Achilles' heel of progressive movements in the United States. It is one of the great ironies of social justice movements that many working within them speak loudly about breaking the chains of oppression, but fundamentally feel safer within a paradigm in which they are marginalized—because it is familiar. Those stuck in this mindset will reject or attack anything that threatens what they know. They will go to great lengths to turn liberatory spaces back into toxic ones, opposing any power that grows large enough to bring about transformative change.

And this, when we don't address it, is why we can't have nice things.

Our discomfort with power shows up in a number of ways. It's there in the fetish for small, scrappy endeavors that have a radical analysis but refuse to amass enough strength to win anything that substantively improves people's lives. It shows up as a penchant for safe, incremental policy goals that are disconnected from a bolder vision of transformative change. It's apparent in the over-focus on railing against the system from the outside instead of wresting the power to govern and using it to the fullest.

There is a lot of movement work that is performative. It's a theater of resistance that doesn't actually seek to transform the status quo. Hammering at the status quo without the force to change it is like pressing our noses to the cage door simply to gain comfort in knowing it is still there.

Authentic movement work, on the other hand, strives to bust open the cage door and destroy the cage once and for all. It's Stacey Abrams responding to the theft of her election by building an organization to protect the voting rights of millions. It's Native organizers like Chrissie Castro, who championed strategies to achieve 100 percent census enumeration in many tribal communities and record turnout among Native voters that created the margin of victory in several key states. The Navajo Nation had voter turnout rates as high as 90 percent in Arizona, New Mexico, and Utah.[1]

It takes strength and courage to fight against oppression. It can take even more to fight for our full freedom and receive our blessings. You can fight against oppression your whole life without ever having to remove your armor. But you can't fight for freedom, you can't fully receive good things, without de-armoring, being vulnerable, and opening your heart—all difficult things for most of us who have survived generational trauma.

Trans WOC risk their lives every day to live in their freedom and full selves. Said Bamby Salcedo, "We are divine people. We are sacred people. We're truthful to ourselves and others and that's one of the reasons the world hates us. Most humans are not able to be truthful to themselves. They navigate the world with masks. When we are fully ourselves as trans people, that is why people hate us and try to kill us. People want to kill our power. Most people are afraid of the light but we are enlightened people."

I often wonder how much potential has gone unrealized for social justice movements because so many within our ranks have developed, as an adaptive skill to generational trauma, a profound inability to welcome opportunity and abundance for fear of losing it. This shows up as fear of failure, fear of being found out as unworthy (impostor syndrome), fear of becoming accustomed to good things and having someone take them away. The impulse to destroy a good thing ourselves, before forces beyond our control can ruin it, is widely prevalent in movement.

For women-led organizations, however, the fear of power is compounded by deeply ingrained social norms that cause people to bristle at a woman who does not know her place. If we are not careful, we will contort ourselves to fit those norms out of an instinct for self-preservation.

Our beloved movement elder Dolores Huerta remembered, "When we started the [United Farm Workers] Union, we were having our first constitutional convention and Cesar was leading the meeting and they were having the nominations for officers. Cesar stepped down from the dais and said, 'You've gotta get someone to nominate you for the vice presidency.' I said, 'Oh, Cesar. I don't have to be an officer; I just want to be supportive and to help.' He said, 'You're crazy. Get someone to nominate you right now.' And so I did. That's an issue we have as women. We've been socialized to support men or other people and never think about supporting ourselves and other women. We don't think that power is something that we need to be able to serve and help others. Women hold back, they feel uncomfortable with power, feel they are overstepping or being too feisty or bold. We need to learn to use our power."

One antidote is to name and describe these norms explicitly—not just when they raise their heads, but in diligent and rigorous political education, so that when they do arise, they are recognizable within an organizational values framework that has clearly disavowed them. Then the boundary setting that needs to happen in each moment cannot be construed as defensive but rather in alignment with existing values that are in place to protect the mission of the organization and the humanity of those working within it.

The Burden of Likability

A certain amount of likability is necessary to lead. The problem is, many of the qualities that are critical to effective leadership—qualities that are valued and respected in cis men—are viewed as unlikable when exhibited by women. Patriarchal gender norms present women with an inverse relationship between positional power and likability. If you dare to be powerful, you are, as Hillary Clinton was called, a "nasty woman." For WOC, who deal with the added layer of the stereotypes around the angry Black or Brown woman, it's even worse. WOC leaders often find themselves walking a tightrope to maintain enough goodwill for their staff team to follow their lead, and enough strong leadership qualities to lead their organizations toward actual impact. One wrong step and you risk being labeled cold, harsh, intimidating, unapproachable, mean, or a bitch, which can become a major barrier to moving work forward. If we're not grounded, proving our "niceness" and our very humanity can become a second job. Instead of asking what more we can do to prove our humanity, WOC leaders need to start asking why we should have to.

When you first face these labels as a leader, most people will wonder, "Am I doing something wrong?" It's advisable to reflect on our actions, and even check in with a member of our squad, to make sure we're not off. Sometimes we will find that we are and course correct. As we become more seasoned, we still do these checks, but are also able to recognize more readily that many labels are other people's projections and stereotypes at work. The more success you have, the more scrutiny you'll receive. Unfortunately, no amount of acrobatics will give these people what they want, which is ultimately for you to step away from the seat of power.

I remember standing on the wooden porch of a rustic retreat center after a hornet's nest of labels were hurled at me by a few staff members who I was meeting in person for the first time and who were crusading in solidarity with a disgruntled staffer. She had been denied a promotion for good reason—an objectively poor job performance—and was exacting her pound of flesh from me. I didn't yet have the skills to cut this off. I felt that if I defended myself against these character attacks, that since I had more positional power, it would read as me coming down on people and only add fodder to their narrative. I had been breaking my back to support the staff team, sacrificing time with my kids to get to know people and support their development, even turning down raises offered me by the board to enable staff to have raises. To be treated like an unfeeling bitch was so hard. By the end of the meeting I was at a breaking point. I waited quietly until everyone except for a couple members of my leadership team and the lead consultant had dispersed, and then I exploded. "That's not who the fuck I am!" To be so unseen is excruciating.

During the twenty-plus years that Chrissie Castro worked as a consultant, she was respected by her many clients. When she became an executive director, however, she noticed a dramatic change in her impact on people she worked with. "The same things that I did as a consultant that were seen as calling in people's power and motivating them were received as harmful when I did them as an ED," she said. "I quickly realized I had to make some dramatic adjustments regarding my pacing, expectations, and overall leadership style."

It's particularly baffling in feminist organizations where leaders are given the dual message, often by their majority-women or even majority-WOC staff, to defy patriarchal expectations and be a bold and confident leader externally, but to conform tightly to these same expectations in order to be liked internally. Purvi Shah spoke of the hypocrisy of how she was treated: "Be smart, on point, but don't be too smart, not aggressive. Zealously advocate, but if you are a woman, do it with a smile. I've had bosses tell me I wasn't nurturing enough. As a student advocate, I was told my personality was too strong. This impossible task of being fierce in front of the enemy and meek in front of my peers has been incredibly destructive to my sense of self. You have to do a thousand calculations about your tone, your words."

When it comes to power, a woman of color leader is ostensibly de-gendered and de-raced in the eyes of staff, who only see her positional power in the micro context of the organization and not her marginalization in the macro context of her field and society at large. There is no awareness of the cumulative effect of the battering she is taking externally and internally.

"You are in this liminal space," described Ai-jen Poo, "of having some power over your little piece, and you are still living in a country defined by structural inequities that disadvantage you. You have to both eat the shit of a misogynist white supremacist society that devalues and exploits your people and take the shit of your people that think you have all this power to abuse or be non-transparent with, or whatever the accusation of the day is."

This next story was one about an attack so rough that I heard about it all the way across the country, from several different people. When I sat down with Alexis McGill Johnson, CEO of Planned Parenthood, she shared her version of what happened: "One of the harder days I've had was around Dobbs. We were pulling together a broader progressive call as part of the coalition table, and leaders of color were running the meeting. We're still in Covid and organizing by Zoom. A racist Zoom bomber calls in and uses the N-word. I was not on the call. I heard about it later, right before a scheduled call the next day with a racially mixed group from our movement table.

"To have no grace or recognition of me as a Black woman in the space. The attacks . . ." Alexis paused. "I've never felt more invisible. I remember hanging up the Zoom and I called another CEO in the coalition and before I could get the words out the tears started. They were so heavy and so much of what I had been carrying for so long. People didn't say, 'I'm going to say some things about your organization but first, I need you to know that I see you, I know it's hard, I do see you're trying.' Instead it felt like, 'I'm upset with one hundred years of history and your position is responsible for fixing white women's mistakes, and every time you resemble that because you are a corporate entity, anytime you fuck up, I'm going to let you know.' There's an expectation of what it means to represent and transform the organization, without recognizing the complexity of managing this size and weight of an organization and without the inside/outside community support to do so. Then you're walking into the next room and getting on the phone with a donor who has a critique coming at you from the other side. Then you go into another room and your white male employee is negotiating really hard on that side. Being the same person but being responsible for all of these pieces without anyone recognizing what a juggle it is, is hard."

So many of us keep the pain and stress of this juggle to ourselves. Should we be doing more to share it with our teams? Would they listen?

And what do we do about direct patriarchal attacks on our leadership?

I have seen many feminist organizations where the majority of women express a strong dislike for a woman leader who seems too decisive, passionate, or direct and where staff show their disapproval through gossip, complaints, refusal to follow work directives, or giving someone the cold shoulder, hammering the leader until she complies with classic patriarchal expectations.

In her 1970 speech at the Congress to Unite Women entitled "Self-Destruction in the Women's Movement," second-wave feminist Anselma Dell'Olio described its manifestation in movement at that time. "These attacks take different forms. The most common and pervasive is character assassination: the attempt to undermine and destroy belief in the integrity of the individual under attack. . . . The ultimate tactic is to isolate her. . . . And who do they attack? Generally two categories," she said. "Achievement or accomplishment of any kind . . . and [those who] have what is generally described as a 'forceful personality' [that does not] fit the conventional stereotype of a 'feminine' woman. . . . If you are in the first category [an achiever] . . . you are immediately labeled a thrill-seeking opportunist, a ruthless mercenary, out to make her fame and fortune over the dead bodies of selfless sisters who have buried their abilities and sacrificed their ambitions for the greater glory of Feminism."

The patriarchal expectations to which WOC leaders are expected to conform boil down to one overarching demand: "Prove you are a nice girl!" This includes the expectations to:

- Qualify all opinions: "I was thinking that maybe we could host it on Tuesday" instead of "Tuesday would be best because . . ."

- Soften all directives: "Do you think you might be able to get this to me by tomorrow?" instead of "Please send this to me by close of business tomorrow."

- Water down statements of strong disagreement until they are indirect: "Interesting. I wonder if you have considered X" instead of "I strongly disagree with that and here's why."

- Appear uncertain, even if you know the answer to a question: "Lobby day is on Monday, right?" "We agree that police brutality is a major problem, right?"

- Behave deferentially to the ideas of others. Many WOC who have been trained as community organizers have had it drilled into them that real leadership is to lead from "the back of the room" and support the leadership of others. As the saying goes, "The best organizers put themselves out of a job." But an ED job is not the same as a lead organizer; it requires the willingness to believe in and act on one's own ideas as well as those of others.

- Never express anger or frustration, no matter how unfairly you are treated.

- Mother and mammy.

- Display your own vulnerability and victimhood to keep people from seeing you as too confident and thus intimidating.

- Never advocate for yourself by challenging the mistreatment you may be subject to as a leader.

"There is a powerful instinct that gets deeply embedded in me and other WOC about navigating expectations," said Miya Yoshitani. "You are deeply aware all the time of how you need to present in order to appear trustworthy or strategic or smart or worth listening to. There is a keen awareness from our own survival and experiences in and outside the movement, maybe within our own families. It's a strength and also a barrier to our own fully dignified humanity."

WOC leaders expend an incalculable amount of energy on the million micro calculations made and micro signals sent to keep people engaged enough for them to move work forward. Often, it's never enough and you are still hit with the stereotype.

Gendered expectations for likability also vary by race. "For Black women, we can whisper something, and people will say we yelled at them," said Fatima Goss Graves. "One of the folks on my senior team after a meeting was like, 'The feedback from that meeting was people are scared of you.' All that happened in the meeting is that I was direct. I said, 'This is a problem and here's why, and if we go down this road this will happen.' My efforts to be direct are often seen as scary."

East Asian women are often hit with a different stereotype. "Part of the Asian American experience in particular is the racial stereotype of just going along to get along," said Miya Yoshitani. "Being pleasing. I always felt there was so little room to make a mistake, to take risks, and to try things completely differently, so little encouragement for that and such a huge expectation of perfection and nonconfrontation. Whenever I contradicted that image, I felt like the fallout was worse than it would have been for someone else. I was contradicting the expectation that I would be always amenable and happy. Happy to get what I was given or grateful to be in the position I was in or have my org at the table instead of really respecting what we were bringing that may have been dramatically different from their expectations of how Asian Americans should show up. It's been treacherous to be in leadership when you are not meeting people's expectations."

The stereotype about aggression impacts Native women as well. "There is definitely an angry Native woman stereotype," said Enei Begaye. "Some girlfriends and I who were all EDs and directors, our code name for ourselves was IAE—Indians Against Everything—[because] we are just telling our opinions and it is being interpreted that way."

So, how should leaders deal with the thorny issue of likability? Sometimes the best way to cope with toxic expectations is to stop trying to meet them. To let go of the need to be liked and normalize the fact that there will inevitably be people who will never like you.

While people don't have to like you, they are required to treat you with respect and to do their work with excellence. "I try to work with people who I enjoy, but I'm also clear around my expectations," said Elle Moxley. "Now I say, 'Ya'll probably not going to like me. Whoever you thought I was, that's not who my job requires me to be.' When you establish boundaries and expectations around deliverables, you get a different response."

Demanding respect rather than likes helps you avoid the tentacles of manipulation.

"I honestly am not motivated by being liked by all people," explained Mona Sinha. "It's not about likability and all about respect. Sometimes women compromise their standards to be liked. That is a dangerous position to be in and a slippery slope because then those people know they can manipulate you. The key fundamentals are: Do your homework, execute with excellence, listen respectfully, and show up authentically. That establishes your credo, and despite themselves, the same people will respect you, not for your likability, but what you show up for. That is different."

The WOC movement leaders who are successful and gain a public profile are often less "likable" too because they are assumed to have the resources and support they need. I've heard people refer to these sisters as "the darlings of philanthropy," "celebrities," and "overexposed." I've sat in rooms where people have actively argued against them getting resources, saying that others could use the dollars more. Having known many of these sisters for ten or twenty years, I know just how false this perception is.

There was a flash flood warning in New York, and I texted Linda Sarsour from the back of the cab I was in to see if she wanted to cancel our breakfast meeting. She texted back, "I apologize on behalf of NYC for this monsoon. We are used to this. We travel when the snow is to the knees." This is very Linda. The rest of my meetings were all canceled. The TV screen in my cab showed news footage of subway staircases that looked like a waterfall and parts of Brooklyn where cars had been abandoned, with water up to their windows. But Linda Sarsour was undeterred. At a classic and crowded diner in SoHo, we talked about the state of the movement, what she has weathered, and how excited she is to own her own home finally. One of the leaders with the largest social media followings, Linda had to spend thirty thousand dollars out of her own pocket one year to put a security detail on her home and her parents' home when they were doxed. She was well into her forties before she could afford to buy a house for her family.

LaTosha Brown, who has been celebrated by Harvard University and is a regular on MSNBC, spent her own retirement savings to finance a leadership program for Black girls in the south that she believed was necessary to meet the moment. She, like so many other leaders, is financially supporting several family members. People love to push leaders out there to take all of the risk, and then abandon them to deal with all of the heat and stress and danger that comes with it. The general discomfort with power that permeates the left, causing people in movement to treat everyone and anything that succeeds, scales, gains power as suspect, hits WOC harder. Men generally, and even men of color, are consistently more strongly flanked by philanthropy and other movement leaders.

Ash-Lee Woodard Henderson, whose Tennessee office was firebombed by white nationalists, said, "I understand what people think the perks are of being in proximity to power. But they don't know what it's like for your kid to be terrified, or your mom to call you because you didn't text her when you landed—or your girlfriend to be frantically screaming at you because some white man is parked in front of her house. Folks don't understand what it's like for folks to be hedging their bets on new leadership."

Freedom comes from getting to a point where, as Teresa Younger powerfully shared, "I will no longer apologize for the power I hold. I want you to like me, but you don't need to be my friend. Do you respect the work I do and the vision we are working with? We are in a (c)(3) structure and a capitalistic structure where the buck stops with me. If you don't like it, you can leave. No one is forcing you to be here. You can make suggestions for how I communicate more effectively, but I'm not giving up the power I hold for you to like me. If the power I hold impacts you to the point where you can't communicate with me, that's on you. If you can't see me as a person in the leadership I am in, that's on you to figure out."

In the end, one of the core things WOC leaders must understand is that no amount of people-pleasing is going to protect you. If you are an effective leader who is making an impact, they will attempt to attack you. Be humble and open to feedback, don't be abusive or harmful—but don't twist yourself into a pretzel trying to prove that you are not a monster. People in movement should stop requiring this of WOC leaders.

16

Haters and Toxic Power

Rape Culture and Leadership

Nothing in my life has come closer to the experience of surviving sexual violence than the immediate aftermath of the attacks I endured as an organizational leader. Having talked to scores of WOC leaders about the sequence of events that typically follows an attack—whether within their organizations or more publicly—the similarities are impossible to ignore.

First, you are attacked. I'm not referring to snide comments and slights but attacks that have the potential to block an organization from accomplishing its mission, demolish a leader's professional reputation, and even endanger the life of a leader and the lives of their family members. Here are a few examples of attacks shared by the leaders I interviewed.

- A staff member with major performance issues became disgruntled about not being promoted and sought revenge by spreading lies about organizational leaders in order to turn other staff against them.

- Right-wingers or people in movement dragged a leader on social media and in the news for baseless accusations. The leader was doxed by news outlets and rival factions of the movement, who published the home addresses of her and her family. She received a visit from FBI agents who warned her that white supremacists had these addresses on a list of houses they planned to bomb.

- A newer staff member with mental health issues had never met the organizational leader in person and had only minimal contact with her via Zoom. The staffer decided to sue the organization and drag the leader online and to funders for allegedly "tearing down younger women."

Second, you are gaslit. The survivor of sexual violence will often be told she is fabricating or exaggerating the violation and its impact on her. She will likely have more than one woman in her life normalize the behavior of her harasser/abuser by quipping, "We've all been there. Boys will be boys. No sense in making a scene. Just ignore it." The woman of color leader will be told another version of this: "That's happened to me. It happens to all of us women leaders. You can't let it bother you. Don't take it personally."

Being too thin-skinned is not sustainable in leadership. At the same time, there are levels of attack that cross the line, and their impact shouldn't be minimized.

The phrase "Don't take it personally" is worth unpacking, as it is said with two different types of intent. Once, when I was being attacked, I had an excellent colleague who happened to be a cis Black man tell me, "You can't take this stuff personally. What's happening is not your fault, and it doesn't mean you're not a good leader." Having worked with many WOC, he was familiar with our propensity to handle any attack by blaming and doubting ourselves. He wasn't minimizing the attack or abandoning me, and he was reminding me not to abandon myself.

Conversely, I was once told, "You can't take this personally. This is par for the course when you sign up to be a leader. You have to toughen up." These kinds of comments minimize and normalize the attack and carry a paternalistic subtext: "Have you considered the possibility that the reason you are bothered by what occurred is that you are just hysterical, weak, ill prepared for your job, or unprofessional?" The rape survivor is asked, "What were you wearing?" and if she says a short skirt, she is asked, "Well, what did you expect?" The woman of color is asked, "What were you doing leading? Well, what did you expect?"

One way to cut through the gaslighting is to bring into focus whether the attack is one that cis men would ever be expected to put up with. During her 2022 U.S. Supreme Court confirmation hearings, Justice Ketanji Brown Jackson was subject to unprecedented levels of grilling by Republicans. Senator Ted Cruz held up Ibram X. Kendi's book *Antiracist Baby,* declaring that it was among the "critical race theory" books found at Jackson's daughter's private school and asked Brown if she believed in the notion that babies are racists. She was also questioned extensively about whether she had gone easy on child porn offenders (her sentences were in fact statistically in line with the mainstream of rulings in these types of cases). Was a white male nominee for the U.S. Supreme Court ever subjected to the level of interrogation, based on baseless rumors, that was leveled at Jackson? The answer is no. And if they had been, they would likely be considered within their rights to challenge what was happening.

Elle Moxley, founder of the Marsha P. Johnson Institute, talked about her journey to reject the gaslighting. "They are Abuser Dynamics 101, but if you don't understand your own cycle of abuse, you won't understand what you are experiencing. I was a child survivor and certain abuses weren't unfamiliar, they were just happening in a new way by people who looked like me and from those I didn't expect."

Third, you are isolated. Many sexual assault survivors describe being treated like pariahs when others find out what happened to them. They are shunned as "sluts" or "dirty" or "ruined." Most WOC leaders who shared their stories of attacks with me described the intense isolation following an attack. One told me, "Everyone treats you like you are radioactive." Another said, "It's like you have a scarlet letter." Some leaders I spoke with were shocked at how quickly they went from being widely respected to being treated like pariahs. It's worth noting that in most of these cases, the attacks were based on false rumors, which were ultimately disproven. A few talked about serious mental health impacts of this phenomenon; one checked herself into an inpatient treatment center for PTSD, and another didn't leave her house or speak to many people in movement for a year. I don't see these leaders as weak or broken. I see them as having a human reaction to the phenomenon of being separated from the pack and left in the wilderness—something that human beings as a species have been genetically hard-wired to regard with terror, as a threat to our survival. Performer Sarah Jones described it as "that core existential terror of being excommunicated from the love that we need to survive." There are many ways in which this isolation is carried out, ranging from those who attempt to blacklist leaders from working in movement to those who simply won't risk anything to stand with them.

Those who assume a woman of color leader who is publicly dragged is probably a bitch who had it coming should consider that until #MeToo, a woman who was raped was assumed to be a slut who asked for it (a norm that still persists in many places).

Said Linda Sarsour, "There are so many reasons why WOC in movement don't stand up for each other and none of them are principled. Anytime we were under attack, people were quiet or wouldn't return our calls." Linda Sarsour recalled her time as cofounder of the Women's March: "The first time it was when the NRA went after us. The NRA put out a video with me, Tamika, and Carmen that said, 'You better meet them with the clenched fist of truth.' Bob [the only white woman among the Women's March leadership] was not in the video. This is how intentional it is. This video went viral. We went to the Fairfax headquarters of the NRA. Our point was, we're not scared. We show up and there were fifty white men with big guns who met us outside. We faced that virtually alone. There was no concept [in the movement] of solidarity with WOC leadership."

"I was dragged on Facebook and Instagram by a former staffer," said one leader who wished to share this story anonymously. "I wasn't their friend, but others were screenshotting things and sending them to me. I was surprised by people in the community who liked her post or wrote something. The community handled it like a rumor, hushed, talking behind my back. Many people told me they didn't believe this person and that they supported me, but I don't know anyone who publicly stuck up for me. Our HR had to let her know that if she didn't take her post down we would open a formal investigation and if she was wrong we would pursue her legally for slander. So she took it down."

Bishop Desmond Tutu famously said, "If you are neutral in situations of injustice, you have chosen the side of the oppressor." Movement people take this to heart when it comes to many of the causes they are working on. But most seem to make an exception for WOC leaders.

One of the clearest pieces I've read about some of the more difficult dynamics that occur in feminist spaces is "Trashing: The Dark Side of Sisterhood,"[1] written in 1976 by longtime feminist and civil rights activist Dr. Jo Freeman (which, along with "The Tyranny of Structurelessness" and "The BITCH Manifesto," comprise three iconic articles she wrote on the topic, which continue to be cited fifty years later). Jo exposed the phenomenon known as "trashing," which she described as "psychological rape," where women eviscerate one another through various public attacks and social exclusion. When I interviewed her, she told me, "In 1970 I plunged into a major depression, which I had not had before then. I knew that the reason was that I had been trashed. I didn't talk about my depression, but I did talk about trashing, including to some of the staff at *Ms.* magazine. They wanted me to write about it. [At the time] Gloria [Steinem] was being trashed and they wanted to expose how common it was to attack leaders and prominent women. One day I sat down at my typewriter and it just came pouring out. I shared it with the *Ms.* staff, but I was reluctant to publish it. I didn't want to air our dirty laundry in public. The *Ms.* staff were gung ho. I finally said yes. *Ms.* got more letters from people in response to that article than they had received from any other article [up until] that time."

In the article, Jo addressed the accountability of the collective for not allowing people to be isolated, writing, "Although only a few women actually engage in trashing, the blame for allowing it to continue rests with us all. Once under attack, there is little a woman can do to defend herself because she is by definition always wrong. But there is a great deal that those who are watching can do to prevent her from being isolated and ultimately destroyed. . . . Many attacks have been forestalled by the refusal of associates to let themselves be intimidated into silence out of fear that they would be next. Other attackers have been forced to clarify their complaints to the point where they can be rationally dealt with."

People perpetuate the isolation of leaders by pretending that a situation that has a clear right and wrong is a he said, she said conundrum that they can't take a side on. In this twilight zone, there is no such thing as evidence, only opinion, and all opinions are equally valid. One leader asked her department manager to take disciplinary action against a staff member, sharing clear documentation proving that this individual had mismanaged over fifty thousand dollars, received several complaints from community members, and publicly attacked the leader. The manager, who wanted to be liked by staff and feared becoming a target by appearing to side with the leader, demurred, saying, "I choose to hold that there are many truths."

People who want to hedge their bets in every direction will express support and empathy to the leader but refuse to back them in public.

Linda Sarsour said, "People will easily allow us to get attacked, and will send a text on the side being like, 'Oh, are you okay?' but are so afraid of the white gaze that they won't actually come out for you publicly." I saw this when Linda was attacked as a leader of the Women's March and many feminists of all colors, who feared the wrath of white women donors, said nothing.

The cognitive dissonance of supportive texts and words said in private, against the abandonment in public, hurts the worst when it comes from your own. I experienced this, on a far less significant scale than Linda, during a time I was being publicly dragged. Several of my WOC staff members sent me lovely gifts with cards attached, asking how I was, declaring their support, and saying how wrongly they felt I was being treated. These same staff then sat in meetings where I was falsely accused of things that they knew to be lies—and didn't stick their neck out an inch to say a word in my defense. Only a couple of staff ever risked anything to defend me in public. I thought about how many sexually abused children have loving mothers and aunties who take them for ice cream or make them their favorite meals to comfort them, while doing nothing to protect them, imploring them to stay quiet and pretend nothing is happening. We know that one of the main reasons rape culture continues is because of the power of bystanders and participation in a norm of silence. This is also one of the reasons WOC leaders continue to be abused in leadership.

In society, rape prevention is too often focused on telling women to practice precautions to avoid being raped. There is far less focus on telling men not to rape. This needs to change. Clearly the emotional abuse WOC leaders face is not equal to the trauma of a physical rape, but the principal of prevention is the same. People in movement need to be educated on how not to abuse WOC leaders.

The grave irony of this cycle is that most WOC leaders in movement have spent our entire lives validating the pain of others who have been wronged, supporting them to reject ongoing mistreatment by speaking out for change. Yet, when it comes to us being mistreated, too many of our movement comrades invalidate our pain, gaslight us, and encourage us to bear our burden in silence. Tragically, too many WOC demand this of one another. Every leader who I talked with about this topic shared that being thrown under the bus or left for dead by your own people is one of the most painful things they have endured in leadership. If we're not careful, this pain can deter us from being bold and powerful.

For many, it becomes too much to bear. Jo Freeman, who would continue to teach, write, and publish extensively, but who stepped away from group spaces, told me, "I finally reach the point where I just walk away. The first time I walked away from the women's movement was in 1969. The second time was in 1979. The third time was in 1989, and after that I never rejoined a feminist group." Jo is a white woman. WOC deal with trashing layered with the compounded pressures of racism.

When one leader told me in a resigned tone about the rampant mistreatment, "We just have to take it. WOC take a lot of shit for movement," I felt a brief pang of heartbreak. Why should we just take it? We have another option. We can change the climate of leadership and make it better for ourselves, our daughters, and future generations.

Relational Aggression

Toxic power expresses itself depending on how people are socialized, which in turn is driven by the ways they are privileged or oppressed. For cis men, it often manifests as a direct frontal attack. For women, it can also appear as relational aggression. According to the American Psychological Association, relational aggression is "behavior that manipulates or damages relationships between individuals or groups, such as bullying, gossiping, and humiliation."[2] In the book *The Development of Relational Aggression,* Sarah Coyne and Jamie Ostrov describe it as "behavior that is intended to harm another's relationships or feelings of inclusion in a group."[3]

Studies show that relational aggression is more prevalent among women and girls and often more damaging to them than it is to men and boys. This makes sense. For centuries, gender norms have prohibited women from expressing anger in their families and communities. As an adaptation, many women resorted to more indirect, passive-aggressive approaches such as social exclusion, icing people out, and destroying their social standing through spreading gossip or rumors.

Women also seek out the social support of others, particularly other women, far more than do men, placing a higher value on these relationships, which in turn can make attacks on their social standing more devastating. "Paradoxically, it is women's trust in other women that makes them easy prey for saboteurs," said Barbara Brock, author of the paper "The Barrier Within: Relational Aggression Among Women."[4] The trust and sharing that enables women to form close relationships also increases vulnerability to being blindsided by women whose intentions are betrayal and sabotage. Brock's 2008 study of women leaders reported that "at the onset of the sabotage, they were unaware of the identity of the saboteur and the person's motivation and confused by what was occurring."

The "trashing" that feminist Jo Freeman explored is, essentially, relational aggression. Hers is one of the clearest accounts of what it feels like to be caught in the swirl of this type of attack. She wrote, "I felt psychologically mangled to the point where I knew I couldn't go on." Freeman continued:

> I have been watching for years with increasing dismay as the Movement consciously destroys anyone within it who stands out in any way. [Trashing] is not disagreement; it is

not conflict; it is not opposition. These are perfectly ordinary phenomena which, when engaged in mutually, honestly, and not excessively, are necessary to keep an organism or organization healthy and active. Trashing is a particularly vicious form of character assassination which amounts to psychological rape. It is manipulative, dishonest, and excessive. It is occasionally disguised by the rhetoric of honest conflict, or covered up by denying that any disapproval exists at all. But it is not done to expose disagreements or resolve differences. It is done to disparage and destroy. . . . These feelings are reinforced when you are isolated from your friends as they become convinced that their association with you is similarly inimical to the Movement and to themselves. Any support of you will taint them.

This was communicated so subtly that I never could get anyone to talk about it. There were no big confrontations, just many little slights. Each by itself was insignificant; but added one to another they were like a thousand cuts with a whip. Step by step I was ostracized: If a collective article was written, my attempts to contribute were ignored; if I wrote an article, no one would read it; when I spoke in meetings, everyone would listen politely, and then take up the discussion as though I hadn't said anything; meeting dates were changed without my being told; when it was my turn to coordinate a work project, no one would help; when I didn't receive mailings, and discovered that my name was not on the mailing list, I was told I had just looked in the wrong place. . . .

My response to this was bewilderment. I felt as though I were wandering blindfolded in a field full of sharp objects and deep holes while being reassured that I could see perfectly and was in a smooth, grassy pasture. It was as if I had unwittingly entered a new society, one operating by rules of which I wasn't aware, and couldn't know. When I tried to get my group(s) to discuss what I thought was happening to me, they either denied my perception of reality by saying nothing was out of the ordinary, or dismissed the incidents as trivial (which individually they were). One woman, in private phone conversations, did admit that I was being poorly treated. But she never supported me publicly, and admitted quite frankly that it was because she feared to lose the group's approval.

WOC leaders are prime targets for this kind of attack, and if we speak out about it, we are often dismissed as petty or taking things too personally. But the cumulative effect gets in the way of moving work forward.

Several EDs have shared examples of a staff member who has performance issues then spins a narrative among their colleagues that the reason that they are receiving critical feedback or being denied a promotion is because management is retaliating against them for bringing reasonable critiques about program and strategy. Within the framework of this narrative, they can then trash certain organizational leaders as power-hungry despots, rallying sympathy by telling co-workers that they live in fear of more retaliation in the form of disciplinary action. This is a half nelson wrestling move of relational aggression, particularly in organizations where there are a lot of new hires and staff aren't able to observe one another's work enough to consider the credibility of the source. It is also a hell of an insurance policy. They gin up fear and anxiety among staff, and then all their supervisor has to do is initiate progressive discipline or fire them the next time they have a major performance issue, and boom! The narrative that the organization retaliates against staff will be fulfilled, lowering staff morale and leaving a mess for management to clean up. In some instances, the staff who work with the person spreading these rumors have even complained to management about having to do their job on top of their own, but are often unwilling to speak out, lest they come off as in cahoots with management. One ED, whose largely remote staff team had always been cheerful and warm with her, described flying across country to meet her team for a training they were hosting. It was a few weeks into this kind of trashing by one employee, and when she walked into the room, every team member averted their eyes and ignored her.

This kind of aggression may feel like middle school pettiness that's not worth one iota of time or attention, but several leaders ignored these dynamics at their own peril. It's one thing to let things go that are personal slights that have no bearing on the work. It's another to let toxicity run rampant, damaging morale and trust and thus the ability to carry out the organization's mission.

Relational aggression is all about bullying and terrorizing someone by separating them from the pack. It can trigger a primal fear, programmed for thousands of years into our DNA, of being left in the wilderness. When this aggression is allowed to run unchecked in an organization, it creates an environment of fear, paranoia, and even panic that causes people to behave out of self-preservation. We know that in moments of panic, people fight, flee, or freeze, and the ways in which they do this aren't always pretty. It's the grown man in a burning building who shoves women and children out of the way to get to the exit first. It's the Gentile in Nazi Germany who folds quickly under questioning, divulging everything they know to the Gestapo about the whereabouts of their Jewish neighbor. Terror reveals what people are made of, and if they lack integrity and courage, their worst and most spineless selves will come to the surface.

I have seen people lobby hard for managers to take action about a negligent co-worker and then when they do, stay tight-lipped when those managers are shredded by other staff. I have seen WOC managers weather intentionally fabricated accusations of transphobia, anti-Asian sentiment, and anti-Blackness, and then, in a desperate attempt to keep the target off their backs, become the biggest cheerleaders for every new weaponized discrimination accusation aimed at someone else. In some cases, I have even seen them disingenuously accuse other people of these same things, the logic being, I suppose, that if the mob is hunting others, it's not hunting them.

The maddening thing is, all of this is quite easy to neutralize if only a small number of people are willing to stay grounded enough in the face of fear, to act with courage and backbone. As Albert Einstein said, "The world will not be destroyed by those who do evil, but by those who watch them without doing anything." Sometimes it takes only one person to stop things from spinning out of control. The organizational leader is often unable to be this person because their positional power makes anything they do potentially suspect and explosive. In the case study above, it took only one grounded senior manager to intervene and put a stop to the staffer who was spreading false rumors, and the entire circus stopped.

The same was true for a woman of color friend of mine, who shared a remarkable story about a teenage girl, a youth group member, who saved an organization from melting down. My friend worked on the staff of a racially homogenous organization where almost everyone, from board to staff to community members, belonged to the same racial group. There were, however, various ethnic subgroups represented, and in a power grab, a single board member complained that the community members of her ethnic group were being discriminated against by the organization's staff members of another ethnic group. The board member had no evidence but had power and clout in the community so people in the neighborhood were hesitant to contradict her publicly.

Many community members told staff privately that they didn't agree with the accusations, but no one was willing to step forward and say as much to the board. As a result, the drama spun on for months, harming the board, demoralizing the staff, and disrupting the organization's programming. Finally, one community member, a teenager from the allegedly discriminated-against ethnic subgroup who cared deeply about the youth program and the organization, asked to meet with the board and told them she thought the claims were bogus. It was enough to give people pause, to compel them to stop spinning based on rumors and ask more questions and listen to the community. The concerns were quickly dispelled, and the drama ended. This youth—a teenager!—was the only person with the backbone to tell the truth, but her lone voice had halted the tailspin of a major organization.

Social media has amplified relational aggression in ways that threaten WOC leaders. The September 2022 *New York Times* piece "How Russian Trolls Helped Keep the Women's March Out of Lockstep" detailed the barrage of social media posts generated by Russian hackers and bots to malign key leaders like Linda Sarsour and Tamika Mallory to deepen racial divisions within the movement. It was relational aggression on a large scale, both in its inception and in the response. The inception was essentially gossip magnified and manipulated through social media to attempt to publicly discredit and isolate the women of color leaders of the Women's March. The reaction was one of fear in which people, terrified of losing their own funding or credibility by being too closely associated with these leaders, did one of two things: joined the attack or stepped away.

The *Times* piece vindicated leaders like Sarsour and speaks volumes about the profound gaslighting these women were subjected to for years. The article also revealed much to me about movement itself. As I read it, I felt my throat constrict with grief and fury. I remembered how these sisters had been treated, not just by some Russians, but by their own. Instead of asking clarifying questions, encircling these sisters with support, helping to talk down the jumpy funders, scores of leftists spread the gossip further and treated these leaders as if they were radioactive, excluding them from meetings, coalitions, and funding. It was so profoundly wrong.

The relentless targeting that Linda and Tamika faced is happening in movements with increasing frequency to WOC leaders—the triple threat of external attack, internal attack, and bystanderism.

No leader is perfect, but so many of the WOC leaders who other people of color are trying to take out are, in fact, high-integrity people who should be valued and protected and who deserve to be engaged in a principled way around critiques or points of disagreement. Holding someone accountable is not the same as trying to destroy them. I don't use these terms lightly because the stakes are high for some of these sisters, not to mention their loved ones, including their children. We're talking about sister leaders who cannot walk down the street next to their children for fear of being attacked. Sisters forced to flee their homes and live in safe houses after being doxed. Sisters with impeccable track records of fighting for their communities who cannot get work in the movement to support their families. Sisters hospitalized from PTSD.

We talk a lot about white people. Yes, some white people have either supported or torn down social justice efforts led by people of color. Yes, attacks on our leaders often originate there, and we need to fight those forces. Yet, from the Black Panthers to many POC-led efforts today, white supremacists and patriarchal attacks from outside have always been most successful in taking out our leaders and obliterating our movements when they were aided by our own people violently expressing their internalized white supremacy and patriarchy toward one another. Movement's overwhelming response to the toxic power directed at WOC leaders is no different.

"I've seen so many leaders ostracized from movement," said Elle Moxley. "People came together to take them down. To watch how people will literally destroy you and oust you. It's almost never white folks. In order to get Black people, you actually need Black folks who say, 'It's okay to get them.'"

A Word on Haters

If you have a hater, chances are you are not the first person they have attempted to tear down, nor will you be the last. It's not personal. Individuals like these aren't wonderful people who win the hearts and minds of everyone and reserve their venom for you; they show their true colors everywhere they go. It's not necessary for you to tell people about them most of the time. It's impossible for you to say anything about them that they are not already saying about themselves with how they show up in the world.

I once crossed paths with another leader who had the same hater that I did. This individual had attempted to take out both of us in the same traumatizing way, and we were able to commiserate about the cleanup and recovery that we both had to do. Another time, I was surprised when senior staff from a large organization pulled me aside to ask my advice on someone they were having major problems with and knew I had worked with.

This person had verbally abused multiple staff at my organization before I learned about it and intervened. I had feared their gossip about the organization would harm us after they left because they held some prominence in the field, but the opposite was true. The people with common sense and maturity saw their dysfunction and took their gossip with a large grain of salt, without me having to do or say a thing. The truth has a way of surfacing.

We must also remember that haters are rarely builders of things that make the world a better place. They talk a lot and do very little and at some point, that will be apparent. As one of my oldest and dearest friends, Jessica Horn, wrote about talkers, "Consider: At some point people will stop focusing on what you are saying and start wondering what you are 'building.' Activism is not just commentary." Trust people to wonder about this.

A movement elder, quoting a saying that is a staple of twelve-step programs, once told me, "You always have the power to keep your side of the street clean." We can do this by not going out of our way to try to trash, destroy, or get even with haters. We can also do this by refusing to participate with haters in relational aggression to drag and exclude other WOC leaders. "There is an ongoing demand from some quarters of our staff and parts of the movement—both white women and women of color—for me to publicly shame other WOC leaders," said Fatima Goss Graves. "My answer is always no. And I have given this speech to my staff a few times—it is not how I choose to lead."

We give away our power to haters when we allow them to occupy space in our thoughts. As Nelson Mandela said, "Resentment is like drinking poison and hoping your enemy dies." It's important to release pain and rage that you feel from the harm that haters caused you. Talk it out with trusted friends, family members, your therapist, and find ways to clear it from your body and mind. Take an honest look at the wounds you carry, often from childhood, that this person may have triggered. Work on healing these so you can release haters from your thoughts. These are toxic people, and as Brené Brown tells us, don't bring toxic people close.

What's helped me to clear haters from my mind is to see them for who they are: individuals who have sustained so much trauma in their lives that they lack the capacity to show love, integrity, and kindness. This allows me to regard them with more empathy.

Beyoncé is a role model for dealing with haters. She doesn't allow them to distract her from her excellence, and she lets the Beyhive (the world's biggest squad) block for her. In an ideal world, you can call on your squad to confront and handle haters offline, getting them to back off without creating a scene online. If their hatred is online and creating damage, your squad can also counter them online without directly rebutting or counterattacking, but by simply offering the alternative perspective and information they have about you. For example, if a leader is dragged by a disgruntled young person on their staff for being "mean" to younger women, other young women can simply offer their testimony on how they have experienced that leader's love and support. This offers the public a fuller picture and context without having to square off and call anyone a liar.

WOC Leaders: "The Real" White Supremacists

When I got my first paid movement job in 2000, white supremacy, homophobia, transphobia, patriarchy and other forms of bias, discrimination, and harassment were commonplace in many movement organizations. Complaints were largely swept under the rug. A legitimate accusation of discrimination carried no real power. A change was sorely needed. My generation continued to organize in the workplace and beyond, just as prior generations had done, to bring that change about. In the summer of 2020, it finally came. Thirty million people marched in the streets around the globe following the murder of George Floyd, and in a testament to the transformative force of grassroots organizing, a tipping point occurred. At last, an accusation of anti-Blackness began to carry the power it should have all along. And just as most wins for Black liberation have a positive ripple effect for other oppressed communities, other terms like "transphobic" and "ableist" began to carry more power too. Yet, power, as we were about to be sharply reminded, is not inherently good or bad; it depends on how you use it.

Most people used this new power constructively, bringing legitimate complaints of bias and discrimination forward to push all kinds of institutions and industries to improve. They mainstreamed the understanding that every one of us living in this country is swimming in the waters of various isms and that if we don't do our work to deprogram certain thinking and behavior, we will inevitably harm one another. More workplaces began taking responsibility for creating an environment of equity and inclusion, where bias and discrimination were not allowed to flourish. It was good to see this progress and there's a need to keep the pedal to the metal on this work.

Other people, however, began using this new power destructively. Movement organizations saw a major uptick in bogus accusations of discrimination and "white supremacy culture" by people who saw it as an easy way to threaten, browbeat, and dominate others into doing what they wanted. By 2022, many, if not most, of the women of color leaders I knew had been accused of perpetuating "white supremacy culture" by someone on their staff—sometimes by people of color and sometimes by white people. This quickly widened to a larger range of accusations of transphobia, xenophobia, antisemitism, ageism, and ableism, among others.

Further complicating matters, in many organizations, constructive and destructive challenges began happening simultaneously. Leaders needed the clarity to parse the two and deal with each accordingly. Constructive grievances deserve an apology, repair, and structural changes to prevent a reoccurrence. Destructive ones must be challenged and disproven. How do you know the difference? You have to examine the evidence. Evidence can be a difficult thing for a leader to insist upon. In the months after George Floyd's murder, the collective pain was so electric, the nation's centuries-old denial of Black suffering so excruciating, that it felt almost unthinkable to challenge any accusation of anti-Blackness. The general sentiment in that moment was that anyone pushing back against an accusation of discrimination of any kind was likely just being defensive and dodging accountability, because why on earth would anyone lie about something like this? This was a fair question, given most people's lived experience up until then. Historically, apart from white women lying in order to turn lynch mobs on Black men, there was little to no incentive for anyone else to lie about these things because the accusations held no power. The risk of speaking out was almost always higher than the potential benefit.

Today we find ourselves at the other extreme. Instead of being ignored, someone charging discrimination at a movement organization will usually garner instant positive attention and support. In many organizations, one person lodging a false claim with zero evidence can easily catalyze an uprising of the entire staff, causing mission-related work to derail, morale to tank, the organization's public reputation to be ruined, and funding to dry up until legal or other processes prove their claims false. That is a lot of leverage.

Here are several reasons why people are misusing discrimination accusations:

To avoid accountability: Don't like receiving fair feedback from your supervisor? Accuse them of disability discrimination. Don't like editing documents? Tell your supervisor that editing is "white supremacist" because it is "worship of the written word." Annoyed by a deadline? Rail about how urgency is a tool of white supremacy. In his article "Elephant in the Zoom: Meltdowns Have Brought Progressive Advocacy Groups to a Standstill at a Critical Moment in World History," journalist Ryan Grim noted that a large number of people of color are taking leadership positions in organizations just as these accusations are on the rise. Grim quotes a Black male organizational leader:

> "I just got the keys and y'all are gonna come after me on this shit? 'It's white supremacy culture! It's urgent!' No, mother-fucker, it's Election Day. We can't move that day. Just do your job or go somewhere else."
>
> Being Black has by no means shielded executive directors or their deputies from charges of facilitating white supremacy culture. "It's hard to have a conversation about performance," said the manager. "I'm as woke as they come, but they'll say, 'He's Black, but he's anti-Black because he fired these Black people.'"

In one case, I watched a staff person who had been making progress to overcome their fragility around feedback do a complete about-face after the uprisings. Abandoning any effort to be accountable, they decided all feedback was racial discrimination and proceeded to attack any supervisor who had given it, including those who were of their same race.

Teresa Younger, a Black woman and CEO of the Ms. Foundation for Women, said, "When I was told I was not Black enough and I was not a feminist because I was saying to someone, 'You don't get to behave that way and represent the organization,' that was a tough conversation."

Some staff use false accusations of discrimination or abuse of authority as an insurance policy. They know they are underperforming and will soon be written up or fired, so they preempt disciplinary action with a public accusation of discrimination so that if the manager follows through on the appropriate disciplinary action, the employee can then frame it to their co-workers, their union, and even the Equal Employment Opportunity Commission, as retaliation.

To gain the upper hand in debates and decision-making: Want the organization to change to a flat structure so that you, as a junior staff member, can feel like you're in charge (whether or not it benefits the organization's mission)? Demand it, then accuse the organization of being anti-Black because you and another Black person asked for it, and not meeting demands from Black people equals anti-Blackness. In one instance, I witnessed a situation like this that was made even more bizarre by another Black woman remaining silent and poker-faced on the Zoom screen while frantically texting the ED, "Please no! I've worked in collectives and they are a nightmare!" (Of course, not all collectives are a nightmare—some work well.)

In an interview with *The New York Times* about his powerful article "Building Resilient Organizations,"[5] Maurice Mitchell of the Working Families Party addressed the rising trend of "identity being weaponized in ways that were not useful for the work." He said, "I'd be in conversation where we were debating ideas and someone would say, 'As the Black son of Caribbean immigrants I think we should support candidate A' and it would shut the debate down when it needed to continue. People use the phrase 'because I have these identities' as a mic drop because my identity in itself establishes the legitimacy of my positions. . . . People are misusing that. I am Black, so is Clarence Thomas, simply elevating my Black identity as a totalizing argument for the legitimacy of my ideas is, I think, a mis-assessment. We run the risk of overcorrecting. As a Black person it does no favors to me for me to say 'as a Black son of immigrants' and for white people to sit on their hands and shut up. I need to be sharpened by the debate. . . . We are just performing while the far right is assiduously organizing to take all of our rights from us."

Now that both accusations and identity markers have a different kind of social capital and power, discernment is a muscle that people on the left must build. As Denise Perry, co-director of BOLD, said, "There is a lot of anti-Blackness, for sure, but just because I am Black and I bring up something and it's not taken on does not mean it's anti-Black. We can disagree."

Increasingly, I saw people assign the label "white supremacy" to whatever they disliked to discredit it and push for a shift to whatever alternative they were demanding. Hierarchy being "white" was a big one. One of my former board members, Chrissie Castro, who is a member of the Navajo Nation, often reminded us that the notion romanticized by many activists—that all hierarchy is white supremacist, and Indigenous people governed themselves through flat social organization—is false. Many Native American tribes, she said, had sophisticated protocols and clear hierarchies for decision-making, which often distributed power in specific ways. Many times, being entrusted with this kind of power was an earned privilege and responsibility for the good of the collective.

Ash-Lee Woodard Henderson

"Whatever is happening with the most ultra-left, which is not the majority—the two people who are like, 'This is just a white supremacist structure.' Okay, so let's have that conversation publicly. Let me tell you how we've essentially doubled salaries, how I didn't take a raise in the first five years, and I started as an executive director at $59,700 as a Black, queer, working-class woman who is the breadwinner and financial caregiver for most of her immediate family. How we inherited a $1.5 million budget (if even that much) for an org that was eighty-five years old and that is a bastion of democracy that is loved and respected by movement practitioners all over the world. Let's talk about how we expanded benefits, went from $1.5 [million] to an over $8 million budget during my tenure. If then you still need a union, please do it. But let's not pretend that this is about BIPOC women not being democratic."

To off-load / ease pain at any cost: Overwhelmed by the weight of your own pain and distress? Off-load it on someone else, or put others at risk to ease your discomfort. In some cases, off-loading happens via confabulation. As defined by Brené Brown, confabulation is a lie told honestly. In these instances, certain individuals—in some cases those struggling with mental health issues—project and scapegoat organizations and colleagues to off-load pain that they no longer feel able to carry, but which did not actually originate with events that happened to them in the organization or movement. Traumatized by COINTELPRO and other forces in the 1970s and '80s, many members of movement organizations became paranoid and began attacking one another, genuinely believing that everyone was an FBI informant. As I watched a modern-day equivalent of this gaining speed, I remembered a TV series I watched as a kid called *The Women of Brewster Place* (trigger warning—sexual violence). One chilling scene shows a lesbian who has been gang-raped in an alley. After her attackers flee the scene, an elderly gentleman tries to help her. Out of her mind with trauma, she mistakes him for one of the attackers and proceeds to beat him to death with a pipe. I thought of that scene on countless occasions as I witnessed staff attack one another with overblown reactions of discrimination against those they had convinced themselves were out to get them.

In other cases, people regress into a state of childlike selfishness and are willing to do things that they know are duplicitous and that compromise the safety of others to ease their discomfort. I once witnessed a normally caring and generous acquaintance of mine put the lives of others at risk. After several devastating events in her personal life, she flew across the country to see some friends. Days later she called me in distress to tell me that everyone she had been hanging out with had tested positive for Covid, that she had all the same symptoms and was sure she had it.

It was the height of the pandemic, before a vaccine was available, and when freezer trucks of bodies were still parked along streets in New York. Most people were still tightly locked down in their homes. The next day she called me from her house. She had boarded a plane full of people and flown home. I was aghast to think she put all those people—elders, immune-compromised folks, children—at risk. It dawned on me that she would have had to lie on the online questionnaire that everyone was being required to fill out at the time to be allowed onto the flight. Registering my shock, she simply said, "I just wanted to be in my own bed." That impulse, to put everyone at risk to ease her own discomfort, would play out next as she publicly dragged a few of her colleagues for discrimination for attempting to hold her accountable for mistakes on the job. The stress of the world had become too much to bear and she was willing to do whatever it took, to whomever was in her way, to ease it.

To aggrandize oneself: Accusations also become a way for power-hungry and attention-seeking individuals to position themselves as victims or saviors to generate visibility and support. This is easily done in most movement organizations, where many staff lack the sophistication to balance solidarity with discernment and will quickly crusade on behalf of anyone who claims to be harmed, and laud anyone who claims to bravely speak out to protect others, as long as the target of their accusation is someone with more positional power.

To seek vengeance: Jealous of another woman of color who has attained a greater level of power, success, or visibility than you? Want to take her down a peg? Lob a made-up accusation of discrimination or engaging in white supremacy. Perhaps the most visible example of this is the many haters who have come at Beyoncé over the years with accusations that she lightens her skin and is trying to be white. After one such incident, in November 2023, her mother, Tina Knowles, defended her daughter, posting,

"I am sick and tired of people attacking her. Every time she does something that she works her ass off for and is a statement of her work ethic, talent and resilience. Here you sad little haters come out the woodwork. Jealousy and racism, sexism, double standards, you perpetuate those things."[6]

To extort money: Tired of your job and want to quit but want to score a payday on the way out? Threaten a lawsuit and collect a settlement. Upset that you didn't receive a promotion and salary hike even though you did nothing to correct the performance issues your supervisor has been telling you about for years? Accuse them of transphobia and organize staff to pressure them until they relent. During my time as an ED, I talked to countless WOC EDs dealing with some version of this situation, though few could talk publicly about it or name names due to the cases getting quickly tied up in legal processes and nondisclosure agreements. In some cases, there were individual employees who were serious grifters moving from organization to organization running the same scam of trumped-up discrimination claims and then cashing in on the payday of a settlement check on their way out. This is possible since even with zero evidence, it is always cheaper for an organization to settle than to undergo the cost and reputational risk of a lengthy trial that could scare away funding for a long period of time before the organization prevails in court and has its name cleared.

Faced with staff who automatically believe accusers regardless of evidence, and laws that block managers from divulging any of the performance issues that often underlie what is occurring, leaders have few tools with which to dispute trumped-up charges in public. This has the added effect of allowing a culture of paranoia to spread throughout the organization, with staff fearing that they will be retaliated against, and managers afraid that they cannot carry out their normal job duties of providing feedback and requiring basic levels of accountability without being attacked by staff.

To block any challenges to false accusations: Someone dares to challenge your false accusations of discrimination using data and facts that disprove what you are saying? Call data itself "white supremacist." I've had people try this on more than one occasion when I brought data and receipts that disproved tired gossip. At which point I wanted to scream, "People of color invented numbers . . . and math!"

The main reason all of these tactics are happening at such an alarming rate is that almost no one is challenging them. As longtime organizer and racial justice leader Libero Della Piana wrote, "Twenty-five years ago, the debate was around whether to address race. Now, the challenge is how to address it."[7] We're slow on the uptake.

We're slow, in part, because we are in incredibly choppy waters. A major whitelash following the progress made after the 2020 uprisings is well underway, with right-wing groups, media, and politicians dismissing any accusations of discrimination and bias as performative "wokeness" and weaponized identity politics. They are waging an assault on critical race theory, affirmative action, ethnic studies, and other hard-won gains. The left has been loath to stoke their narrative and so has largely held its tongue instead of having the necessary nuanced and courageous conversation about what is occurring within its own ranks. There is an urgent need for people in movement to simultaneously confront and drive out actual bias while strongly rejecting false accusations.

When people use terms like transphobia, ableism, or anti-Blackness in righteous ways, we must support them. But when they use them to intimidate and dominate others, we cannot sit idly by—we must intervene. I have been stunned by the bystanderism and silence of movement folk in the face of this type of misuse—as if they think it's not possible for these terms to be cheapened and once again be rendered powerless, setting back decades of work. Far from protecting hard-won gains, our silence is jeopardizing them. There is a real need for honesty about the individuals who are using identity in duplicitous ways. As LaTosha Brown so wisely put it, "People who believe that they deserve a pass on hurting others because they are from a more oppressed group are not just lacking in political education, they are lacking in values."

The weaponization of identity and discrimination accusations is hitting women of color leaders hard. Because of the already thin margin of error we are allowed, the professional reputations of women of color leaders don't weather false accusations of discrimination as well as those of white women or men. I've seen several talented people leave positions of leadership despite zero evidence of their wrongdoing because they feared staff would make good on threats to drag them on social media for made-up discrimination claims and that the public would not care about proof. As she left my organization, one of these women told me, "I just don't think my career would survive it."

Many of the Black women I interviewed had been accused of anti-Blackness and engaging in white supremacy culture by Black members of their staff who became angry with them, usually after the leader tried to draw an appropriate boundary with problematic performance or behavior on the job. Black women leaders are dealing with this while also dealing with more identity-based attacks than any other demographic group.[8]

Several non-Black WOC leaders who have been stalwart supporters of Black struggle and Black leaders have been falsely accused of anti-Blackness for similar reasons. The prevailing sentiment I heard from these leaders about the impact they believed public accusations would have on their ability to work in movement was captured by one of my interviewees: "If you are accused of anti-Blackness," she said, "you're done."

One non-Black woman of color leader who wanted to remain anonymous told me, "There was a Black leader who got furious with me and engaged in a lot of bad behavior. I tried to handle it myself. But no one came towards me to try to help. I was immobilized because I felt like shit. Then my anger grew towards leaders on my staff or friends in the movement. Nobody figured out how to get in there with me." In my observation of situations like these, many Black folks who disagree with the accusations will stay silent because they don't want the headache of being accused by other Black people of being an Uncle Tom or a sellout. Non-Black people of color will stay silent because they don't want to volunteer as next to be called anti-Black, and white people stay quiet because they are generally in a perpetual state of terror about saying the wrong thing.

How did it get this bad?

There are many reasons, but one key contributing factor is a 1999 paper on "white supremacy culture" written by a white woman, Tema Okun. One of the most widely circulated texts associated with diversity, equity, and inclusion throughout movement, academia, and other sectors, it lists a set of fifteen traits and behaviors as white supremacist, including "perfectionism, urgency, defensiveness, worship of the written word, quantity over quality, only one right way, either-or thinking paternalism, power hoarding, fear of open conflict, progress is bigger and more, objectivity, right to comfort, and individualism."

There are grains of truth in what Okun offered. It is true, for example, that most white-led foundations will open their doors to an organization with a well-written proposal and close them to an organization whose positive impact on the lives of the community it serves is widely reported through oral narratives. But by and large, the piece paints with large and damaging broad brush-strokes.

Countless WOC leaders have dealt with staff members of all races brandishing the paper and charging them with perpetuating white supremacy culture by expecting that people meet deadlines (urgency!), produce high-quality work (perfectionism!), use proper grammar and punctuation in external communications (worship of the written word!), and mobilize the number of votes needed to win an election (quantity over quality!). And if they push back on these accusations, they are even more white supremacist because then they are disagreeing (defensive!). WOC have found ourselves in a double bind: White male mediocrity is not an option for us. To succeed, we and the organizations we lead must be excellent. But now, when we hold our teams to the bar that they need to meet, many staff refuse and accuse us of white supremacy.

My elders taught me that Black and Brown excellence, like that of Toni Morrison, was not about playing to the white gaze or meeting some standard that white folks had set; it was about pride in ourselves and the joy of giving our communities a level of excellence and quality that they so dearly deserved. Whiteness was fundamentally not at the center. This was true, even as there is an inherent tension in the United States that people of color must navigate to hold on to the wisdom and grounding of our cultures of origin while also learning to use tools of Western society. Growing up, I was surrounded by people of color who managed this tension masterfully to survive and thrive. An Indigenous person may practice a traditional ceremony to retain their language and culture while also mastering U.S. law to fight in the courts to protect tribal sovereignty. A Black person may excel at ballet but also expand the art form, making it more inclusive for people of color. Alvin Ailey and Sheila E. and Bruce Lee are excellent. So are Maya Angelou, Cherríe Moraga, Arundhati Roy, and Deb Haaland.

I was also raised with an acute understanding of the difference between someone like Clarence Thomas, who assimilates into the white power structure by selling out his own people; and someone like Haaland, who uses her education and position within mainstream institutions to fight for the rights of Native people.

Most people of color who have excelled in practically any field in the United States have had to deal with three fronts of attack. The first are white people who actively oppose us accessing certain tools and achieving excellence. During slavery, reading and writing were punishable by death. It wasn't that long ago that top-tier universities like Harvard, Princeton, and Yale refused to admit people of color. The second are white people who don't believe people of color are capable of excellence. Too many youth of color continue to languish in public school classrooms where white teachers hold them to a lower bar of expectations and standards than white students. The third front is a segment of our peers: other people of color, who out of fear of the unfamiliar or jealousy, or both, accuse us of being sellouts. Most students of color who excelled academically as children can remember at least one peer of color admonishing us with "You think you white? You think you better?"

Recalled longtime reproductive justice leader Silvia Henriquez, "I remember seeking out WOC who became my mentors— Wilma Montanez, Elsa Ríos, Adisa Douglas—most of them in the funding community. I'll never forget the first time I sent in a proposal to a foundation. I got called into Adisa Douglas's office. She said, 'This is not well written. This is not how you write to ask for money.' She literally walked me through how to do it. I had a model, I had a template. I was twenty-seven years old. I had never worked in an organization where I had to write a proposal. She took the time to tell me you need to learn how to write this way to ask for money. Then it was my first funders meeting and it was Wilma saying, 'I gotta review this PowerPoint and what are you wearing.' Yes, it's a double standard. She's like, 'White ladies can show up with their long dresses and their hair all crazy but not you.' I never thought of it as being called in. I literally thought, *These people are trying to help me do what I'm trying to do.* Fast-forward, I'm one of these [older] WOC, and [younger] people think it's like, 'Silvia is bought into white supremacist culture because she's showing up with her suit and her hair pulled back and with makeup,' but that's who I am! That's how I was taught and that's how I was raised in the movement by WOC."

WOC who attain positions of power in organizations are often those who have beaten the odds to obtain higher education, who know how to code-switch in order to navigate white spaces, who have a certain command of academic written and spoken communication styles, and who know how to navigate and push things through Western systems and bureaucracies. It is true that we must all be careful not to reify the harmful behaviors of white supremacist culture.

It is also true that not every code-switch or use of deadlines, grammar, or other tools is problematic, abusive, or white supremacist. "Was Toni Morrison white supremacist because she used grammar and punctuation?" I recall asking a group once in frustration. Some of the things that WOC leaders have gained by navigating white institutions are adaptive skills that are not in and of themselves bad or white supremacist, as long as they are balanced by a respect for and accountability to communities of color.

The "you think you're white" accusations are nothing new for WOC leaders, but the Okun paper supercharged them. At a leadership retreat I attended, each of Okun's fifteen traits was printed on its own piece of paper and spread out on the floor. Participants were asked by a woman of color trainer to stand next to the one that they could admit shows up in their behavior. Two of the largest groups were women of color—the first standing around the word "perfectionism," the second near "worship of the written word." One colleague whose work had helped power scores of major policy wins said quietly, "It's hard because writing is my superpower." Another lamented that her white staff were using accusations of white supremacist perfectionism to push back on her efforts to raise the quality of the team's work. She could not get her team to understand that the mediocrity that funders and allies accepted from the white male ED who had preceded her would never be accepted from her, a woman of color; nor did she want to deliver at that level for the community the organization served.

What is perhaps most dangerous about Okun's piece is that it links certain traits exclusively to white people. The notion that urgency is always white supremacist is ahistorical. Some of the most gradual, nonurgent people on the planet are white supremacists resisting equity. One of the central calls of the Civil Rights and Black Power movements was to turn away from gradualism and toward urgency. In "Mississippi Goddam," Nina Simone famously sang, "Do things gradually, *too slow!* Will bring more tragedy, *too slow!*" Dr. King preached, "This is no time to engage in the luxury of cooling off or to take the tranquilizing drug of gradualism."

On the notion that urgency and timeliness is white supremacist, Denise Perry of BOLD said, "People lift up and honor Harriet Tubman. A key lesson is how to be a commitment to our word. Harriet showed us that our commitment to be on time and in coordination was the path to freedom. We like to say that when Harriet said meet at the gate at ten, you had to be there at ten, not ten-thirty, because that could be the difference between freedom and bondage. We have greatness in our lineage to use in this work, the stars guided our ancestors' use of time not as oppressive but as a tool to create collective coordinated action toward freedom if you moved with Harriet."

There is also a national chauvinism that shows up in Okun's arguments. Bigger and better is white? How then do we explain the Egyptians with their pyramids, or the Chinese with their Great Wall, the Indians with their Taj Mahal? Perfectionism comes from white people? I was truly baffled. I wondered if Okun had ever met any immigrant parents or heard of Richard Williams, father of Venus and Serena Williams. Americans are perfectionists? Really? Because we are increasingly failing to be competitive globally in many areas, from industry to education. Compared with the math, science, and literacy scores of students in seventy-one other countries, the United States ranks thirtieth in math and nineteenth in science.[9]

And is worship of the written word white? Some of the oldest texts ever discovered were from the Middle East and Africa.

What Okun's piece reveals more than anything else is one of the great symptoms of white supremacy, which is the gravitational pull white people feel to center themselves and their ownership of things. Ironically, just as Okun wrote a piece meant to help dismantle white supremacy, she centered white people in wildly essentialist and damaging ways.

It's baffling to see the respect and uptake that Okun's piece has received, given its lack of rigor and her own attempts, via her website, to respond to the rising complaints. She herself shared one such complaint received: "Another, a skilled facilitator, reports that 'I could not possibly tally the number of hours I have spent over the last three years dislodging people from the reductive stance they construct based on the tool. In its current form, just to name one area, it tilts people towards a behavioral and ahistorical frame. And because it couches things in a way that can be read as absolutist, it can generate almost ridiculous orthodoxies of exclusion. I worked in one situation where the communications function had come to a grinding halt because a segment of the staff had decided that editing was white supremacist and, while yes, there are elitist and racist frames around proper language, the organization was locked in an either/or frame that was incredibly unhealthy and unproductive.' "[10]

Despite apparently registering the significant ways the piece has been used to damage organizations—particularly those led by WOC—Okun has offered only the non-apology that she is sorry that others have misinterpreted her words and intentions. In a 2023 interview with *The Intercept* reporter Ryan Grim, she responded to his question about whether, if she had it to do over, she would write the piece again, and she answered yes.

It would be unfair, of course, to put the entire problem on Okun. People in movement, including many people of color, need to take accountability for their uncritical adoption of her piece and use of it as a weapon with which to bludgeon one another. Embarrassingly, and yet another sign of the way quick and dirty meme culture prevails over rigorous engagement with texts, many people of color using her piece assumed Okun was a person of color and that the scholarship was sound—something that critical thinking or a quick Google search would easily have disabused them of. Her paper was also carried on the wave of a larger cultural zeitgeist of callout and cancellation.

Without nuance and detail, charges of white supremacy become just another weapon that people use to dominate one another, to attack Black and Brown excellence, and to tear down WOC in leadership. Unchallenged they undermine the fight to protect hard-won gains like affirmative action, ethnic studies, and a climate in which real discrimination claims are treated with the seriousness they deserve.

17

Recovering from Attack and Burnout

One of the first things I did after my last day at Groundswell was to call a plumber to fix the drain in my shower. It had become clogged with my hair, which had been falling out in chunks from stress. It was like a bad joke, a bizarre metaphor for the whole situation. The tools that had worked for me as a leader my entire career had failed and so had the tools from my local hardware store that I had used to clear a million drains before. After fifteen years of relatively smooth sailing, with a fairly normal amount of hiccups and conflict among staff, the last eighteen months—2020 through 2021—had been brutal. For the first time since I had entered movement when I was fifteen years old, I considered leaving it entirely. It was a shocking thought since this work had always felt like a calling, the only thing I'd ever wanted to do.

The hits that WOC leaders take within movement organizations are vicious, and the recovery time is real. I have seen countless sisters, strong and resilient people, leave movement organizations in bad shape. Some with levels of exhaustion so deep that they were unable to work for months. Others beset with severe health problems that would plague them for years. A few experienced full-blown nervous breakdowns that landed them in institutions.

Surviving abuse, family abandonment, and racial othering required me to be mentally tough. I consider myself a strong person—mentally and physically. I have both an acute sensitivity and a thick skin. I have always been able to navigate extremely challenging environments and dynamics without being intimidated or rattled—which is partly what made me so successful in building the organization I built, requiring me to navigate difficult white spaces in the donor world and act as a bridge to people of color at the grassroots level.

But the force of the attack that was directed at me from other WOC during my last few months at Groundswell was unlike anything I had ever experienced. It gutted me on every level: physically, mentally, and spiritually. It also hit me at a time when, like many leaders, after four years of Trump and Covid, my exhaustion levels were at an all-time high. Due to immune issues in our household, my co-parent, Tricia, and I had spent eleven months of 2020 at home, homeschooling our nine-year-old and caring for our one-year-old with no outside childcare. It had been a tour of duty on top of the ED load I was carrying, and I was still recovering from it.

I knew when I left that to keep from falling into a deep depression or succumbing to the long list of stress-related health ailments I was managing, I would need to put as much energy into my healing and recovery as I had into keeping the organization afloat. Tricia had the foresight to book me a weeklong solo trip to Kauai. I flew there just weeks after my last day at the organization.

The Airbnb I booked was small and dated but had a beautiful ocean view. For five glorious days I followed my intuition on what I needed to heal. I slept, meditated, journaled, wept, read spiritual and self-help books, and watched Thich Nhat Hanh YouTube videos on anger, forgiveness, and healing. I did yoga on the lawn downstairs, looking out at the sailboats and surfers. I drove my rental car around the island to hike in the mountains and kayak rivers until I was sweaty and smeared with the island's red soil. I swam in the ocean until it felt like the poison of all the trauma and pain began to pour out of my body. I stopped at fruit stands and ate mangoes and papayas in the sun, letting the juice run through my fingers and down my chin. I cooked clean meals for myself, full of veggies, detoxing my system. I called a few loved ones to reconnect, but mostly I recharged alone. I got quiet. I had always focused most of my prayers on my loved ones, movement comrades, and my organization. Now I prayed for myself, for my own healing. I hadn't anticipated it and still struggle to adequately describe it, but the spirit that I felt in the red earth, lush green hills, soft beaches, iridescent ocean waves, and breathtaking waterfalls held me and healed me in a powerful way. It felt like mercy.

A picture a passerby took of me at the start of the trip was alarming when I saw it later. My face was strained, my jaw clenched, my eyes almost wincing. I couldn't muster a smile. I looked like something the cat had dragged in. By the end of the trip, my mood was noticeably lighter. A friend I called remarked that I sounded less on edge than I had been in months.

When I returned home, I knew the road to full recovery was long, but I felt I was off to a good start. My mental health was not where I wanted it to be. I had always been an upbeat person, but

I struggled to get out of bed in the morning. My doctor diagnosed me with situational depression and anxiety and prescribed medication.

I went to therapy weekly. I resumed swimming two to three times a week—a routine I had started a few months earlier when I felt I might break under the stress at work. In the water, everything is lighter—it holds your weight for you, giving you a break. As I glided from one side of the pool to the other, I felt like the water was pulling the stress, anxiety, and grief off my body. I began running and biking in nature a couple of times a week as well, taking in the beauty of trees and rivers, of red-tailed hawks and bald eagles. Strengthening my body felt good, like an affirmation of life and rejection of despair. I hiked regularly in forests with old-growth trees, whose majestic presence calmed me at a cellular level. I spent time with my kindred people and played with my kids and my beloved dog. I began meditating for longer stretches, listening more intently to the guidance that was there for me. I was diligent about getting seven to eight hours of sleep a night. If my anxiety kept me up, I would take a nap during the day. Staying disciplined and consistent was uncomfortable but critical. I noticed I was able to keep my mental health above water. On the days I didn't do these things, my mood tanked, and so I stayed vigilant.

At the advice of my friend Sayra Pinto, I also prioritized play as a key part of my healing. ED life is not just about the sheer amount of time the tasks of the job require—it's also about the real estate the organization takes up in your brain. It's the waking up at 2:00 A.M. to write something down that you can't forget to do for the organization. It's your mind flashing onto a work thing while you're in line at the grocery store, or playing with your kids, or on a date with your partner. It's space that could be used for other things. As soon as I was able, I set about reclaiming this space by filling it with things that brought me joy. This included passions I had pursued before ED life, including music, singing, dancing, writing, paddleboarding, and hiking, as well as new things I had always wanted to try but didn't have the time for, like training for sprint triathlons, improv theater, organizing backyard barbecues with the queers in my neighborhood, and giving my most cherished relationships the full time and presence they deserved.

After several months I began to gingerly reach out to a few people in movement whom I felt I could trust. This was difficult. When you have been beaten down by a few rotten people, while others you thought you could trust refuse to defend you, it does something to you. Some of the greatest harm I sustained was to my ability to trust my own judgment about people. I seriously wondered if something was wrong with me. Two years later, over breakfast, a friend shared with me what an elder former staffer had told her years before: "Vanessa has the wrong people around her." I seriously wondered if my powers of discernment were broken altogether. But over my time of healing, I'd realized my gut instincts were fine. I just needed to stop overriding them. This realization let me contemplate a return to movement work with the knowledge that I was now wiser than I had been. I knew I could do things differently.

I made a list of the people in my life I could count on, starting with people who had shown up over the years by telling me the truth—not just what I wanted to hear—and had my back in good times and bad. I thought about the expression "Surround yourself with people who fight for you in rooms you aren't in" and why I had struggled to do this. I did deep work to repair my sense of self-worth until I could honestly say, "I deserve people around me who have kindness, integrity, and backbone, who see me and protect me." Slowly and gingerly, I began to redefine my inner circle.

I also began to let go and forgive. As John Lewis reminds us, "You have to have the capacity and ability to take what people did, and how they did it, and forgive them and move on." This is not a linear process. Each day I felt less and less bothered by the lack of capacity others had to show up well. Forgiving myself for my errors was, in many ways, even harder but day by day I made progress.

MINI MASTER CLASS

Dolores Huerta

"It's important not to hold grudges. We have to put things behind us. If we load up our bag with too many hurtful memories it burdens us. One thing I've learned from men is they can be bitter enemies and then you'll see them laughing and joking and working together. This is something that is really hard for women. We have to remember that what we are trying to accomplish is bigger than a grudge."

Slowly, I began to reengage in various movement meetings on Zoom or in person, but I was jumpy. I was hypervigilant when choosing my words. On more than one occasion I called someone I knew and trusted to see if I had come off as abrasive. Each time, they were puzzled, reassuring me that I hadn't been, and that everyone had appreciated my contributions. Still, the slightest sign of tension among people in a group would trigger my anxiety. For a while I was diligent about only entering rooms with "adults," by which I meant people who had enough emotional maturity and regulation to be about the work and not engage in nonsense.

It took two years to be able to relax and enjoy being with movement comrades again. Now I am finally enjoying diving in fully to movement spaces.

Sarah Jones has some thoughts on healing from attack following her one-woman show and recent film *Sell/Buy/Date,* which waded into the highly polarized conversation about the sex industry to invite people into a more nuanced conversation. She shared, "When I and my original collaborators—three WOC—and mama Meryl Streep went to make a film that tried to honor the range of conversations [about the sex industry] the attack I received was so merciless on social media it was a near cancellation. My goal was to say, I'm here to fight the system, not you, sisters. I was attacked from both sides—women from the sex worker community, and those in the anti-trafficking space. They went to Ford Foundation and said, 'Take her funding.'" She sighed as she recounted the pain of this experience. "It was extremely traumatizing for me and in some ways I have not fully recovered. I was in hiding. I was in so much pain. I felt there was nowhere to turn. After that I needed spiritual chiropractic. My goal was to be a facilitator of more unifying dialogue. That part happened as much as I hoped was possible. To watch women who might normally attack one another on Twitter instead being together in person talking with each other—that was the dream, and it happened."

Jones is not alone. I've talked to many leaders who describe going into various degrees of hiding or isolation following an attack, before beginning the work of healing. For Jones, healing required being present with her grief of what happened. She shared, "I'm sitting shiva to allow space for the grief. Trauma breaks us down, but grief puts us back together. It is the reintegration. We are not in a society that allows us to grieve even the micro traumas. You have to go through the grief work."

Ashindi Maxton encouraged people to take the time off to heal, sharing, "I didn't do anything for seven months, other than taking care of my mom and dad, who were sick. I did some journal writing, not a whole lot. I spent hours on the phone with my closest friends, people who really believe in me. I slept ten hours a night. I cooked. I rested." We must give ourselves the permission to take the time off that we need.

In the freezing cold of January 2022, my daughter Ifetayo and I put on our winter coats and gloves and hats and walked across the crunchy frost of the front lawn. We kneeled down in the dirt at the edge of the yard and dug holes in the frosty earth, near the fairy garden. It was uncomfortable work. Inside our home behind us, the warmth of the fireplace and couch where we could curl up and watch a movie beckoned. Yet this is where we wanted to be. Into each hole we dropped a smooth, brown bulb, covering it over carefully with fluffy brown earth. "Tucking it into its bed for winter!" Ife said cheerfully. The discomfort of that work in the bitter cold of winter would all be worth it in the spring when we would delight in the blooming of colorful tulips and alliums. Keeping an open heart is not always spa days and relaxing by the pool. Sometimes it is the hard, generous, and patient work of unearthing the pain and bitterness to heal, of planting love, hope, and vision so we can enjoy their beauty in the coming season.

The Right to Fail

Dolly Parton has written some three thousand songs. Most of them were never hits. Malcolm Gladwell talked about how it typically takes ten thousand hours of doing something to become excellent at it, with many of those hours spent making mistakes.

Mistakes teach you lessons, and learning from failure makes you stronger, smarter, and more resilient. Said actress Lupita Nyong'o, "It's only when you risk failure that you discover things. When you play it safe, you're not expressing the utmost of your human experience." What, then, do we do with the fact that so many WOC leaders feel they have little to no margin for error?

I have yet to find a woman of color who doesn't agree with the spirit of what Miya Yoshitani conveyed here: "I always felt that there was so little room to make a mistake, to take risks and to try things completely differently [instead of] such a huge expectation of perfection."

What do we do with the fact that most WOC leaders believe they have to be far better than their white male counterparts to be taken seriously and that they risk being discarded the minute they fail?

"When I was in college and we were all stressed out by looking for jobs, I started putting my rejection letters on the dining room wall," Mona Sinha recalled. "Others started doing it too—taking away the shame and laughing about the rejections together. We need to learn to share failure so that it is not a symbol of shame."

This, in turn, can widen the margin for error that is available to WOC leaders. Ash-Lee Woodard Henderson believes we need more spaces to celebrate victories and be honest and accountable about what didn't work. "Perfection isn't required to lead, but accountability is," she said. "Accountability as an abolitionist is not punishment. Accountability without grace is punishment. Grace without accountability is being complicit. A lot of us get accountability without grace."

I struggled with self-compassion and self-forgiveness as a leader. I had no problem giving people on my staff grace with their mistakes, but I was my own worst critic. My inner critic, which had begun as an adaptive tool to help me survive in a world that required me to be excellent in order to survive and advance, had become a weight that was dragging me down. I took accountability to the extreme, often blaming myself for anything that went wrong, even things that were out of my control. I went over mistakes in my mind, learning from them, but I was often unable to let them go and forgive myself.

But failure is a human experience, a right. When we are afraid to fail, we become afraid to risk, afraid to be bold, which is our superpower.

1. When you fail, talk about it. Normalize failure as a part of success.

2. Take responsibility with accuracy: Be accountable for what is yours, let others deal with what is theirs, and acknowledge the factors that were out of your control. On the things you are accountable for, make amends and repairs as needed and learn the lessons.

3. Offer yourself compassion and forgiveness. As Maya Angelou advised, "Forgive yourself for not knowing what you didn't know before you learned it."

18

Playing Big

One of the things I love most about the wins WOC leaders deliver is how they reflect a conviction to play big for our communities. Celebrating these big wins and encouraging bold leaps is essential for our boldness and recovery from leadership challenges.

In August 2022, President Biden signed the Inflation Reduction Act, authorizing $370 billion to combat climate change and support disadvantaged communities. This included caps on insulin costs, Medicare drug price negotiations, and $1 billion for public housing green upgrades. Initially, two bills existed: a stripped-down infrastructure bill and the robust Build Back Better Act. Over time, leaders favored the former, but the Congressional Progressive Caucus, chaired by Pramila Jayapal, ensured that essential elements from Build Back Better were included.

Jayapal, driven by her experiences as a woman of color, and supported by WOC-led grassroots groups, fought to include provisions for housing, childcare, and environmental justice. This leadership prioritized community needs over political expediency. She said, "Everything that we fought for in Build Back Better was stuff that wasn't being brought to the table because there weren't the right people at the table until we did it: housing, the care economy, environmental justice—with solutions shaped by the participation of groups historically left out, like domestic workers and environmental justice activists. These are all issues I've worked on and lived as an immigrant woman in movement."

Jayapal and her colleagues fought to ensure that language and provisions within Build Back Better made it into the final legislation. "The infrastructure bill was going to get moved without Build Back Better," she said. "We didn't support splitting them because of course then it becomes easier to say, 'We'll pass the low-hanging fruit of hard infrastructure but we're going to forget about getting women back into the workplace, primarily WOC in the care economy, or getting housing for people who are ending up houseless in cities across the country.'

"All the progressives in the Senate voted for the [stripped-down] infrastructure package and sent it down to the House," said Jayapal. "The big moment was saying no to the president, to the speaker, and all of these powerful leaders, but doing it as a collective of sixty-plus members that were strong enough to say 'No, we won't move this forward without both pieces of legislation.' We insisted that we were not going to pass it unless we drafted the legislation for the rest of it: housing, childcare, paid leave—all the things that mattered to women and families across the country. We had to hold up three times with the president calling us, the speaker calling us. Our language was added, and we were able to get all Democrats in the House to vote for it."

What Jayapal did exemplifies the bold leadership of so many WOC. As a leader, she refused to leave the most vulnerable behind. She calibrated her efforts based not on political calculations of what was palatable or expedient, but on what the communities she represents actually needed to survive and thrive. This boldness among WOC leaders helps change the destinies of millions of people.

Similarly, in *Allen v. Milligan,* the U.S. Supreme Court ruled in favor of Black plaintiffs who accused Alabama of violating the Voting Rights Act by redrawing the congressional map to dilute Black voting power. This win, preventing a major blow to democracy, was due to the fearless advocacy of Black female plaintiffs and organizers, including Letetia Jackson, a plaintiff in the case. Letetia, a lifelong civil rights activist from Dothan, Alabama, exemplifies the leadership that helped achieve this significant victory. "They see the writing on the wall," she said of Alabama racists. "They are full of fear for the change."

Many in Alabama have long sought to restore Jim Crow–era policies. In 2013, *Shelby County v. Holder* led to the gutting of Section 5 of the Voting Rights Act. In *Allen v. Milligan,* Alabama aimed to strip away Section 2, the only remaining teeth of the Act. Letetia and other activists fought hard. Black people make up 27 percent of Alabama's population, and their growing political muscle was undeniable in the 2017 election of Doug Jones. Letetia noted, "Black women turned out 98 percent in this election; they could not explain his win any other way." Despite ongoing challenges, Letetia's leadership underscores the transformative impact of WOC.

Letetia is an active member of the Black Women's Roundtable, advocating for political commitments to Black women. In *Allen v. Milligan,* she was present as Justice Ketanji Brown Jackson dismantled the state's race-neutral argument. "When they started the arguments and she started talking, I knew we had a chance," Letetia said. Justice Jackson asked, "Do you understand how the Fourteenth Amendment originated?" She highlighted its purpose to give freed Black men equal voting opportunities. Letetia observed, "She came educated, unafraid, and unapologetically

Black." Letetia concluded, "No one thought we would win since Alabama has led the charge in destroying the Voting Rights Act and anything else that would be fair representation for Black folks in this state."

Letetia's credo on leadership exemplifies how Black women play big: "Never back down, never settle, stay true to what you think is best for you and your community and what you are fighting for. . . . It is Black women in this state who are leading this charge. We are going to change the face of Alabama."

WOC have also been responsible for the greatest gains in immigrant rights. Leaders like U.S. representative Judy Chu of California have spearheaded much of the strongest legislation, including the Dream and Promise acts. It was young, undocumented WOC who led the chant "Yes you can!" at a press conference protesting Obama's stance that he couldn't act on DACA. Young immigrant WOC, like Greisa Martínez Rosas of United We Dream, were the vanguard on the ground, organizing to build the political pressure that allowed new laws, like DACA, to be passed. There are many who attribute the DACA win to the willingness to take these kinds of direct actions, as well as WOC working in different movement sectors leading efforts to lock arms in solidarity for immigrant rights.

At the state and federal level, WOC are also leading the fight around the care economy, which encompasses demands for paid family leave, childcare, eldercare, and fair working conditions for domestic workers. In one of the most glaring examples of how labor laws can discriminate, domestic and agricultural work were the only sectors excluded from the labor protections within Franklin D. Roosevelt's New Deal because these jobs were done almost exclusively by Black workers. Today these workforces are predominately Black and Brown, and they continue to fight for basic labor protections that every other class of worker has enjoyed for nearly a century. Having been a union organizer myself, with SEIU's home care division, I know firsthand how incredibly difficult it is to build connection and unity with workers who lack centralized worksites. At one point I was the only organizer for a turf of two thousand workers, each working in a different house for a different family. It was tough. Under the tireless leadership of Ai-jen Poo, one of the best organizers of our time, the National Domestic Workers Alliance has become the largest membership-based WOC-led organization in the country. Responding to the organizing power of NDWA, ten states,[1] two cities,[2] and the District of Columbia have passed domestic workers' bills of rights. The Domestic Workers Bill of Rights, federal legislation[3] that would benefit 2.2 million workers, is now working its way through Congress.[4]

Katherine Grainger, a lawyer and managing partner at Civitas Public Affairs Group, said of the New Deal exclusions, "Anytime you do policy organizing like that and a group of people get cut out, it is those who have the least political power, and it is almost impossible for them to get it back. The fact that Ai-jen and others have been able to mobilize folks that often don't have documentation, are marginalized because of race and language barriers—as well as economic barriers—and turn them into a political force, is almost impossible and would only be done by women of color who recognize the nuances of stealth, on-the-ground organizing that builds up a power base to push on the status quo." Throughout history, domestic workers were treated as largely invisible by the mainstream male-dominated labor movement. As Grainger said, "Even being able to *see* the organizing potential of domestic workers is only something that WOC would be able to identify." She's absolutely right. And that is playing big.

I'm always amazed at the degree to which the labor of WOC is erased in some of the most historic wins. There has been very little press coverage of the epic battle that resulted in Deb Haaland, of the Laguna Pueblo tribe, becoming the first Native American secretary of the Department of the Interior. It wouldn't have happened without Native women. Their work began years before, painstakingly registering, educating, and turning out voters in Native communities—many of whom had never received so much as a phone call or a door knock from the major political parties. Said Judith LeBlanc, longtime movement leader and executive director of Native Organizers Alliance, "Political parties and academics and government agencies have always considered Native people statistically insignificant." In fact, Native people are capable of deciding elections in several key states, but also, as Judith pointed out, they are "politically significant because of our treaties and because we are the only people with a collectively owned land base that has been self-governed since the beginning of time as sovereign nations." She refers here to the fact that treaties are protected by the Constitution such that if and when they are violated, it opens the door to erode constitutional rights for all people. Therefore, all people who care about their rights in the United States should care about Native people having an equal opportunity to engage in the democratic process.

It took until 2018 for the first Native women to be elected to Congress. Said Judith, "We never had our Maxine Waters and Barbara Lee for our children to grow up with. Native women's leadership was [finally] being acknowledged on the national political stage. This was a result of the momentum gathered at Standing Rock—a camp of ten thousand people where women played a critical role—which successfully interrupted the dominant narrative on who Native people are in the twenty-first century."

That momentum continued into the 2020 election, when despite enduring the worst Covid rates in the country, Native people also delivered some of the highest levels of voter turnout. Said

Judith, "We had one hundred moccasins on the ground in five battleground states—overwhelmingly women. The Navajo people had 80 percent voter turnout, with the majority of the organizing led by women. The Menominee Reservation is located in the most infectious county in the state of Wisconsin and yet achieved a 23 percent increase in voter turnout."

After being elected, Biden appointed more Native people to the administration than ever before and became the first president to say "states and tribal nations" in his speeches. But there had never been a Native in the cabinet, and Biden was looking to appoint to those positions his longtime political friends, who tended to be older white men. Tom Udall, U.S. senator from New Mexico, was being considered to lead the Department of the Interior. As Judith described, "The Department of the Interior is the most important department for Indian communities, overseeing our land, healthcare, schools, everything that is critical to life for Native people is housed in that department."

Native women at the helm of organizations such as IllumiNative and the Native Organizers Alliance brought together a group of leaders to promote the nomination of Deb Haaland for secretary of the Interior. Haaland had been a community organizer in New Mexico. She had once been homeless, living in her car with her daughter. She had a long track record of fighting with integrity for the rights of Native people and if she won, she would understand that she would not have been there without Native women and grassroots organizing. They began a push and mobilized over two hundred tribes to send letters to the transition team and gathered nineteen thousand signatures on a petition. Biden put her nomination forward. Native women didn't let up, leading another push for her confirmation, this time with over forty thousand letters sent to the Senate—a scale of organizing that Judith said "has never been done for any nomination."

One of the historic actions Deb Haaland took once confirmed was to form a committee around the use of the racist, misogynistic term "squaw" and eliminate it from over seven hundred federal geographical locations that used that name.

Said Judith, "It never would have happened without her. And we began to see, in Indian Country, why grassroots political power is important. Representation of Native women in the cabinet was not a destination, it was the beginning of structural reforms, of Native people sitting at the table alongside all the others who have the right to share in democratic governance. It is a magical movement moment, a grassroots upsurge, where WOC are taking our place in the governance of the whole."

A wealth of stories highlighting the importance of WOC to the 2020 election and the electoral landscape can be found in the book *Power Concedes Nothing: How Grassroots Organizing Wins Elections,* edited by Linda Burnham, Max Elbaum, and Maria Poblet.

Minnesota state senator Erin Maye Quade exemplifies the courage required to dismantle harmful systems. She led the fight to remove her state's abortion restrictions, saying, "I wasn't going to go into the legislature and carry the bill to remove [restrictions] and just be like, 'Well, we'll just see what we can get.' It was an extensive bill with a lot of laws that had to be repealed, and I carried a binder around and sat down so many times with so many members for really heartbreaking conversations to explain who it was harming and how. I cried more about this bill than I have about anything else. I don't think there was anyone else who cared as much from this intersectional place as I did."

Playing big requires rejecting gender and race norms and often creating your own platform. "At the beginning, when I was in the movement and talking about limited things, I was palatable," said Linda Sarsour. "When I started broaching things like abolition, equal pay, and race, I was isolated and marginalized by many white women as well as more mainstream civil rights spaces. Now I have my own platform. I say what I want when I want. I'm the woman who is going to ask you a hard question that you haven't thought about, who is going to say, 'Okay, cool, I see what you're doing here—are you willing to pass this piece of legislation that is going to exclude Black Africans and Middle Eastern people and Muslim folks? And if that's not the case, then explain it to me, because I'm here to understand.'" Playing big also requires taking risks. Fatima Goss Graves said, "Having the courage to not be afraid of power was the biggest gift. I haven't forgotten that lesson." Nor should any of us.

PART FIVE

Superpower #3 Generosity

19

Rising by Lifting Others

When I was new to philanthropy, an elder named Adisa Douglas saw me speak and engage at a few meetings. "You are absolutely incredible!" she told me. "And I'd like you to be my protégé." I was stunned. I was not used to receiving praise, much less glowing words from someone I admired as much as Adisa. Adisa had grown up in North Carolina during Jim Crow and was active in the Civil Rights Movement. In the bizarre world of philanthropy, which in the early 2000s was populated mostly by affluent white people, Adisa was a grounding force. One of my first interactions with her was at the annual conference hosted by a large network of reproductive rights funders. We were in a massive ballroom, and we were seated with six other people at the same round table. The speaker at the podium threw out an icebreaker for each table to discuss: What was the first movie you ever saw in a theater as a child?

The room was abuzz as people began to share. Matter-of-factly, Adisa said that she never went to the movies as a child because Jim

Crow segregation required Black people to sit in the rafters in the back, and her father wouldn't abide his family spending money in a place that treated them as second-class citizens. The table fell silent. She didn't say it with a chip on her shoulder, but she didn't soften it to make the white people comfortable either. She just let them sit with the facts. I loved her for it. Particularly since, when you looked at where this room full of mostly white funders was moving their money, they had created the equivalent of rafter seating for WOC-led grantees, who received less than 5 percent of the dollars granted by that network annually.

Adisa gave me one of the most precious gifts an elder can give a young person: She saw and believed in my brilliance and potential way before I could see it in myself. Each time she spoke with me, she poured so much love and encouragement into me. One day I was feeling down for some imperfection in a speech I had delivered, and I critiqued myself harshly in her presence. "Don't talk about my Vanessa like that!" she said. "No one is allowed to talk about Vanessa like that, not even you." When she and her partner moved into a retirement community, she sent me a set of boxes that were filled with first editions and signed copies of some of the most iconic texts about Black history, Black feminism, and ethnic studies: James Baldwin, Angela Davis, Audre Lorde, bell hooks. Many of these were books that had been a lifeline for me as a teenager, written by authors who meant a great deal to me. I recalled my undergrad days when I had spent hours in my professor's office cataloging, arranging, and poring over many of these same volumes.

Another day, a large, flat, square package arrived. I opened it and saw a beautiful framed painting of Rosa Parks by Clyne E. Cunningham. To this day, I have hung it in every apartment and house I have lived in. When my kids were born, as soon as they could point and talk, it was one of the first images they asked about. Throughout their childhoods, they would point and ask again and again to hear us tell the story of Miss Rosa Parks and the legacy of freedom fighters that was part of their lineage.

Adisa was so adamant, so fierce, so clear about her belief in me and the good I had to offer the world, that over time I began to entertain the possibility that she might be right.

The other gift Adisa gave me was a keen sense of my place in the arc of history. I knew the story didn't begin with me, that the work I did must build on and honor the generations of work that came before—and that it wouldn't end with me. This gave me perspective. Throughout my movement journey, I have thought regularly about the sacrifices that went into giving me the platform for my leadership: the people of color in the 1960s, '70s, and '80s who organized sit-ins and demonstrations that resulted in the first ethnic studies departments, where I would eventually learn about the history and experiences of people of color and our movements. The people who ran grassroots organizations in communities of color for decades, on an entirely volunteer basis, before there was a drop of funding. I thought about the WOC in philanthropy who toiled for over ten years before I ever came into the reproductive rights space, diligently tilling the soil to change hearts and minds with few returns, so that future generations could finally see the fruit of money flowing to our communities.

I am grateful for this perspective. There is a grounding in it, a humility, and a sense of purpose and responsibility that is far greater than myself. It is a widely held sentiment among mid-career WOC in movement today. As Miya Yoshitani, co-director of the Movement Innovation Collaborative, said, "So many of our stories of how we got to this work come from our own grandmothers, mothers, aunties, the other WOC movement leaders who brought us in and created a sense of belonging for us. We are part of a legacy of shared leadership, shared over generations."

She recalled, "Some of the very first people in the environmental justice movement to make space for me and to make me feel welcome and like I had a legitimate place in the movement were all WOC. It was Dana Alston from the Panos Institute who, when I was twenty years old, invited me to the First National People of Color Environmental Leadership summit. I would never have had the organizing life and career I have had without her extending that. Later it was the graciousness with which Peggy Saika, my first boss at APEN [Asian Pacific Environmental Network], thought there was something valuable for me to contribute. There was reluctance in various environmental orgs to share leadership because people felt their positions would be threatened, but a lot of the women who were part of the [environmental justice] movement in the early days were the exact opposite of that."

Rajasvini Bhansali, one of the warmest and most welcoming friends and movement colleagues I know, recalled of the women who brought her into movement, "When I was young, an intergenerational crew of queer WOC in Austin, Texas, took me in. They politicized and developed me as an organizer and helped me have a lot more joy and flirtation and fun in my life than I had before then. I'm forever grateful for that group of people. I think I was so deeply imprinted by those older mostly Afro Latina and Black women who took me in and loved me up so good that I assumed that existed everywhere. It was my big disappointment to see that in the big cities like the Bay Area and New York, people are a lot more cautious and it's a lot harder to break into cliques. You have to prove yourself, your politics, your way of being. That caused me some pain but it taught me an important lesson about how I want to move in the world. I'm proud of being open-hearted."

Others talked about their blood lineage in movement. "I was born and raised in movement," said Dara Cooper, former ED of the National Black Food and Justice Alliance. "It wasn't a question of whether, but how I would be in movement."

There is also, of course, support, sisterhood, and solidarity in movement. Fatima Goss Graves recalled, "When I came into the National Women's Law Center, we had a couple of events to say farewell to the co-founders who had led for forty-five years, to honor their legacy and welcome me. The balance between that was always hard. Ai-jen Poo reached out, and a year later she threw me a giant welcome party with a committee of amazing women of color and invited everyone. She was like, 'You need to be introduced on your own, and it's really important for us to send a collective statement that women of color are embracing you as the leader of this organization.' We were in the midst of the world being on fire. I was like, 'We don't have time for a party!' And she said, 'We are definitely making time for a party.' When there is a Black woman who is new to [a leadership] role, whether I've known them forever or not, I reach out, I make them have a coffee with me, I tell them as many secrets and tricks about donors and leading that I know and introduce them to donors where I can."

I have often sent welcome flowers to sisters taking the helm of organizations, and I have received them as well. The leaders I spoke with expressed such deep appreciation for the sisterly support they had received.

"We must keep the spirit of solidarity and support alive," said Teresa Younger. "I felt incredibly lonely the first few years I was in this role. What I want other WOC leaders to do is to pick up the phone and call each other. I find myself calling new EDs in movement space to say, 'Congratulations, welcome, and if you need anything, call. I'm a good listener.'" Teresa is authentic to her word and she is one of the sisters in movement who have, in many moments, helped me feel less lonely.

In my own journey, while my greatest support has come from WOC, I have also been supported by many white women. This is important for me to acknowledge because the world I want to create and see for my daughters is one where they give and receive support to and from all kinds of people. It's important for white folks to know that it's not just the job of people of color to support one another—that they can extend and receive that support too.

Two dear colleagues, Teresa Younger, CEO of the Ms. Foundation, and Surina Khan, former CEO of the Women's Foundation California, are each at the helm of what are among the largest women's funds in the country. There was a time when our three foundations were fundraising from many of the same donors, and funding many of the same grantees. We could have easily competed with one another, but we refused to. We referred donors to each other and invited one another to speak at various events we hosted. It was Teresa who encouraged me to do the Rockwood *Leading from the Inside Out* Yearlong Fellowship, saying it was life-changing for her and reminding me that I should value myself enough to allow my organization to invest in my leadership. It was Surina who served on my board and had my back during some of the formative years of my organization.

One time, an ally of Groundswell tried to boost us by standing up in a room of donors and disparaging the Ms. Foundation. Teresa called me. I immediately called the person, asked them to cease and desist, and then worked to repair the damage as best I could by lifting Ms. whenever I spoke with the staff or members of that donor group. Once, when Surina alerted me that one of their donors had defunded her organization, saying they decided to fund Groundswell instead, I immediately picked up the phone and called that donor and asked them to reverse that decision. In the end, the funder found the money to support us both without reducing anyone's grant. In the process, they learned a valuable lesson: We were not interested in scoring gains at one another's expense.

No one can pit us against one another when we refuse to allow it.

Showing Up for WOC Leaders

For those readers who are not WOC leaders, and who care about making leadership less treacherous for those who are, take in what is here in this book, use it diligently, and share it widely with others. For WOC leaders, let this be a reminder that we could do every bit of self-work possible and employ all the best strategies, and it would still not be enough to make the leadership positions we occupy fair and just if there is not also an uptick in right action from others. We have a right and a responsibility to demand more, for ourselves and for the leaders who will come after us.

If we had a magic wand, what would WOC leaders change about how others treat us? Below are a few things we wish the people who work with us would do. And as Ashindi Maxton reminds us about WOC, "When we are doing well, everyone is doing well. You never go wrong by doing right by us."

Have empathy. Try your best to see what a woman of color leader is up against every single day. Understand how hard she has had to work to get where she is. Be cognizant of the barriers she faces in every room she enters. Have compassion for what it is like to be underestimated, undervalued, tokenized, demonized, viewed with suspicion and mistrust, given no room for error, treated as disposable. Her struggles don't entitle her to be unkind to others, but if she is a kind and just leader, she deserves a generous amount of your compassion, grace, and support. Ash-Lee Woodard Henderson said it beautifully: "Love us. Love us in practice. Love us when we fuck up. Love us when we're great. If leadership really was as dope as people say it is then everyone would sign up to do it. Love us enough to be disciplined and principled enough to call us in, to give us comfort."

Notice the lens. Become acutely aware of the patriarchal and white supremacist lens through which WOC in leadership are often viewed. Educate yourself about the common stereotypes and biases behind this lens. The next time you hear a woman of color leader described as incompetent, shrill, angry, mean, or unfeeling, separate facts from gossip and ask yourself if the same things would be said about someone who was white or a man.

Don't be a bystander. If you notice that people's views are skewed by bias and stereotypes, don't let them go unchecked. Intervene! Challenge them! Say something! If you witness a takedown of a woman of color leader, stop and think about your experience with this leader and whether it matches the accusations. If it doesn't, speak up to share your positive experience as another data point for people to consider. As Ashindi Maxton put it, "When you hear (unfair) criticism of a leader, stand by them. Use your power and your social and political capital to stop harm."

Stand in solidarity with trans women. If you are a cis woman, don't be a TERF (trans-exclusionary radical feminist). Know that trans women are real women too. Educate yourself about their lived experiences, the brilliance they are bringing to society, and the barriers they face. Advocate strongly for the inclusion of trans women in women's rights spaces and urge other cis women in that space to do the work in advance to ensure that the environment is trans inclusive. When a trans woman enters a space, welcome her, and act in solidarity. Ensure that her voice, issues, and ideas are not marginalized, correct misgendering, and don't allow transphobic comments to pass unchecked.

Open doors. There are many rooms from which WOC are essentially barred but that we need to enter to fight for a better society. Help open these doors, brokering introductions, vouching for leaders, inviting them in, and supporting them once they have entered. Proactively ask the WOC leaders you know if there are any doors they have been trying to get through that you could help open.

Think and strategize intersectionally. Show up wherever you go as a feminist and looking through an intersectional lens that takes into account race, class, gender, and colonization.

Don't be a hater. Check your impulse to speak to or about a leader out of jealousy, projection, or an attempt to boost your own power and visibility by bringing down someone who you perceive as having more. Remember that WOC with positional power sustain much more damage to their reputations and careers when attacked than others. Engage in principled struggle by bringing legitimate critiques and call-ins to a leader one-to-one, in a direct meeting, rather than via email or text or via a public callout.

Support her right to fail. Talk to those who judge her harshly about how important it is to not reify cultural norms that hold WOC leaders to higher standards and give them less margin for error. Remind others to put her failures in the context of her broader track record of success, acknowledge failure as a necessary part of success, and treat her as they would want to be treated, with grace and kindness. Remind her of these things too!

Support her growth and have her back. Give her honest and constructive feedback from a place of wanting to help her grow and succeed. Don't withhold these things out of your own fear of being labeled unsupportive or racist.

Encourage her to think big! Offer to lighten her load so that she has the space she needs to build out her big-picture vision, ask her to share it, and (if you agree it's a good idea) encourage her to try it and have her back with the skeptics.

There are so many ways to step up with greater awareness, empathy, and solidarity to have the back of WOC leaders.

20

Advice for Our Younger Selves

A
s I closed out each interview with the leaders I spoke to for this book, I asked them what advice they would give to their younger selves about leadership. Five responses showed up again and again in their answers. As I read them over, I recalled a lovely member of my staff who once told me that she put a picture of herself as a child on her altar, where she meditated daily. She said that looking at the picture was a way of remembering to treat her adult self with kindness and compassion.

WOC leaders are so hard on ourselves. When the world is forever siding against you, this can feel like an act of self-preservation. You catch the errors before they do. You protect every vulnerability before they can lampoon you. You dazzle with an excellence so undeniable that they think twice about questioning your competence. Our self-critique can be harsh and even cruel. We do this to protect ourselves from others, but then we are left with another dilemma:

Who is going to protect us from ourselves? When leaders responded to this question, their voices softened as they thought about their younger selves, and about the young people they are nurturing in their lives today: their daughters, nieces, and mentees.

My hope is that WOC in leadership can embrace these five pieces of advice with the love and care that every one of us deserves.

Trust yourself. Trust your gut, intuition, and big ideas. Tune out the doubt, jealousy, and hate coming from others and learn to hear yourself. Devote time to the things that allow you to clearly hear your inner voice.

Build your squad. Find the colleagues and mentors who *really* know and love you enough to celebrate your success and tell you the truth. Invest time in those relationships.

Protect yourself. Keep people with backbone around you. Draw strong boundaries with the things that don't serve your highest purpose: overwork, toxicity, things that are outside of your power to fix, and even with major sacrifices that you do not, in your heart, really want to make (such as not having kids or giving up an important hobby). Understand that "No" is a complete sentence and can be said unapologetically. Never abandon yourself or allow yourself to be mistreated. When toxic or abusive behavior is coming your way, cut it off.

Shine your light fully and unapologetically. As Ash-Lee Woodard Henderson said, "Don't pansy around leadership." Walk in your full power. Be ambitious, be assertive, put your biggest, boldest vision out there.

Know that you are enough. Know you are enough to deserve good people around you, to be treated and to treat yourself with kindness, compassion, and respect, to let go of shame, to claim credit for your good work, to ask for the help you need. You are strong enough to take valuable feedback without spiraling into shame, to take accountability for and learn from your mistakes, and to also forgive yourself.

Another spring has come and my children are growing and blooming along with the flowers we planted together in our yard. Ife bounds from plant to plant in the fairy garden, squealing with delight at each new bud and blossom, remembering the ones we planted in the hard winter ground. "Mommy Vanessa, look at this one! Come look!" she exclaims. I follow her until we've seen them all and then watch her wander to the corner of the yard to chat with the fairies. A neighbor stops to say hello and I remark offhandedly to her that I think the Japanese elm tree I planted just before the pandemic may not have survived the winter. "I think it might be dead," I say, running my fingers over its bone-dry leaves. Ife overhears me and looks stricken. She looks at the tree and begins to weep, really weep, like from the depths of her little soul. I had no idea how much love she felt for this tree. It dawns on me that she is still so whole, so integrated in her being, so much in harmony and right relationship with the earth, other beings, her feelings, and magic. She grieves the dead tree and delights in each new flower with her entire heart. She hasn't been fractured by society and life. Both she and her big sister, Kwali, have this. This wholeness. They have so much less trauma than I had at their tender ages. Tricia and I have loved and protected them since they were born with the warmth and ferocity of two lionesses. Wholeness is their birthright. I know they are going to be incredible in whatever they decide to do in life, with even more potent superpowers of 360-degree vision, boldness, and generosity than previous generations.

I want them to do whatever their hearts desire to the absolute fullest. If their passion never brings them into social justice movements and they find other ways to cultivate beauty and joy in the world, that's fine. But if they ever decide to lead in work for social change, I'm clear on one thing: I want them to have exponentially less shit in their way. And I don't want to wait for *their* future for this. I want it now, for the WOC leaders of this moment. The future of democracy and the planet is uncertain, but of one thing I am sure: Humanity has an embarrassment of riches in WOC MVPs of social change. I know the work will always be hard—changing the status quo always is. Social justice work is going to be treacherous externally due to the backlash of those who cling to the old oppressive systems and fear a freer world. My fervent hope—for my sister movement leaders, for my daughters, and by extension for all of humanity—is that the positions from which leaders do their essential work to change the world will cease to be treacherous internally due to mistreatment from those who work within movements.

I wish for every good-hearted woman of color leader to reclaim the massive amount of time and energy we spend every day buffering and navigating archaic stereotypes and expectations, and pivot it into supercharging movements and their ability to win. I want us to win!

And I want us to thrive.

Acknowledgments

This book has taken a village to come into being. My deep gratitude and heartfelt thanks to: My co-parent and best friend, Tricia Speid, for her tremendous encouragement and support. My kids: Kwali, Ifetayo, and Cuddles the dog, for cheering me on and giving me space to write and reminders to take breaks to play! My mother, who stood by me when I was a child and instilled in me a love of courage, freedom, and the value that we are put on this earth to both fulfill our own potential and lift others. Those who gave me feedback on the draft manuscript: My beloved mentor Adisa Douglas, and my friends and movement comrades Jessica Horn, Katherine Grainger, Ash-Lee Woodard Henderson, LaTosha Brown, Chip Giller, and Tricia. My brother John Scott for getting me out from behind the computer and onto the biking trails, where inspiration could strike, and my sister Kumi for her support. Dear friends Dana Ginn Paredes and Lillian Ortiz, Shaw San Liu and Kawal Ulanday, Cathy Lerza, and Connie Cagampang Heller, for believing in me in this endeavor, and for our many conversations about movement dynamics and leadership. My friend Edgar Villanueva, for his generous advice and encouragement about a first book. My phenomenal agent, Tanya McKinnon, and my brilliant editor, Jamia Wilson, whose combined insight and generous thought partnership have been incredible. And most of all, my heartfelt thanks to those who graciously allowed me to interview them for this book. I am forever changed and uplifted by your wisdom and heart:

Ai-jen Poo, National Domestic Workers Alliance

Akaya Windwood, author and social activist

Alexis McGill Johnson, Planned Parenthood

Alicia Garza, JPB Foundation

Amisha Patel, formerly of Grassroots Collaborative

Andrea Mercado, Florida Rising

Ash-Lee Woodard Henderson, formerly of the Highlander Research and Education Center

Ashindi Maxton, co-founder, Donors of Color Network

Bamby Salcedo, TransLatin@ Coalition

Chrissie Castro, Native Voice Network

Cindy Wiesner, Grassroots Global Justice Alliance

Colette Pichon Battle, Gulf Coast Center for Law and Policy

Dara Cooper, formerly of the National Black Food and Justice Alliance

Denise Perry, Black Organizing for Leadership and Dignity

Dolores Huerta, Dolores Huerta Foundation for Community Organizing

Elle Moxley, Marsha P. Johnson Institute

Enei Begaye, Native Movement

Erin Maye Quade, Minnesota State Senate

Fatima Goss Graves, National Women's Law Center

Gina Clayton-Johnson, Essie Justice Group

Gloria Walton, The Solutions Project

Greisa Martínez Rosas, United We Dream

Jessica Byrd, Black Campaign Strategies

Jessica González-Rojas, New York State Assembly

Jo Freeman, author

Judith LeBlanc, Native Organizers Alliance, citizen of the Caddo Nation

Katherine Grainger, Civitas Public Affairs Group

Kim Jackson, Georgia State Senate

Layal Srouji, Columbia University Apartheid Divest coalition

Letetia Jackson, Tandeka LLC

Linda Burnham, movement elder, mentor, and strategist

Linda Sarsour, MPower Change

Loretta Ross, Smith College

Maryam Alwan, Columbia University, Gaza Solidarity Encampment

Miya Yoshitani, Movement Innovation Collaborative

Mona Sinha, Equality Now

Nikki Fortunato Bas, Oakland City Council

Pramila Jayapal, U.S. House of Representatives

Purvi Shah, Movement Law Lab

Rajasvini Bhansali, Solidaire Network

Sarah Audelo, Open Society Foundations

Sarah Jones, writer, actor, director

Shaw San Liu, Chinese Progressive Association

Silvia Henriquez, Ford Foundation

Surina Khan, formerly of the Women's Foundation California

Teresa Younger, Ms. Foundation for Women

Viviana Rennella, Windcall Institute

Notes

Chapter 1: The MVPs and Their Three Superpowers

1. Alexandria Ocasio-Cortez of New York, Ilhan Omar of Minnesota, Ayanna Pressley of Massachusetts, Rashida Tlaib of Michigan, Cori Bush of Missouri, Summer Lee of Pennsylvania, Delia Ramirez of Illinois, following the 2022 elections.

2. Electoralizing: to translate issue fights into electoral power by galvanizing voters to turn out to the polls and cast their ballots.

3. Shaun Harrison, Shanteal Lake, and Sam Abbott, "How Black Activists Spurred the U.S. Government to Expand School Meal Programs, Addressing Child Hunger and Boosting Future Productivity," Washington Center for Equitable Growth, February 22, 2022, https://equitablegrowth.org/how-black-activists-spurred-the-u-s-government-to-expand-school-meal-programs-addressing-child-hunger-and-boosting-future-productivity/.

4. Matthew Ballew and others, "Global Warming's Six Americas across age, race/ethnicity, and gender," Yale Program on Climate Change Communication, Climate Note, April 5, 2023, https://climatecommunication.yale.edu/publications/global-warmings-six-americas-age-race-ethnicity-gender/.

5. Sylvia Chi, "IRA: Our Analysis of the Inflation Reduction Act," Just Solutions Collective, 2023, https://justsolutionscollective.org/solution/ira-our-analysis-of-the-inflation-reduction-act/.

6. Intersectionality: "the complex, cumulative way in which the effects of multiple forms of discrimination (such as racism, sexism, and classism) combine, overlap, or intersect especially in the experiences of marginalized individuals or groups," https://www.merriam-webster.com/dictionary/intersectionality.

7. Jamila Taylor, "Eliminating Racial Disparities in Maternal and Infant

Mortality," Center for American Progress, May 2, 2019, https://www
.americanprogress.org/article/eliminating-racial-disparities-maternal-infant
-mortality/.

8. Janice Gassam Asare, "Black Women in DEI Are Under Attack," *Forbes,*
March 11, 2024, https://www.forbes.com/sites/janicegassam/2024/03/11
/black-women-in-dei-are-under-attack/.

9. Wesley Lowery, "AOC's Fight for the Future," *GQ* magazine, September 7,
2022, https://www.gq.com/story/alexandria-ocasio-cortez-october-cover
-profile.

10. UN Meetings Coverage and Press Releases, Security Council: "With Highest
Number of Violent Conflicts Since Second World War, United Nations Must
Rethink Efforts to Achieve, Sustain Peace, Speakers Tell Security Council,"
January 26, 2023, https://press.un.org/en/2023/sc15184.doc.htm.

Part Two. Superpower #1: 360-Degree Vision

1. Bernice Johnson Reagon, "Coalition Politics: Turning the Century," in *Home
Girls: A Black Feminist Anthology,* ed. Barbara Smith (New York: Kitchen
Table: Women of Color Press, 1983), p. 363.

Chapter 3: The Whole Truth

1. Natalie Orenstein, "Oakland Home Histories: Living in a Long Lost Lesbian
Bar," *The Oaklandside,* May 2, 2022, https://oaklandside.org/2022/05/02
/oakland-home-histories-living-in-a-long-lost-lesbian-bar/.

2. Manny Fernandez and Mitch Smith, "Houston Voters Reject Broad
Anti-Discrimination Ordinance," *The New York Times,* November 3, 2015,
https://www.nytimes.com/2015/11/04/us/houston-voters-repeal-anti-bias
-measure.html.

3. Amy Casso, "Oregon Didn't Forget Anyone When Fighting for Abortion
Access and That's Why It Won," *Bustle,* August 10, 2017, https://www
.bustle.com/p/oregons-fight-for-abortion-access-didnt-leave-anyone
-behind-75607.

Chapter 4: The Power in Belonging

1. Ejeris Dixon, "Building Community Safety: Practical Steps Toward
Liberatory Transformation," Transform Harm: A Resource Hub for
Ending Violence, December 12, 2018, https://transformharm.org/tj

_resource / building-community-safety-practical-steps-toward-liberatory -transformation /.

2. Bernice Johnson Reagon, "Coalition Politics: Turning the Century," in *Home Girls: A Black Feminist Anthology,* ed. Barbara Smith (New York: Kitchen Table: Women of Color Press, 1983), p. 364.

3. Anand Giridharadas, *The Persuaders: At the Front Lines of the Fight for Hearts, Minds, and Democracy* (New York: Alfred A Knopf, 2022), pp. 53–54.

4. Tristan Harris, *What Now? with Trevor Noah* podcast, December 19, 2023, Spotify.

5. Laura Hülsemann, "Democracy in Decline Worldwide, New Report Says," *Politico,* November 2, 2023, https:/ / www.politico.eu / article / democracy -decline-worldwide-new-report-says /.

6. Johnson Reagon, "Coalition Politics: Turning the Century," *Home Girls,* p. 364.

7. Deepak Bhargava, Shahrzad Shams, and Harry Hanbury, "The Death of 'Deliverism': Economic Policy Success Isn't Enough. We Need a More Holistic Approach to Addressing People's Fears and Anxieties," *Democracy: A Journal of Ideas,* June 22, 2023, https:/ / democracyjournal.org/ arguments / the-death-of-deliverism /.

8. Priya Parker, *The Art of Gathering: How We Meet and Why It Matters* (New York: Riverhead Books, 2018), p. 71.

Chapter 5: Barriers to Bring Down

1. Maggie Bullock, "The #MeToo Case That Divided the Abortion-Rights Movement," *The Atlantic,* March 2020, https:/ / www.theatlantic.com / magazine / archive / 2020 / 03 / the-abortion-doctor-and-his-accuser / 605578 /.

2. "Jon Ronson Quotes," BrainyQuote.com, BrainyMedia Inc., January 12, 2024, https:/ / www.brainyquote.com / quotes / jon_ronson_864710.

3. "Emotional Contagion," *Psychology Today,* https:/ / www.psychologytoday .com / us / basics / emotional-contagion.

4. Jeffrey Zaslow, "Surviving the Age of Humiliation," *The Wall Street Journal,* May 5, 2010, https:/ / www.wsj.com / articles / SB10001424052748703612804575222580214035638.

5. Bernice Johnson Reagon, "Coalition Politics: Turning the Century," in *Home Girls: A Black Feminist Anthology,* ed. Barbara Smith (New York: Kitchen Table: Women of Color Press, 1983), p. 359.

6. Caitlin Breedlove, "The Threshold Series: 1," *Medium,* March 28, 2021, https:/ / caitlinbreedlove.medium.com / the-threshold-series-1-cc9fc9d5849f.

7. Bonnie Rose, "Othering and Belonging: Highlights from Awakin Call," *Service Space,* July 16, 2020, https://www.servicespace.org/blog/view .php?id=31313.

Chapter 6: Two Generational Shifts

1. Michael Andor Brodeur, "Toni Morrison in Her Own Words: 'The Function of Freedom Is to Free Someone Else,'" *The Boston Globe,* August 6, 2019, https://www.bostonglobe.com/arts/2019/08/06/toni-morrison-her-own -words-the-function-freedom-free-someone-else/OS8quuie2VF355fuKC wzDJ/story.html#:~:text=%E2%80%9CThe%20function%20of%20 freedom%20is,Barnard%20College%20commencement%20speech%2C %201979.

Chapter 8: Burnout

1. Cathleen Clerkin, "More Women Work in Nonprofits. So Why Do Men End Up Leading Them?," *Harvard Business Review,* April 26, 2024, https://hbr .org/2024/04/more-women-work-in-nonprofits-so-why-do-men-end-up -leading-them#:~:text=Overall%2C%2062%25%20of%20nonprofit %20CEOs,money%2C%20power%2C%20and%20prestige.

Chapter 10: Setting Boundaries

1. Hailey Paige Magee (@haileypaigemagee), "In order to break the people-pleasing pattern . . . ," Facebook, June 16, 2021, https://www.facebook .com/haileypaigemagee/photos/pb.395090373886163.-2207520000 ../4194979250563904/?type=3&eid=ARDQwod7-hkZwPgq_wf8tUwEQU _qca00XWfSNx1mtQBMl1g4hWaP85nf_cV5UJ53IGbsw57floS6t4nG&paipv =0&eav=AfYV2qKn16BHMb0J1M89-dTF1Z0iLl7Mnqj_dvBCh5Q027zrv NMPz21llE9IIfKbMa0&_rdr.

Chapter 11: Healing Ourselves

1. Bilal G. Morris, "LaTosha Brown Is a Black Joy Blazer Who Has Dedicated Her Life to the Cause," NewsOne.com, August 1, 2023, https://newsone .com/4648323/latosha-brown-is-a-black-joy-blazer-who-has-dedicated-her -life-to-the-cause/.

2. *James Baldwin: Collected Essays: Notes of a Native Son / Nobody Knows My Name*

/ *The Fire Next Time* / *No Name in the Street* / *The Devil Finds Work* / *Other Essays,* ed. Toni Morrison (Library of America, 1998).

3. Gisselle Bances, "Meet the 'Undocumented' and Unafraid Latina Leading the Immigrant Justice Movement: 'I Am Here to Stay,'" Yahoo!Life, October 6, 2020, https://www.yahoo.com/lifestyle/undocumented -unafraid-latina-leading-immigrant-justice-movement-173605563.html?.

Chapter 13: We Are Not a Monolith

1. Bernice Johnson Reagon, "Coalition Politics: Turning the Century," in *Home Girls: A Black Feminist Anthology,* ed. Barbara Smith (New York: Kitchen Table: Women of Color Press, 1983), pp. 357–58.

Chapter 15: Feminism's Problem with Power

1. "Celebrating the Native American Vote in the 2020 Election," First Nations Development Institute, News, accessed July 15, 2023, https://www .firstnations.org/news/celebrating-the-native-american-vote-in-the-2020 -election/.

Chapter 16: Haters and Toxic Power

1. "Trashing: The Dark Side of Sisterhood," by Joreen, accessed July 15, 2023, https://www.jofreeman.com/joreen/trashing.htm.

2. "Relational Aggression," *American Psychological Association Dictionary of Psychology,* accessed July 15, 2023, https://dictionary.apa.org/relational -aggression.

3. Sarah M. Coyne and Jamie M. Ostrov (eds.), "The Development of Relational Aggression: An Introduction," *The Development of Relational Aggression* (Oxford Scholarship Online, May 24, 2018), accessed August 30, 2023, https://doi.org/10.1093/oso/9780190491826.003.0001.

4. Barbara L. Brock, "The Barrier Within: Relational Aggression Among Women," *Journal of Women in Educational Leadership,* University of Nebraska at Lincoln, Department of Educational Administration (October 2010), https://digitalcommons.unl.edu/cgi/viewcontent.cgi?article=1252 &context=jwel.

5. Maurice Mitchell, "Building Resilient Organizations," *The Forge,* November 29, 2022, https://forgeorganizing.org/article/building-resilient -organizations.

6. Elena Chabo, "Tina Knowles Slams Trolls Accusing Beyoncé of Skin Bleaching or 'White-Fishing,'" *Harper's Bazaar,* November 30, 2023, https://www.harpersbazaar.com/celebrity/latest/a45998954/tina-knowles-beyonce-skin-bleaching/.

7. Daniel Martinez HoSang, LeeAnn Hall, and Libero Della Piana, "To Tackle Racial Justice, Organizing Must Change," *The Forge,* January 4, 2022, https://forgeorganizing.org/article/tackle-racial-justice-organizing-must-change.

8. Dhanaraj Thakur and DeVan Hankerson Madrigal, "An Unrepresentative Democracy: How Disinformation and Online Abuse Hinder Women of Color Political Candidates in the United States," Center for Democracy and Technology report, October 27, 2022, https://cdt.org/insights/an-unrepresentative-democracy-how-disinformation-and-online-abuse-hinder-women-of-color-political-candidates-in-the-united-states/.

9. Drew DeSilver, "U.S. Students' Academic Achievement Still Lags That of Their Peers in Many Other Countries," Pew Research Center, February 15, 2017, https://www.pewresearch.org/short-reads/2017/02/15/u-s-students-internationally-math-science/.

10. Tema Okun, "White Supremacy Culture Characteristics," White Supremacy Culture, accessed October 4, 2024, https://www.whitesupremacyculture.info/characteristics.html.

Chapter 18: Playing Big

1. California, Connecticut, Hawaii, Illinois, Massachusetts, Nevada, New Mexico, New York, Oregon, and Virginia.

2. Philadelphia and Seattle.

3. Cosponsored by Senators Kirsten Gillibrand and Ben Ray Luján and Representative Pramila Jayapal.

4. "Domestic Workers Bill of Rights," National Domestic Workers Alliance, accessed July 15, 2023, https://www.domesticworkers.org/programs-and-campaigns/developing-policy-solutions/domestic-workers-bill-of-rights/.

Index

abandonment of WOC leaders, 14, 27, 151

abortion access/justice, 8, 79, 81, 83, 96, 155, 375

Abrams, Stacey, 139, 154, 307

Abu-Jamal, Mumia, 54

accountability, 114, 155, 174, 179, 219, 341–42, 366–67

accusations, false, 348

ACLU, 81

Advance Native Political Leadership, 157

advice for younger selves, 389–92

affirmative action, 19, 348

"Age of Anti-Ambition, The" (Malone), 158

aggression, relational, 328–36, 337

Ailey, Alvin, 352

Albany State College, 144–45

Albany State University, 144–45

All* Above All, 82–83, 96, 155, 208

Allen v. Milligan, 370–71

Alliance for Youth Action, 211–12

Alston, Dana, 382

Alwan, Maryam, 146–48, 158–59

American Psychological Association, 328

American Rescue Plan, 8

amygdala, 93–94

Angelou, Maya, 30, 352, 367

anti-hierarchy streak, 157

anti-leader streak, 157

Antiracist Baby (Kendi), 322

anti-war demonstrations, 80–81

Anzaldúa, Gloria, 53

APEN (Asian Pacific Environmental Network), 382

apologies, 26–27, 232

Art of Gathering, The (Parker), 113

Asian community, 58–59, 122–23, 248–49, 316

Asian Pacific Environmental Network, 9

attacks
on leaders, 320–21
recovering from, 358–67

Audelo, Sarah, 211–12, 244

authenticity, 103–4

authoritarianism, 20, 27, 97

Babybuds, 70, 71

back-stabbing, 27–28

Bailey, Essie, 152–53

Baker, Ella, 125, 203

Baldwin, James, 22, 53, 235, 380

Bareilles, Sara, 230

"Barrier Within: Emotional Aggression Among Women, The" (Brock), 329
barriers
case study involving, 122–24
emotional contagion, 120–21
empathy, 117–20
fragility, 129–34
narcissistic individualism, 134
othering, 140–42
performative cheerleading, 128–29
performative wokeness, 124–28
perpetual deconstructionism, 138–40
projection, 116–17
scapegoating, 116–17
360-degree vision and, 116
trauma bonding, 121–22
victim cloaking, 134–38
withholding feedback, 128–29
Bas, Nikki Fortunato, 204, 272
Bass, Sandra, 139, 243
Batiste, Jon, 290–91
battles, picking, 213–14
Beattie, Melody, 230
beauty, white standard of, 50–51
Begaye, Enei, 272, 284, 316
Bell, Simone, 278
belonging
creating, 99–105
power in, 86–115
toxic, 88–89
Beyoncé, 338, 346–47
Beyond Neutrality, 179
Beyond Survival (Dixon), 178
Bhansali, Rajasvini, 6, 129, 165, 222–23, 238, 291, 382
Bhargava, Deepak, 108
bias, countering, 18–19
Biden, Joseph, 248, 368, 374
big picture, keeping sight of, 295–96, 388
Bipartisan Infrastructure Law, 9

"BITCH Manifesto, The" (Freeman), 325
Black Campaign School, 149, 154
Black feminist politics, 78
Black liberation movements, 78
Black Lives Matter, 7, 153
Black Lives Matter Network, 191
Black National Anthem, 46
Black nationalism, 78
Black Organizing for Leadership and Dignity (BOLD), 114, 127, 165, 241, 343, 355
Black Panther free breakfast program, 9
Black Panther Party, 55, 57, 74, 78, 93, 128
Black Power movement, 55, 354
Black Pride, 51
Black Voters Matter, 91
Black Wall Street, 55
Black Women's Roundtable, 370
Boggs, Grace Lee, 227
bold demands, power of, 81–85
boldness
author's experience of, 34
feminism's problem with power and, 300–319
introduction to, 265
playing big as, 368–76
recovery/healing and, 358–67
staying on-key and, 269–99
as superpower, 12
toxic power and, 320–57
boundaries
advice regarding, 296–97
healthy, 174, 198
lack of, 165
mothering/mammying and, 213–16
porous, 221
problems setting, 112–13
rejection and, 117
setting, 166, 217–25

Bradshaw, Doris, 59
BRAVE, 83
Breedlove, Gina, 241
bridges needed
    developing core strength, 172–82
    early intervention, 170–72
    inoculation and education, 169–70
    updated intake filters, 167–69
Brock, Barbara, 329
Brown, Adrienne Maree, 177
Brown, Brené, 189, 207, 225, 338,
    344–45
Brown, LaTosha, 91, 160, 230–33, 289,
    318, 349
Build Back Better Act, 368–69
"Building Resilient Organizations"
    (Mitchell), 342–43
Burke, Tarana, 15
Burnham, Linda, 6, 164, 172–73, 176,
    177, 198, 240, 241, 245, 375
burnout, 185–201, 358–67
Butta (club), 56
Byrd, Jessica, 149, 154, 209, 223
bystanderism, 335, 349, 386

Cáceres, Berta, 99
cage, oppression as, 304–9
California Native Vote Project, 157
Calling In (Ross), 95, 177
cancel culture, 23, 95, 357
care economy, 371
caretaking, assumptions of, 14, 25,
    202–16
Carter, Lynda, 32
Casso, Amy, 84
Castellanos, Lisa María, 244
Castro, Chrissie, 157, 307, 311, 343
character assassinations, 313–14
Chavez, Cesar, 59, 125, 143, 156, 309
cheerleading, performative, 128–29
Child Tax Credit, 8
childhood, author's, 32–43

Chinatowns, burning of, 55
CHIPS and Science Act, 9
Christopher Street Liberation Day
    rally, 140
Chu, Judy, 371
Civil Rights Movement, 17, 78, 140,
    144–45, 354, 379
Civitas Public Affairs Group, 84, 207,
    372
class differences/classism, 249–50
Clayton-Johnson, Gina, 152–53, 213,
    305
cleaning up after others, 210–16
climate action, women of color
    and, 9
climate change, 94, 108, 146, 151
Clinton, Bill, 98
Clinton, Hillary, 139, 309–10
Club Mango, 56
Club Papi and Mami, 56
coalition building, 102–3
"Coalition Politics" (Reagon), 92, 132,
    170, 246–47
coat check, unspoken, 76–78
codependency, 218, 219–20, 229–30,
    234
Codependency No More (Beattie), 230
code-switching, 49, 52–53, 353
co-director models, 199
Cofield, Bola, 235
COINTELPRO, 93, 242, 345
collaboration, balancing with
    top-down decision-making,
    279–89
colonization, 74, 250
colorism, 50–52, 124–25
Columbia University, 146–47
Combahee River Collective, 9, 78
comfort, false expectations of, 132
community organizing, 57–60
compassion, 92, 391
confabulation, 344–45
conflict, capacity to navigate, 168

conformity, 91
Congress to Unite Women, 313
Congressional Progressive Caucus, 8,
    368
context, importance of, 119
Cooper, Dara, 154–55, 157–58, 160,
    205, 221, 244, 382–83
core strength, developing, 172–82
courage, 296
course correction, 174
Covid-19, 94, 105, 107, 120, 148, 242,
    345–46, 359
Covid-19 Hate Crimes Act (2021), 248
Coyne, Sarah, 328–29
Crenshaw, Kimberlé, 9
critical race theory, 19, 322, 348
Critical Resistance, 252
critical thinking, 168
Crucible, The (Miller), 120
Cruz, Ted, 322
Cuban Revolution, 55
culture of humiliation, 125–27
Cunningham, Clyne E., 380–81

DACA, 371
Daddy-Daughter Dance, 69, 75
Daily Show, The, 119
Dalkon Shield, 95
Davis, Angela, 173, 380
"Death of 'Deliverism,' The"
    (Bhargava), 108
death threats, 20, 26, 34, 162, 266, 293
deconstructionism, perpetual, 138–40
Delgado, Gary, 57–58, 149
Della Piana, Libero, 348
Dell'Olio, Anselma, 313
DelValle, Alexandra, 194
Democracy Alliance, 187, 212–13
destigmatization, 84–85
*Development of Relational Aggression,
    The* (Coyne and Ostrov), 328–29

Diallo, Amadou, 54
differences, working across, 102
discomfort, learning to sit with, 220
discrimination accusations, misuse of,
    341–57
diversity, equity, and inclusion,
    rollback of, 19
diversity within movement, 246–62
division, Trump administration and,
    93–94
Dixon, Ejeris, 92, 178
dominance, 65
Donors of Color Network, 273, 303
Douglas, Adisa, 17, 144, 220, 290,
    352–53, 379–81
Doyle, Glennon, 282–83
Dream Act, 371
due process, 174

E., Sheila, 352
East Bay Alliance for a Sustainable
    Economy, 204
education
    inoculation and, 169–70, 216
    political, 176–78
Einstein, Albert, 333
Ejerie Labs, 178
Elbaum, Max, 375
Election Administration Fund,
    212–13
Electoral Justice Project, 149
"Elephant in the Zoom" (Grim), 341
elitism, 91
Embodiment Institute, The, 218
EMDR (Eye Movement
    Desensitization and
    Reprocessing) therapy, 234
EMILY's List, 154
emotional contagion, 120–21, 123–24
emotional labor, 25
emotional maturity, 168

emotional regulation, 177
empathy, 78, 117–20, 121, 123, 176,
    385–86
entitlement, 156
environmental justice, 8, 59, 382
Equal Employment Opportunity
    Commission, 342
Equality Now, 284
Essie Justice Group, 152–53, 213, 305
expectations
    gendered, 315–16
    list of, 24–28
    managing, 214–15
    need for, 112–13
    placed on WOC leaders, 314–15
    setting clear, 170, 182
external focus, 215–16
extortion, 347–48

Facebook, 324
failure, right to, 365–67, 387–88
family, author's separation from,
    34–37
Family Dance, 75, 76
Fanon, Frantz, 128
fear
    abundance of, 308
    during author's childhood, 37–38
    collaboration and, 283
    frenzy of, 93–95
    silence due to, 22–24
    of success, 306–7
    Trump administration and, 93–94,
        120
feedback
    ability to receive, 168, 391
    fragility around, 341–42
    generational shifts and, 154–55
    providing, 388
    timely, 171
Fey, Tina, 158

fight-or-flight response, 93, 124
finding your no, 221–22, 223–24
FIRE (Feminist Intercultural
    Revolutionary Encounter), 54
First National People of Color
    Environmental Leadership
    summit, 382
501(c)(4)s, 286–88
flank, people on your, 224–25
flat organizations/structures, 157,
    181, 342
Florida Rising, 114, 205, 274
Floyd, George, 94, 131, 224, 247–48,
    339, 340
Fonda, Jane, 13
Ford Foundation, 208, 364
Forward Stance, 241
Forward Together, 83, 241
fragility, 129–34, 154–56, 222, 223,
    304, 341–42
fragmentation, 64, 76–77, 79
*Freedom: Medicine Words for Your Brave
    Revolution* (John), 222
Freeman, Everette J., 144
Freeman, Jo, 325–26, 328, 329–31
Freire, Paulo, 128

gaslighting, 14, 229, 236, 321–23, 335
Gay, Claudine, 135
gay rights movement, 84
Gaza solidarity encampments,
    146–48
Gen X, 144, 156, 157, 158
Gen Z, 144, 158–59
gender binary, rejection of, 144, 145
gender norms
    busting of, 9
    partriarchal, 309–10
gender pay gap, 77
gender-affirming health care, 104
gendered expectations, 315–16

generational shifts
  mentality shifts and, 159–63
  organizational development (OD)
    firms and, 165–66
  outdated intake filters and, 163–65
  younger generation and, 143–59
generosity, 12, 57
George Floyd Justice in Policing Act,
  248
Gilligan, James, 126
Giridharadas, Anand, 96
Gladwell, Malcolm, 365
glass cliffs, 25
Global State of Democracy, 97–98
González-Rojas, Jessica, 306
"gotcha culture," 91–92
gradualism, 354
Grainger, Katherine, 84–85, 207, 372
Grassroots Collaborative, 189
Grassroots Global Justice Alliance, 98,
  150
grassroots organizing, 178–79
Grassroots Power Project, 175
Graves, Fatima Goss, 133, 202, 276,
  315, 337, 376, 383
greed, 65
Green New Deal, 7–8
Grim, Ryan, 341, 355
Groundswell Action Fund, 16, 255–56
Groundswell Fund
  author's departure from, 358
  belonging and, 100–105
  corrections within, 303
  early days of, 90–91
  founding of, 16, 60
  funding and, 384
  problems at, 105–11, 301–2
  racial tensions and, 122–23, 130–31,
    247–48
  reflection on author's experience
    at, 112–15, 194
gun violence, 72, 74, 148–49
Gunn-Wright, Rhiana, 7

Haaland, Deb, 352, 373–75
Haley, Nikki, 6
Hamer, Fannie Lou, 125, 131
Harding, Vincent, 233
Harris, Kamala, 10–11, 139
Harris, Tristan, 97
hate crimes, 120
haters, 336–38, 387
Hawaiian independence, 55
healing
  expectations of, 202–3, 205
  within organizations, 240–45
  of ourselves, 226–39
health and well-being, 185–91
health insurance, 70, 104
health outcomes, racial disparities
  in, 15
Heller, Connie Cagampang, 126, 197,
  270, 290
Hemphill, Prentis, 218
Henderson, Ash-Lee Woodard, 17,
  20, 118, 152, 172, 242, 262, 318,
  344, 366, 386, 390
Henriquez, Silvia, 155, 195, 208, 292,
  352–53
Hernandez, Cindy, 89–90
Hicks-Wilson, Della, 134
Highlander Research and Education
  Center, 17, 156, 242
Holding Change (Brown), 177
Hollywood, racism and misogyny
  in, 15
home care workers, union for, 80
hooks, bell, 49, 53, 301, 380
Horn, Jessica, 21, 290, 337
"How Russian Trolls Helped Keep
  the Women's March Out of
  Lockstep," 96, 334–35
Hubert, Janet, 283
Huerta, Dolores, 10, 17, 59, 125,
  140, 143, 156, 197, 203, 308–9,
  363
Hughes, Langston, 53

humiliation, culture of, 125–27
humility, 178–79
Hurston, Zora Neale, 24, 53
Hyde Amendment, 251

iceberg effect, 119
identity, weaponization of, 342–43,
    348, 349
identity politics, 150, 156, 348
IllumiNative, 374
IMF (International Monetary
    Fund), 54
immigrant rights marches, 153
immigrants, undocumented, 239
income inequality, 20
incompetence, assumptions of, 14,
    24–25
incrementalism, 82
Indian Health Services, 251
Indigenous communities, 63, 66
individualism, 160
individuality, 246–62
Inflation Reduction Act (2022), 8, 9,
    368
inner critic, 366–67
inner enemy, 111–12
inner voice, 276
inoculation and education, 169–70,
    216
Instagram, 324
instincts, trusting, 236
insulin, capping cost of, 8
intake filters
    outdated, 163–65
    updated, 167–69
Intercept, The, 355
internal focus, 215–16
International Institute for Democracy
    and Electoral Assistance (IDEA),
    97–98
intersectionality, 9, 12, 52, 387
intervention, early, 170–72

intrauterine insemination (IUI)
    procedures, 70
Iraq war, 80–81
islands, avoiding being, 238
isolation, 323–28

Jackson, Ketanji Brown, 322–23,
    370–71
Jackson, Kim, 273, 277, 279, 306
Jackson, Letetia, 370–71
Jamison, Judith, 46
January 6 insurrection, 20, 93
Japanese Americans, internment
    of, 55
Jayapal, Pramila, 8, 17, 278–79,
    368–69
Jeffersons, The, 37
Jess-Cook, Carolyn, 14
Jim Crow, 379–80
John, Jaiya, 222
Johnson, Alexis McGill, 189, 207,
    312–13
Jones, Doug, 370
Jones, Sarah, 14–15, 17, 86–87, 276,
    324, 364
Jordan, Michael, 46
"just burn it all down" mentality,
    152
Justice40 Initiative, 9

"Karens," 163, 164–65
Kendi, Ibram X., 322
Kerr, Steve, 13
Khan, Surina, 180–81, 211–12, 276–77,
    384
Kim, Helen, 233, 237
King, Gayle, 289
King, Martin Luther, Jr., 17, 156, 200,
    354
King in the Wilderness, 17
Knowles, Tina, 346–47

Kochiyama, Yuri, 63, 203
Krishnamurthy, Kalpana, 83

land acknowledgments, 124
Latinx farmworkers, 59
leadership positions, toll taken by,
    15–16
Leading with Joy (Bhansali and
    Windwood), 129, 238, 265
LeBlanc, Judith, 250–51, 373–75
Lee, Barbara, 271, 373
Lee, Bruce, 352
Lee, N'Tanya, 177
lens, paying attention to, 386
Lerza, Cathy, 90–91, 290
Lewis, John, 363
LGBTQ community. *See also* trans
    people
    author's children and, 73
    having children and, 69–71
    marriage equality and, 84–85
    support from, 55–57
Liberation Fund, 287
lifting others, rising by, 379–88
"Light Shines Brightest in the Dark,
    The," 290–91
likability, 25, 309–19
limit setting, 25–26
listening skills, 178
Liu, Shaw San, 290
long-term organizing, 153–54
Lopez, Destiny, 82–83
Lorde, Audre, 21, 49, 59, 81, 111, 380
lynchings, 120, 134–35, 224

Magee, Hailey, 220
Mallory, Tamika, 96, 190–91, 324,
    334
Malone, Noreen, 158
Mandela, Nelson, 337
mantras, daily, 234–35

March on Washington, 140
margin of error, lack of, 14, 23, 25,
    366, 387–88
Markle, Meghan, 9–10
marriage equality bills, 84–85
Marsha P. Johnson Institute, 191, 323
Martínez Rosas, Greisa, 239, 371
martyrdom mindset, 144, 158
maternal mortality rates, 15, 101
Maxton, Ashindi, 212–13, 273–74,
    303, 365, 385, 386
Medicaid, 8, 101
Medicare, 8
Mercado, Andrea, 114, 205, 274, 299
#MeToo, 7, 15, 324
microaggressions, 41–42, 73–75, 261,
    273–74
millennials, 144
Miller, Arthur, 120
Mills, Nicolaus, 125
mission schools, 55
"Mississippi Goddam" (Simone), 354
mistakes, 365–66
Mitchell, Maurice, 342–43
mobilizations, one-off, 153–54
Montanez, Wilma, 352–53
Moraga, Cherríe, 53, 352
Morrison, Toni, 53, 162, 351, 353
mother figures, staff dynamics and,
    209–10
mothering/mammying, 14, 25,
    202–16
Movement for Black Lives, 130, 149,
    196
movement influencer syndrome, 244
Movement Innovation Collaborative,
    203, 381
Movement Law Lab, 196, 274
movement spaces/work. *See also*
    generational shifts; *individual
    organizations and leaders*
    belonging and, 86–88
    infrastructure for, 152–54

Moxley, Elle, 191, 303, 316–17, 323, 336
MPower Change, 266
Ms. Foundation for Women, 181, 211–12, 342, 384
Ms. magazine, 325
mud settling, patience for, 237–38
multi-issue approach, 10
mutuality, 63

NAACP, 156
NARAL, 81, 82, 83
narcissistic individualism, 134
National Association of Black Journalists, 11
National Black Food and Justice Alliance, 154, 160, 205, 383
National Domestic Workers Alliance, 8, 198–99, 240, 280, 372
National Domestic Workers Bill of Rights, 372
National Latina Institute for Reproductive Justice, 155
National Women's Hall of Fame, 95
National Women's Law Center, 133, 276, 383
nationalism, 247
Native Americans, 58, 157, 250–51, 316, 343–44, 373–75
Native Movement, 272
Native Organizers Alliance, 250, 373, 374
Native Voice Network, 157
New Deal, 371–72
New York Times, 96, 158, 334–35, 342
9/11 attacks, 80, 271
Noah, Trevor, 119
nondiscrimination ordinances, repeal of, 79
nondominance, 174, 175
NRA, 324

nurturing, assumptions of, 14, 25, 202–16
Nuyorican Poets Café, 14
NY Renews, 9
Nyong'o, Lupita, 366

Oakland, California, author's move from, 69–70, 71–72
Obama, Barack (and administration), 213, 275, 371
Ocasio-Cortez, Alexandria, 7, 8, 20
Occupy Wall Street, 153
off-loading, 344–46
Okun, Tema, 350–51, 354–57
Omar, Ilhan, 293–94
OneAmerica, 278
oneness, 63
opening doors, 387
oppression, internalization of, 21
organizational culture, 112, 170, 182
organizational development (OD) firms, 27, 113, 165–66, 172, 258
organizing
    grassroots, 178–79
    movement organizations and, 88
Ostrov, Jamie, 328–29
othering, 140–42
overcorrection, 172, 173, 180
overpreparing, 195–99
overwork, culture of, 189–91, 193–95, 197, 205
Owens, Candace, 13
Oya, Kumi, 290

Palestinians, support for, 146–48
Panos Institute, 382
paranoia, culture of, 347–48
Paredes, Dana Ginn, 83, 290
Parker, Priya, 113
Parks, Rosa, 17, 156, 380–81
Parton, Dolly, 365

Patel, Amisha, 189–90, 206–7, 219, 282
patriarchy
    gender norms and, 309–10
    internalization of, 21
    internalized, 283–84
Pelosi, Nancy, 293–94
People Could Fly, The, 44
performative cheerleading, 128–29
performative wokeness, 124–28, 150, 177, 348
perpetual deconstructionism, 138–40
Perry, Denise, 114, 127–28, 165, 205, 213–14, 240–41, 343, 355
Persuaders, The (Giridharadas), 96
physical well-being, 185–91
Pinto, Sayra, 132, 361
Planned Parenthood, 81, 189, 207, 312
play, healing and, 361
playing big, 368–76
Poblet, Maria, 375
Poehler, Amy, 158
political education, 176–78, 182–83
Politico, 97
Pollyanna, 42
Poo, Ai-jen, 198–99, 240, 280, 297–98, 306, 312, 372, 383
powell, john, 140
power
    comfort with, 168
    feminism's problem with, 300–319
    toxic, 328
Power Concedes (Burnham, Elbaum, and Poblet), 375
Prakash, Varshini, 7–8
prescription drug costs, 8
projection, 26, 116–17
Promise Act, 371
protecting yourself, 390
protection, deserved, 236–37

Psychology Today, 120
Public Service Center, 139
Puerto Rican independence, 55
purism, 99

Quade, Erin Maye, 291–92, 375
queer community. *See* trans people
quiet quitting, 158

race and racism. *See also* white supremacy
    author's childhood and, 40–60
    author's children and, 73–75
    author's experience of, 253–54
    conflicts involving, 257–61
    gender pay gap and, 77
    gendered expectations and, 315–16
    institutional, 272
    internalized, 283–84
racial justice movements, 9
rape culture, 320–28
Reagon, Bernice Johnson, 17, 65, 92, 102–3, 132, 144–45, 170, 246–47
recovery from burnout or attacks, 358–67
relational aggression, 328–36, 337
relational leadership praxis, 203
Rennella, Viviana, 145–46, 198, 252–53
reproductive freedom, 81
Reproductive Freedom for All (formerly NARAL), 81, 82, 83
reproductive health care, 70, 77, 82, 104
Reproductive Health Equity Act, 81
reproductive justice movement, 7, 8, 58, 82–83, 94–95, 96–97, 155
respect, 317
Riera, Sylvia, 140
right relationship, concept of, 63

rigor, 174
Ríos, Elsa, 352
Rockwood Leadership Institute, 142
Rockwood *Leading from the Inside Out*
    Yearlong Fellowship, 384
Roe v. Wade, 98
Ronson, Jon, 119, 126
Roosevelt, Franklin D., 371
Ross, Fred, 156
Ross, Loretta, 94–95, 118, 177
Roy, Arundhati, 53, 352
Russian troll farms, 96
Rustin, Bayard, 140

sabbatical policies, 199
Sai Baba, 45
Saika, Peggy, 382
Salcedo, Bamby, 141, 191–93, 210,
    213, 214–15, 308
Sankofa, 150, 290
Santos-Lyons, Aimee, 83
Sarsour, Linda, 96, 190–91, 265–67,
    293–94, 303, 305–6, 317–18, 324,
    326–27, 334–35, 375–76
scapegoating, 116–17, 345
Scarlet Letter, The, 27
Schaff, Libby, 272
Scott, John, 233, 290
self-aggrandizement, 346
self-critique, 389–90
"Self-Destruction in the Women's
    Movement" (Dell'Olio), 313
self-doubt, 284
self-perception dysmorphia, 275
self-worth, 215, 295
Sell/Buy/Date (Jones), 364
Sen, Rinku, 89
Serenity Prayer, 198
Service Employees International
    Union (SEIU), 80–81, 89–90,
    149–50, 372

Set Boundaries, Find Peace (Tawwab),
    221
sexual abuse, author's experience of,
    33–34
Shah, Purvi, 196, 205, 274, 292, 311
Shah, Seema, 97–98
Shakur, Assata, 49, 53
shame, 125–27
Shelby County v. Holder, 370
Shen, Eveline, 58, 83, 241
silence, price of, 22–29
Simone, Nina, 354
single-executive-director model, 199
single-issue struggles, absence of, 81
Sinha, Mona, 284, 317, 366
slash-and-burn tactics, 150
Smith, Ms. (teacher), 41–42
Smith, Will, 283
Smith College, 54
So You've Been Publicly Shamed
    (Ronson), 119, 126
social disconnection, 108
social exclusion, 87, 100, 105
social justice movement. *See also*
        individual organizations and
        leaders
    arts and, 14
    author's work in, 5
    fragmentation and, 64–65
    women of color in, 7, 15–16
social media
    attacks on leaders and, 324–25
    attention spans and, 119
    barriers and, 96–98
    emotional immaturity and, 134
    generational shifts and, 151
    relational aggression and, 334
    shortened attention spans and, 149
    social justice movement and,
        147–48
Solidaire Network, 6, 129
solidarity, 78, 90, 96, 297, 386–87

Solis Policy Institute, 212
Solutions Project, 18–19
somatic practitioners, 240–41
soul retrieval, 234
Southern Black Girls and Women's
    Consortium, 91
Southerners on New Ground, 139
squad, building your, 289–99, 390
"Squad, the," 7
"squaw," elimination of use of, 375
Srouji, Layal, 146–48, 151, 152, 153,
    158–59
Standing Rock, 373
Steele, Claude M., 18
Steinem, Gloria, 325
stereotype threat, 18
stereotypes
    common, 249
    fear and, 18
    impact of, 275
    public discourse and, 22
strategy, 174–75
Streep, Meryl, 364
structural changes, 199–201
Sunrise Movement, 7–8
superpowers, 12
Surface Transit, 14
Sweet Honey in the Rock, 17

Tao Te Ching, 66
Tawwab, Nedra, 221
Texas Organizing Project, 286
Theater of the Oppressed, 233
Themba, Makani, 130, 133–34, 243
Thich Nhat Hanh, 360
Thomas, Clarence, 352
Three Point Strategies, 149, 154
360-degree vision
    introduction to, 63–67
    as superpower, 12
    whole truth and, 69–85

Time's Up, 15
tokenizing, 28
top-down decision-making, balancing
    with collaboration, 279–89
toxic belonging, 88–89
toxic power, 328
trans justice and inclusion, 255–57
trans people, 79, 100, 386–87. *See also*
    LGBTQ community
Transdisciplinary Leadership and
    Creativity for Sustainability,
    132
transgender healthcare, 77
TransLatin@ Coalition, 141, 191–92,
    213
trashing, 325–26, 329–30
"Trashing: The Dark Side of
    Sisterhood" (Freeman),
    325–26
trauma
    healing and, 242–43
    unrepaired, 226–27
trauma bonding, 121–22, 177
Tremillo, Michelle, 286
tribalism, 97, 262
Trump, Donald
    demographics of supporters
        of, 13
    fear and, 93–94, 120
    Harris and, 11
    impact of, 87, 148, 157, 161
    inauguration of, 6–7
    January 6 insurrection and, 20
    opposition to, 12–13
    response to election of, 286–88
trust in yourself, 390
truth telling, 24
Tubman, Harriet, 46, 49, 162, 290,
    355
Tutu, Desmond, 325
"Tyranny of Structurelessness, The"
    (Freeman), 325

Udall, Tom, 374
underestimation, 186, 274
undocumented immigrants, 239
unionization, 179–81, 182
United Farm Workers, 10, 140, 143, 308–9
United We Dream, 239, 371
unity, 88
University of Washington, 53, 54
UnRestrict Minnesota, 292
Untamed (Doyle), 282–83
Urban, Melissa, 221, 225
us-versus-them sentiments, 105

vacation time, using, 194–95
values, clear, 170, 174, 182
vengeance, 346–47
Vibration of Grace (Breedlove), 241
victim cloaking, 134–38, 150
victim narratives, 135–37
Violence Against Women Act, 141
virtue signaling, 96–97
vision, long-arc, 174–75
Vision Change Win, 178
voter suppression, 212–13
voter-turnout rates, 7, 307, 373–74
Voting Rights Act, 370–71
vulnerability, 207–9

Walton, Gloria, 18–19, 193–94, 196, 241, 250, 271–72, 285
Washington State, author's move to, 71–73
Waters, Maxine, 373
We Will Not Cancel Us (Brown), 177
Weahkee, Laurie and Sonny, 58
Western medicine, 64
Western States Center, 83–84
What It Takes to Heal (Hemphill), 218

What to Do When He Won't Change, 29–30
When No Thing Works (Wong), 66
Whistling Vivaldi (Steele), 18
white fear, 18
white guilt, 128
White House Environmental Justice Advisory Council, 9
white supremacy. *See also* race and racism
   culture of, 26, 339, 349, 350–51, 354–57
   internalization of, 21
   Trump administration and, 120
   WOC leaders and, 338–57
wholeness, 63–64, 66, 76–77, 79
Wiesner, Cindy, 98–99, 150, 197–98, 219, 221, 244, 284
Williams, Richard, 42–43, 355
Williams, Serena, 355
Williams, Venus, 42–43, 355
Windcall Institute, 145–46
Windwood, Akaya, 129, 142, 172, 238, 265, 285, 291
Winfrey, Oprah, 289
witch trials, 120
withholding feedback, 128–29
Wiz, The, 46
wokeness, performative, 124–28, 150, 177, 348
Women of Brewster Place, The, 345
Women of Color Resource Center, 173, 241
Women's Foundation California, 180, 211–12, 276, 384
Women's March, 87, 96, 153, 190–91, 266, 324, 326
Women's Policy Institute, 212
Wonder Woman, 32–33
Wong, Norma, 65–66, 118, 130, 174, 175, 241

work ethic, 158–59, 204
Working Families Party, 342
workplace norms, generational shifts
  and, 144, 145–46
World Bank, 54
WTO (World Trade Organization), 54

X, Malcolm, 63

Yoshitani, Miya, 203, 214, 215, 219,
  315, 316, 366, 381
Young, Don, 278–79
Younger, Teresa, 181, 211–12, 253,
  318–19, 342, 383, 384

Zeldin, Lee, 293
Zinn, Howard, 53

ABOUT THE AUTHOR

VANESSA PRIYA DANIEL has worked in social justice movements for twenty-five years as a labor and community organizer and funder. She founded and served for seventeen years as executive director of Groundswell Fund, a leading funder of women of color–led grassroots community and electoral organizing. She is a recipient of the Smith College Medal, was featured by *The Chronicle of Philanthropy* as one of fifteen "Influencers" who are changing the nonprofit world, and was recognized by *Inside Philanthropy* as one of the "Top 100 Most Powerful Players in Philanthropy." Daniel has written for *The New York Times* and other publications.

vanessapriyadaniel.com
Instagram: @vanessapriyadaniel
X: @vanessapdaniel

ABOUT THE TYPE

This book was set in Dante, a typeface designed by Giovanni Mardersteig (1892–1977). Conceived as a private type for the Officina Bodoni in Verona, Italy, Dante was originally cut only for hand composition by Charles Malin, the famous Parisian punch cutter, between 1946 and 1952. Its first use was in an edition of Boccaccio's *Trattatello in laude di Dante* that appeared in 1954. The Monotype Corporation's version of Dante followed in 1957. Though modeled on the Aldine type used for Pietro Cardinal Bembo's treatise *De Aetna* in 1495, Dante is a thoroughly modern interpretation of that venerable face.